Gilbert Simondon

Being and Technology

Edited by Arne De Boever, Alex Murray,
Jon Roffe and Ashley Woodward

EDINBURGH
University Press

Edinburgh University Press Ltd
22 George Square, Edinburgh EH8 9LF

First published in hardback by Edinburgh University Press 2012

www.euppublishing.com

Typeset in 10.5/13 pt Sabon
by Servis Filmsetting Ltd, Stockport, Cheshire, and
printed and bound in Great Britain by
CPI Group (UK) Ltd, Croydon, CR0 4YY

A CIP record for this book is available from the British Library

ISBN 978 0 7486 4525 1 (hardback)
ISBN 978 0 7486 7721 4 (paperback)
ISBN 978 0 7486 4525 1 (webready PDF)
ISBN 978 0 7486 5079 8 (epub)
ISBN 978 0 7486 5078 1 (Amazon ebook)

Contents

Abbreviations v

Editors' Introduction: Simondon, Finally vii
Arne De Boever, Alex Murray, Jon Roffe and Ashley Woodward

1. Technical Mentality 1
Gilbert Simondon, translated by Arne De Boever

Explications

2. 'Technical Mentality' Revisited: Brian Massumi on Gilbert Simondon 19
With Arne De Boever, Alex Murray and Jon Roffe

3. Identity and Individuation: Some Feminist Reflections 37
Elizabeth Grosz

4. Crystals and Membranes: Individuation and Temporality 57
Anne Sauvagnargues, translated by Jon Roffe

Implications

5. The Question of Anxiety in Gilbert Simondon 73
Igor Krtolica, translated by Jon Roffe

6. Infra-Psychic Individualization: Transductive Connections and the Genesis of Living Techniques 92
Marie-Pier Boucher

7. '*Du mort qui saisit le vif*': Simondonian Ontology Today 110
Jean-Hugues Barthélémy, translated by Justin Clemens

8. The Aesthetics of Gilbert Simondon: Anticipation of the Contemporary Aesthetic Experience 121
Yves Michaud, translated by Justin Clemens

Resonances

9.   Gilles Deleuze, a Reader of Gilbert Simondon   135
     Sean Bowden
10. Science and Ontology: From Merleau-Ponty's 'Reduction'
     to Simondon's 'Transduction'   154
     Miguel de Beistegui
11. The Question of the Individual in Georges Canguilhem and
     Gilbert Simondon   176
     Dominique Lecourt, translated by Arne De Boever
12. The Theatre of Individuation: Phase-Shift and Resolution
     in Simondon and Heidegger   185
     Bernard Stiegler, translated by Kristina Lebedeva

     Glossary: Fifty Key Terms in the Works of Gilbert
     Simondon   203
     Jean-Hugues Barthélémy, translated by Arne De Boever

     Notes on Contributors   232

     Index   235

Abbreviations

Abbreviations used to refer to Simondon's published works

CI   *Communication et information* [Communication and Information] (Chatou: Editions de la Transparence, 2010) (collection of texts)

CSI   'Cours sur l'instinct' [Course on Instinct], in Simondon, CI (see above)

CSP   *Cours sur la perception* [Course on Perception] (Chatou: Editions de la Transparence, 2005) (course from 1964 to 1965)

FIP   'Forme, information, potentiel' [Form, Information, Potential] (lecture from 1960, added by the publisher), in Simondon, ILFI and IPC (see below)

HNI   'Histoire de la notion d'individu' [History of the Notion of the Individual] (text added by the publisher), in Simondon, ILFI (see below)

IGPB   *L'Individu et sa genèse physico-biologique* [The Individual and its Physico-Biological Genesis] (Grenoble: Jérôme Millon, 1995) (this book contains the first two-thirds of ILFI, as well as its introduction and conclusion)

ILFI   *L'Individuation à la lumière des notions de forme et d'information* [Individuation in Light of the Notions of Form and Information] (Grenoble: Jérôme Millon, 2005) (Simondon's main thesis for the *Doctorat d'Etat*, written between 1954 and 1958)

IMIN   *Imagination et invention* [Imagination and Invention] (Chatou: Editions de la Transparence, 2008) (course from 1965 to 1966)

IPC   *L'Individuation psychique et collective* [Psychic and Collective Individuation] (Paris: Aubier, 1989 and 2007) (this book

	contains the last third of ILFI, as well as its introduction and conclusion)
IT	*L'Invention dans les techniques* [Invention in Technics] (Paris: Seuil, 2006) (collection of texts)
MEOT	*Du mode d'existence des objets techniques* [On the Mode of Existence of Technical Objects] (Paris: Aubier, 1958) (Simondon's secondary thesis for the *Doctorat d'Etat*, written between 1954 and 1958)
MT	'Mentalité technique' [Technical Mentality], *Revue philosophique de la France et de l'Etranger*, 3 (Paris: PUF, 2006)
NC	'Note complémentaire sur les conséquences de la notion d'individuation' [Additional Note on the Consequences of the Notion of Individuation] (text added by the publisher), in Simondon, ILFI and IPC (see above)

Editors' Introduction: Simondon, Finally

Arne De Boever, Alex Murray, Jon Roffe and Ashley Woodward

Gilbert Simondon: Being and Technology is the first book in English dedicated entirely to the work of this French philosopher. Although the importance of Simondon's thought for twentieth- and twenty-first-century continental philosophy is clear – his work is foundational for Gilles Deleuze and Bernard Stiegler, and resonates in the writings of other prominent thinkers, such as Jean Baudrillard, Paolo Virno, Giorgio Agamben and Roberto Esposito – relatively little attention has been paid to Simondon in the English-speaking academy. The few scholars writing about Simondon in English who have contributed to this collection – Brian Massumi, Elizabeth Grosz and Miguel de Beistegui, amongst others – are, next to some philosophers not included here (Alberto Toscano, Bruno Latour and Isabelle Stengers for example), the exceptions that confirm the rule.

Born in 1924, Gilbert Simondon was a doctoral student of both the French philosopher and physician Georges Canguilhem and the French phenomenologist Maurice Merleau-Ponty. By 1958, he had finished both his main thesis, *L'Individuation à la lumière des notions de forme et de l'information* [Individuation in Light of the Notions of Form and Information], and his supplementary thesis, *Du mode d'existence des objets techniques* (*On the Mode of Existence of Technical Objects*), for the French doctoral degree. While *Du mode d'existence* was immediately published in France and quickly turned into an influential book, it would take until 1964 for the first part of Simondon's main thesis to be published. This text was later republished in 1995. The second part of the thesis, on which the forthcoming English translation *Psychic and Collective Individuation* is based,[1] was not published until 1989, the year of Simondon's death. This part was later republished in 2007. Due to a rising interest in Simondon's swork in recent years, a number of other (French) volumes have begun to appear, including a collection of texts on 'communication and information' and Simondon's 1964–5 course on 'perception', as well as the course on 'imagination and invention' and the collection of texts on 'invention and technics'. With the English translation of *Du mode d'existence* and the second part of Simondon's thesis well under way,[2] the early twenty-first century interest in Simondon is taking off in the English-speaking world, and the fact that translations into German, Russian, Korean, Italian and several other languages are in progress suggests a quickly growing interest in Simondon worldwide.

This book developed out of the first English-language special journal issue – published by *Parrhesia: A Journal of Critical Philosophy* – dedicated entirely to this important thinker.[3] The dearth of English-language criticism on Simondon is no doubt largely due to a lack of English translations of Simondon's writings,[4] and it was on the occasion of the forthcoming publication of the translation of Simondon's *Psychic and Collective Individuation* and *On the Mode of Existence of Technical Objects* that *Parrhesia* decided to put together a special issue on Simondon's work. Several of the features, articles and interviews that were published in *Parrhesia*'s special issue are reproduced here with only minor modifications. However, this book has also been expanded significantly with several other contributions from emerging and established scholars of Simondon's work. *Gilbert Simondon: Being and Technology* thus hopes to contribute further to English-language scholarship on Simondon, and function as a guide as this scholarship continues to expand.

As well as (somewhat playfully) alluding to some of the major texts of twentieth-century philosophy (by Martin Heidegger, Jean-Paul Sartre and Alain Badiou), the subtitle of this book has been chosen to reflect the two topics central to Simondon's philosophy: ontology and technology. Scholars have also suggested that the field of psychology and the human sciences should be added as a third area of investigation. (In fact, Simondon was elected to the chair in psychology at the Sorbonne in 1963.) Although the latter is also represented here – Marie-Pier Boucher and Dominique Lecourt's contributions, for example, reflect on this – the book's main areas of interest are, as its subtitle indicates, 'being' and 'technology'. The notions of ontogenesis, individuation (a near-synonym for ontogenesis, as Barthélémy explains in his glossary) and technics (which is not exactly technology) are thus central to this book's project. By gathering contributions that address all these areas of Simondon's thought, the book ultimately hopes to stimulate reflection on how these different elements of Simondon's philosophy fit together.

As a whole, this book aims to introduce readers to Simondon's thought, as well as pursue some of its implications for contemporary philosophy. It includes an important piece of Simondon's own work: his text 'Technical Mentality', which was published in English for the first time in *Parrhesia*'s special issue. Because of the highly technical nature of Simondon's thought, as well as the intricacies of his writing, this book includes a number of contributions that help to explain Simondon to the reader ('Explications'). This first section of the book begins with an interview with Brian Massumi which aids a reading of 'Technical Mentality', while helping to locate Simondon in the contemporary theoretical scene. It then follows with an explanation of his theory of individuation and its practical import for feminism and political thought in general (Grosz), before further clarifying this theory by way of an examination of his discussion of crystals and membranes as models for individuation (Sauvagnargues). In an attempt to think not simply *with* but also *after* Simondon, the book also explores the 'Implications' of Simondon's thought for contemporary philosophical reflection about anxiety, science, technology and aesthetics (Krtolica, Boucher, Barthélémy, Michaud). In addition, several of the contributions in the book explore the 'Resonances' of Simondon's thought in the work of other thinkers: Deleuze (Bowden), Maurice Merleau-Ponty (de Beistegui), Georges Canguilhem (Lecourt) and Martin Heidegger (Stiegler).

The book also includes an extensive glossary by Jean-Hugues Barthélémy, one of the most important Simondon scholars working in France today, which explains fifty key notions in Simondon's work. Importantly, the works referenced in this glossary include not only those works by Simondon that are soon to appear in English, but also all of Simondon's published works. Thus, the glossary provides something like a 'legend' to the map of Simondon's thought that this book lays out. As is the case with several of the other texts that are collected here, the glossary extends beyond the immediate scope of this book by helping the reader to situate *Psychic and Collective Individuation* and *On the Mode of Existence of Technical Objects* in relation to Simondon's numerous other publications, many of which will hopefully one day become available in English as well.

We cannot conclude our introduction before briefly considering the questions, Why Simondon?, and more specifically, Why Simondon today? Both Brian Massumi and Elizabeth Grosz address these questions directly in their chapters, but we may briefly indicate the following. Simondon is a philosopher of technology whose works anticipate in fascinating ways the subsequent developments of the technical world with which we are now dealing, such as the internet, and technologies of information and communication more generally.[5] Simondon's originality as a philosopher of technology is indicated, first, by his critical rejection of cybernetics and attempt to formulate an alternative perspective, and second, his inscription of this theory of the nature of technical objects within a highly original, generalized ontology. This ontology describes the emergence and individuation of beings as such, delineating technical objects in terms of both their commonalities with and their differences from other types of beings.

Simondon provides a theory of being that is significantly inspired by the natural sciences; as Simondon's close relation to Canguilhem might suggest, his work establishes a bridge between philosophy and the sciences. Heavily influenced by developments in physics in his time, Simondon found himself – like his teacher Canguilhem, and like Canguilhem's own teacher Gaston Bachelard – in between these two disciplines. Simondon's ontology, which in its positive orientation towards the sciences was significantly at odds with Heidegger, was also an important inspiration to Deleuze. For these reasons, Simondon must be read as an interesting philosopher of technology and an ontologist in his own right, while also being situated at a number of historically significant points of contact with other major developments in twentieth-century thought.

More than this, however, Simondon's work is of particular value for the currents of thought now developing in the early twenty-first century. As Massumi and Grosz both note, over the last decades intellectual currents in the humanities have shifted from a context unreceptive to Simondonian thought to one in which the moment seems ripe for his (re)discovery. As Massumi glosses this, it has entailed a move from the prevailing acceptance of 'constructivism' to what he calls 'inventivism'. While constructivism focuses on the cultural construction of reality while remaining sceptical towards the claims of the natural sciences, inventivism seeks to think the natural processes involved in any and all constructions. Grosz suggests that constructivism (which she associates with structuralism and poststructuralism) was a necessary corrective to essentialist forms of thought, but one which overcompensated. Moreover, contemporary philosophical thought is increasingly engaged in explicitly ontological investigations. In the wake of Deleuze, philosophers like Badiou, Quentin Meillassoux and certain strains of speculative realist thought have once again posed the goal of thinking in terms of being. In this regard too, the arc of contemporary thought has brought it back into the terrain mapped out in such a powerful way by Simondon himself.

We are now in a position to think in a more balanced way the relation between the processes which have previously been designated the natural and the cultural, and perhaps, with Simondon, to question this distinction itself. Fighting relentlessly against the classical oppositions of the vital to the mechanical, Simondon always tried to think further than what the traditional delimitations of disciplines allowed. This is, no doubt, part of the reason why his thought has proved to be so extraordinarily stimulating for the writers who have contributed to this volume, and which we hope it will also prove to be for its readers. As Friedrich Nietzsche famously suggested, some people are born posthumously.[6] In our view, contemporary coordinates suggest that the time is right for Simondon's (second) 'birth'.

NOTES

1. This translation is forthcoming with the University of Minnesota Press.
2. This translation is forthcoming with Semiotext(e).
3. The special issue is available at: http://www.parrhesiajournal.org/past.html#issue07.
4. To our knowledge, excerpts from Simondon's work have previously been published in English in: Jonathan Crary and Sanford Kwinter (eds), *Incorporations* (New York: Zone, 1992), Joke Brouwer and Arjen Mulder (eds), *Interact or Die!* (Rotterdam: V2_, 2007) and *Parrhesia*.
5. In addition to the chapters by Massumi and Grosz, see Henning Schmidgen, 'Thinking Technological and Biological Beings: Gilbert Simondon's Philosophy of Machines', *Revista do Departamento de Psicologia – UFF*, 17.2 (2005), pp. 11–18 (www.scielo.br/pdf/rdpsi/v17n2/v17n2a02.pdf).
6. Friedrich Nietzsche, 'Preface' to *The Anti-Christ*, in Aaron Ridley (ed.), Judith Norman (trans.), *The Anti-Christ, Ecce Homo, Twilight of the Idols, and Other Writings* (Cambridge: Cambridge University Press, 2005), p. 3.

Chapter 1

Technical Mentality[1]

Gilbert Simondon, translated by Arne De Boever[2]

This chapter is not concerned with ontology but with axiology. It aims to show that there exists a technical mentality, and that this mentality is developing, and is therefore incomplete and at risk of being prematurely considered as monstrous and unbalanced. It requires a preliminary attitude of *generosity* towards the order of reality that it seeks to manifest, because this incomplete genesis brings into play values that a general refusal [of this mentality] would condemn to ignorance and would risk negating.

We will try to show that the technical mentality is coherent, positive, productive in the domain of the cognitive schemas, but incomplete and in conflict with itself in the domain of the affective categories because it has not yet properly emerged; and finally, that it is without unity and is almost entirely to be construed within the order of the will.

COGNITIVE SCHEMAS

The theoretical domain was the first to emerge in Western civilizations, the first to have been theorized, systematized and formalized. It has led to productive constructions and it presents in itself a method of discovery and interpretation that can be generalized. In this sense, the technical mentality offers a mode of knowledge *sui generis* that essentially uses the analogical transfer and the paradigm, and founds itself on the discovery of common modes of functioning – or of regime of operation – in otherwise different orders of reality that are chosen just as well from the living or the inert as from the human or the non-human.

Leaving Antiquity[3] aside, technology has already yielded in at least two ways schemas of intelligibility that are endowed with a latent power of universality: namely, in the form of the Cartesian mechanism and of cybernetic theory.

In the Cartesian mechanism, the fundamental operation of the simple machine is analogous to the functioning of logical thought capable of being rigorous and productive. A simple machine is a transfer system that, in the particular case in which the movement is presumed to be reversible, in the state of equilibrium, establishes the identity of a work that puts into motion and a work that resists. If each piece of the machine carries out this transfer rigorously, the number of pieces can be whatever; what changes is merely the direction of forces – as with the pulley – or the factors (force and movement) of a product that remains constant, as in the case of the pulley-blocks. The rational mental process returns the essence of the customary technical objects to this transfer schema: a chain is an enchainment of links, with the second link being fixed to the first just as the first is fixed to the anchoring ring. The transfer of forces goes from link to link, so that if each link is welded well and there are no gaps in the enchainment, the last link is fixed to the anchoring point in a more mediated but also more rigorous way than the first. A building, stone upon stone, row upon row, is a transfer of the 'certum quid et inconcussum' – the resistance of the stone of the foundations – all the way to the top, through successive levels that each acts as the foundation for the immediately following higher level. This intelligibility of the transfer without losses that mechanizes ideally and analogically (but also in reality, by virtue of the Cartesian conception of knowledge) all the modes of the real, applies not only to the RES EXTENSA but also to the RES COGITANS: the 'long chains of reasons' carry out a 'transport of evidence' from the premises to the conclusion, just like a chain carries out a transfer of forces from the anchoring point to the last link. The rules of the method are not only inspired by mathematics; they also perfectly conform to the different stages of fabrication and technical control. Thought needs an anchoring point that is the operative equivalent of the stone under the building, or of the ring that is attached to the origin of the chain: *certum quid et inconcussum*: it is *evident* what remains after all attempts at deconstruction, even after hyperbolic doubt. The conduct of reasoning requires an analysis – a division of the difficulty into as many parts as possible and as needed in order to better solve the difficulty – because each piece of the intellectual montage must play a simple, univocal role – like a pulley, a lever of which the mechanical function in the whole is simple and perfectly clear. The third rule (of the synthesis or the order) is the arrangement according to the schema of the completely unified whole of the machine. Finally, the fourth rule, that of control, is the unification of the placement of the different pieces and the adaptation of the machine as a whole to the two realities at both ends of the chain.

What is carried out in both the rational study of machines and in the conduct of thought is the *transfer without losses*: science and philosophy are possible because the transfer without losses is presumed to be possible. Consequently, the only domains that are accessible to philosophical reflection are those with a continuous structure. It will therefore be clear why Descartes has wanted to consider living beings as machines: if they were not machines *ontologically*, they would have to be so at least *analogically* in order to be objects of science.

Cybernetics, which was born from the mathematization of the automatic regulation apparatuses [*dispositifs*] – particularly useful for the construction of guidance technologies of airplanes in flight – introduces into this the recurrence of information on a relay apparatus as the basic schema that allows for an active adaptation to a spontaneous finality. This technical realization of a finalized conduct has served as a model of intelligibility for the study of a large number of regulations – or of regulation failures – in the living, both human and non-human, and of phenomena subject to becoming, such as the species equilibrium between predators and objects of prey, or of geographical and meteorological phenomena: variations of the level of lakes, climatic regimes.

In this sense, technology manifests in successive waves a power of analogical interpretation that is *sui generis*; indeed, it is not hemmed in by the limits of repartition of essences or of domains of reality. It does not have recourse to categories, leaves aside generic relations, special relations and specific differences. None of the schemas exhausts a domain, but each of them accounts for a certain number of effects in each domain, and allows for the passage of one domain to another. This transcategorical knowledge, which supposes a theory of knowledge that would be the close kin of a truly realist idealism, is particularly fit to grasp the universality of a mode of activity, of a regime of operation; it leaves aside the problem of the atemporal nature of beings and of the modes of the real; it applies to their functionings; it tends towards a phenomenology of regimes of activity, without an ontological presupposition that is relative to the nature of that which enters into activity. Each of the schemas applies only to certain regimes of each region, but it can in principle apply to any regime of any region.

The application of such schemas of intelligibility requires two main conditions, which can be presented as postulates of the 'technical mentality':

1. *The subsets are relatively detachable from the whole of which they are a part*. What technical activity produces is not an absolutely indivisible organism that is metaphysically one and undissolvable. The

technical object can be repaired; it can be completed; a simple analogy between the technical object and the living is fallacious, in the sense that, at the moment of its very construction, the technical object is conceived as something that may need control, repair and maintenance, through testing and modification, or, if necessary, a complete change of one or several of the subsets that compose it. This is what one calls anticipated 'maintenance', to use the Anglo-Saxon term.

This postulate is extremely important when one questions the way in which one can engage with a living being, a human being or an institution. The holistic postulate, which is often presented as an attitude of respect for life, a person or the integrity of a tradition, is perhaps merely a lazy way out. To accept or reject a being wholesale, because it is a whole, is perhaps to avoid adopting towards it the more generous attitude: namely, that of careful examination. A truly technical attitude would be more refined than the easy fundamentalism of a moral judgment and of justice. The distinction of the subsets and of the modes of their relative *solidarity* would thus be the first mental work that is taught by the cognitive content of the technical mentality.[4]

2. The second postulate is that of the levels and the regimes: *if one wants to understand a being completely, one must study it by considering it in its entelechy, and not in its inactivity or its static state.*

The majority of technical realities are subject to the existence of a threshold to start up and to maintain their own functioning; above this threshold, they are absurd, self-destructive; below it, they are self-stable. Very often, the invention consists in supposing the conditions of their functioning realized – in supposing the threshold problem resolved. This is why the majority of inventions proceed by condensation and concretization, by reducing the number of primitive elements to a minimum, which is at the same time an optimum.

Such is the case, for example, with the stato-reactor of Leduc. On the ground, it is merely an absurd structure, incapable of providing a push in a determinate direction; but starting from a certain speed of movement, it becomes capable of maintaining its speed – in other words, its pushing forward – and of furnishing a usable energy of movement.

The GUIMBAL group – which is held entirely in the forced conduct of a dam – originally seemed absurd. The alternator is of such small dimensions that it seems that the armature must be destroyed by the Joule effect. But it is precisely this small dimension that allows for the alternator to be lodged completely within the canalization, on the turbine axis itself. This ensures a cooling that has a considerably greater effect than that of an alternator placed in the air. This disposition is made possible by putting the alternator in a casing filled with oil, which heightens the isolation and improves the thermal exchanges, all the while ensuring the lubrication of the different levels and preventing water from coming in; here, the multifunctional character of the oil of the casing is the very schema of concretization that makes the invention exist, as a *regime* of functioning.

Analogically, it is possible to anticipate the existence, within different orders of reality, of certain *effects* (used here as in the expressions 'the Raman effect', 'the Compton effect') that for their existence require determinate thresholds to be crossed. These effects are not *things*; they imply, as their condition, the existence of certain *structures*. An internal combustion engine that is turned off is in a stable state and cannot turn itself on; it needs a certain amount of energy coming from outside, it needs to receive a certain angular speed in order to reach the threshold of self-maintenance, the threshold beyond which it functions as a regime of automatism, with each phase of the cycle preparing the conditions of completion for the following phase.

From these few observations, we can conclude that the technical mentality already offers coherent and usable schemas for a cognitive interpretation. With the Cartesian mechanism and cybernetics, it has already yielded two movements of thought; but in the case when there is an awareness of the systematic use of the two postulates presented above, it also appears to be capable of contributing to the formation of larger schemas.

AFFECTIVE MODALITIES

The picture is much less clear, however, as soon as one tries to analyse affective contents. In this case, one encounters an antagonism between the artisanal and the industrial modalities, an antagonism that is paired to an impossibility of completely separating these two aspects. The craftsman's nostalgia traverses not only the industrial life of production, but also the different daily regimes of the consumption of goods coming from the industrial world.

It is difficult to return a bundle of perfectly coherent and unified traits to the opposition between the artisanal and the industrial modality when one wants to account for the genesis of affective modalities. However, we will propose a criterion that, after several attempts, seemed to be the least problematic: in the case of the craftsman, all conditions depend on the human being; the source of energy is the same as that of information. The two sources are both in the human operator. There, energy is like the availability of the gesture, the exercise of muscular force; information simultaneously resides in the human operator as something learned, drawn from the individual past enriched by education, and as the actual exercise of the sensorial equipment that controls and regulates the application of the learned gestures to the concrete materiality of the workable material and to the particular characteristics of the aim [of the work]. The manipulation is carried out according to continuous schemas on realities that are of the same scale as the operator. Correlatively, the distance between the act of working and the conditions of use of the product of the work is weak. The shoemaker has directly taken the measurements, the saddler knows for which horse he is working. Recurrence is possible; the speed with which the object wears off, the types of deformation of the product during usage are known to the craftsman, who not only constructs but also repairs.

Moreover, in the case of the craftsman, the relation between the Human Being and Nature is immediate, because it lies in the choice of the materials and of the work that is done on them. In the artisanal modality, work is artifice; it orders and makes act differently workable materials that are almost primary materials, but that remain close to the natural state, like leather or wood. Artisanal work is generally not preceded by a complete transformation of these primary materials. The latter would require the investment of sources of energy taken from outside of the human body. In this sense, such a transformation comes – even in the pre-industrial state – from an industrial schema: namely, that of metallurgy, which is industrial through the transformation of the mineral into metal, even if it remains artisanal because of the way it produces objects.

The industrial modality appears when the source of information and the source of energy separate: namely, when the Human Being is merely the source of information, and Nature is required to furnish the energy. The machine is different from the tool in that it is a relay; it has two different entry points, that of energy and that of information. The fabricated product that it yields is the effect of the modulation of this energy through this information, the effect that is practised on a workable material. In the case of the tool, which is handheld, the entry of energy and the entry of information are mixed, or at the very least partially superimposed. Of course, one can guide the chisel of the sculptor with one hand, and push it with the other, but it is the same body that harmonizes the two hands, and a single nervous system that appropriates their movement into such detail from the material and for the set aim. Moreover, the potter's work, which is moved by his feet, is still of the same kind, but it allows one to anticipate the birth of the machine. Glass-making is artisanal in so far as the glass-maker furnishes the energy that dilates the initial bubble by blowing, and in so far as he regulates through the rhythm of his blowing the speed of the plastic deformation of the glass. But it becomes industrial when the energy is borrowed from a compressor.

When he borrows energy from a natural source, the human being discovers an infinite reserve, and comes to possess a considerable power. For it is possible to set up a series of relays, which means that a weak energy can lead to the usage of considerable energies.[5]

Unfortunately, the *entry of information* that comes into the work is no longer unique in the way it is with the artisanal gesture; it happens through several moments and at several levels. It takes place a first time with the invention of the machine – an invention that sometimes implies the bringing into play of considerable zones of knowledge and the gathering of a large number of human beings. It happens a second time with the *construction* of the machine and the regulation of the machine, which are modes of activity that are different from the machine's usage. Finally, it happens a third and a fourth time, first in learning to work with the machine, and then in the machine's usage. Whereas the machine constitutes a complete technical schema, as the relation of nature and the human being, as the encounter of information and energy operating on material, none of the four moments of information contribution is organically linked to and balanced out by the others. The act of information contribution becomes dissociated; it is exploded into separate moments taken on by separate individuals or groups. In order for the craftsman to recognize his equivalent in the industrial modality, the same human being must be inventor, constructor and operator. However, the effect of this amplification and complication of the industrial world is to spread out the different roles from each other: not only the source of information from the source of energy and the source of primary material, but even the different tasks of information contribution. It is thus a weaker part of the total capacities of the human being that is engaged in the industrial act, both when s/he is operator and in the other roles of information contribution. The iterative and fragmentary regime of the task of the operator in industrial production is an 'anatomy of work' that provokes different effects of industrial fatigue. But it is also exhausting to have only invention as a task, without also participating in construction and operation. The figure of the unhappy inventor came about at the same time as that of the dehumanized worker; it is its counter-type and it arises from the same cause. To put itself at the dimension of the machine's energy entry, the information entry complicates itself, becomes divided and specialized, with the result that the human being is isolated not only from nature[6] but also from himself, and enclosed in piecemeal tasks, even as inventor. He thus encounters the discontinuous through work.

However, trying to return to directly artisanal modes of production is an illusion. The needs of contemporary societies require not only large quantities of products and manufactured objects, but also states that cannot be obtained by means of the human body and by the tool. This is because the temperatures, the pressures, the required physical reactions, the scale of the conditions do not match those of human life. The workplace, on the other hand, is a *human environment.*

It is in this very emphasis on industrial production, in the deepening of its characteristics, that an overcoming of the antithesis between the artisanal modality and the industrial one can be studied with a greater likelihood of success. And this not only generally and superficially but also by means of what, within the industrial organization of the production, has pushed to its extreme limits the specialized fragmentation of human information contribution: the rationalization of work through a series of methods of which Taylorism was the first.

VOLUNTARY ACTION: A STUDY OF NORMS

But we must cut short here the consideration of the affective modalities in order to investigate norms of voluntary action, and thus to complete this construction of the technical mentality. Indeed, the technical mentality can be developed into schemes of action and into values, to the point of yielding a morality in human environments that are entirely dedicated to industrial production. But in so far as these environments remain separated from the social field of the usage of products, in so far as they themselves remain fragmented into several specialized groups by their different functions of information contribution to machines – mastery, technicians, workers – they cannot elaborate a value code that is capable of becoming universal because they do not have the experience of technical reality as a whole. The technocratic attitude cannot be universalized because it consists of reinventing the world like a neutral field for the penetration of machines; constructing a metal tower or an immense bridge undoubtedly means making a pioneer work and showing how industrial power can leave the factory in order to gain in nature, but there is something of the isolation of the inventor that subsists in this activity in so far as the tower or the bridge does not become part of a network covering the Earth in its mazes, in accordance with the geographical structures and living possibilities of this Earth. The Eiffel Tower and the Garabit viaduct must be considered as the arrival of the end of the industrial concentration around sources of energy or primary material sources: that is to say, not as spectacularly isolated centres and successes, but as the first maze of a virtual network. The Eiffel Tower, which was entirely designed and fabricated in the factory and only assembled on site, without a single correction, has now become the carrier of aerials; it interconnects with hundreds of pylons, masts and stations by which Europe will be covered. It becomes part of this multifunctional network that marks the key points of the geographical and human world.

It is the standardization of the subsets, the industrial possibility of the production of separate pieces that are all alike, that allows for the creation of networks. When one puts railroad tracks over hundreds of kilometers, when one rolls off a cable from city to city and sometimes from continent to continent, it is the industrial modality that takes leave from the industrial centre in order to extend itself through nature. It is not a question here of the rape of nature or of the victory of the Human Being over the elements, because in fact it is the natural structures themselves that serve as the attachment point for the network that is being developed; the relay points of the Hertzian 'cables', for example, rejoin with the high sites of ancient sacredness above the valleys and the seas.

Here, the technical mentality successfully completes itself and rejoins nature by turning itself into a thought-network, into the material and conceptual synthesis of particularity and concentration, individuality and collectivity – because the entire force of the network is available in each one of its points, and its mazes are woven together with those of the world, in the concrete and the particular.

The case of information networks is, so to speak, an ideal case where the success is virtually complete, because here energy and information are united again after having been separated in the industrial phase. At the same time, the assemblages and the substructures of the industrial gigantism return in a more manageable way, in a lighter form; electronics and telecommunications use reduced tonnages, moderate energies, dimensions that are not crushing. The factory rediscovers something of the workplace when it is transformed into a laboratory. It is no longer for the individual user, as in the artisanal modality, but for the simultaneously collective and individual user – nature itself – that the laboratory anticipates a made-to-measure assemblage. Such lines of pylons, such a chain of relays constitute the harness of nature. Only the fabrication of separate pieces remains industrial. At the same time, the distance between the inventor, the constructor and the operator is reduced; the three types converge towards the image of the technician, this time both intellectual and handy, who knows at the same time how to calculate and how to install cabling.

Very close to the case of information networks is that of networks of *energy distribution*. Electric energy is at the same time information and energy; on the one hand, it can be indefinitely paired down without a loss of productivity. A vibrator, which is a motor, can be located in the point of a tool as light as a pencil and feed on the network. A human being can easily manipulate with a single hand a 1/3 horsepower engine. This energy can, at the very moment of usage, entirely be modulated by information of which it becomes the faithful carrier. On the other hand, the very standardization of the conditions of energy production, which allows for the interconnection and normalized distribution, turns this energy into the carrier of information; one can ask the alternative network to make function (as the source of energy) a watch whose workings it regulates as carrier of information. The simultaneous usage is concretized in the synchronic motor.

Communication and transportation networks are, by contrast, less pure. They do not succeed in revealing themselves in their true function, and the technical mentality does not succeed in making itself heard in any preponderant way – first of all, because social or psychosocial inferences put a considerable burden [on these networks]; second, because, unlike information or energy networks, they are not entirely new and without functional antecedents. The railway enjoyed a privileged situation because it was relatively clearly distinct from the road, which meant that it could develop in an almost autonomous way. In the case of these other networks, however, the social begins to manifest itself in the form of *obsolescence*, the kind of disuse that is linked to the aging of convention and the transformation of social habits rather than a wearing-off or a loss of functionality of the technical object. A wagon with merchandise or a tender of a locomotive ages less quickly than a passenger car, with its ornaments and inscriptions; the one that is most overloaded with inessential ornaments is the one that goes out of fashion the most quickly.

But it is in the technical objects suited for the road network that the resistance opposed to the development of the technical mentality is the clearest. Obsolescence hits the passenger car much faster than the utility vehicle or the agricultural tractor, which nevertheless are its close cousins; the car ages faster than the plane, whereas the plane has technically gone through more important transformations than the car. This is because the plane is made for the runway and for the air. It is necessarily a *network reality* before being a separate object. The car is conceived not only as a network reality – like trucks – but as a social object, an item of clothing in which the user presents himself. It thus receives characteristics like the ones one used to wear on clothes and that overburdened them with lace and embroideries . . . these scale-like ornaments of psychosocial life – here, they become paint, chrome, aerials. The social importance can also express itself through mass, volume and the size of the vehicle.

To bring about the production of the technical mentality in the domain of voluntary choice, one could try to apply the categories of a common ethics of the relation between human beings: for example, the category of sincerity. A car deteriorates quickly because it was made to be seen rather than to be used; the space taken up by the width of the doors is not protected against rust; the underside is not treated according to the principles of aerodynamics whereas the visible parts are abundantly profiled.

But the essential is not there, and the introduction of a dualist moral system of good and evil, of the hidden and the manifest, would not lead one very far. To find real norms in this domain, one must return towards the cognitive schemas that have already been drawn out, and ask oneself how they can respond to the exigency manifested by the pressing incoherence of the affective modalities.

The reason for the inessential character of technical objects, which is at the same time the cause of this inflation of obsolescence that has hit the population of produced objects, is the absence of an industrial deepening of production.

A car becomes obsolete very fast because it is not one and the same act of invention, construction and production that simultaneously makes the road network and the cars appear. Between the network – this functional harness of the geographical world – and the cars that traverse this network, the human being inserts himself as a virtual buyer; a car only comes to function if it is bought, if it is chosen, after it has been produced. There is a recurrence that comes into play on the basis of this mediation. The constructor, who has to produce serially, needs to calculate the possibilities of sales; not only must he simultaneously construct the network and the cars, but he also has to anticipate this sales option. In order to be valuable, a car must be bought after having been constructed, like the Roman child who was put into the world by the mother but was only admitted to life after *elevatio*. One could also compare this alienated condition of the produced object in the situation of venality to that of a slave on the market in Antiquity, or to that of a woman in a situation of social inferiority; the introduction to active existence happens through means that are inadequate to the real functions. It takes place against entelechy and thus creates a duality, a prevalence of the inessential, a distortion of true nature; choice is made under the dubious influence of charm, prestige, flattery, of all the social myths or of personal faiths. In the inessential situation of the buyer – who is neither a constructor nor a user in act, the human being who chooses, introduces into his choice a bundle of non-technical norms. It is the anticipation, in the project of production, of the play of these norms that creates the mixed character of the venality of the industrial product, and that is the main source of obsolescence. The *distance* between the act of production and the act of usage, this lack of real information, allows for the introduction of the inessential, which creates obsolescence. Because it is judged once and for all, accepted or rejected in full in the decision or the refusal to buy, the object of industrial production is a closed object, a false organism that is seized by a holistic thought that was psycho-socially produced; it allows for neither the exercise nor the development of the technical mentality at the level of voluntary decisions and norms of action.

But how is it possible to pass to a structure of the object that would allow one to draw out the technical mentality? First of all, and generally speaking, a position of ascetism allows one to get rid of the artificial and unhealthy character of social burdens, which expresses itself through hypertelic developments or developments that in reality do not function. A contemporary transatlantic liner – a fake floating city rather than an instrument of travel – slowly tends towards the recruitment of lonely, idle ones; the cargo ship is more pure. This proliferation of the inessential already takes hold of the commercial aeroplane: the companies flatter the traveller; the plane grows bigger and heavier. But the essential lies in this: in order for an object to allow for the development of the technical mentality and to be chosen by it, the object itself needs to be of a reticular structure. If one imagines an object that, instead of being closed, offers parts that are conceived as being as close to indestructible as possible, and others by contrast in which there would be concentrated a very high capacity to adjust to each usage, or wear, or possible breakage in case of shock, of malfunctioning, then one obtains an *open* object that can be completed, improved, maintained in the state of perpetual actuality. An electric machine that is not provided with an organ of protection, whether a fuse or a circuit breaker, is only in appearance more simple than a protected machine. When there is an overload, the system of protection kicks in, and the machine becomes absolutely comparable to what it was before the accident, once the system of protection has been returned to its initial state. This return to the initial state presupposes standardization, normalization. The more rigorous this normalization, the more perfect the machine; this is the case with calibrated fuses, or also with electronic tubes that one replaces in a machine. This is the key point: the post-industrial technical object is the unity of two layers of reality – a layer that is as stable and permanent as possible, which adheres to the user and is made to last, and a layer that can be perpetually replaced, changed, renewed, because it is made up of elements that are all similar, impersonal, mass-produced by industry and distributed by all the networks of exchange. It is through participation in this network that the technical object always remains contemporary to its use, always new. However, this conservation in a state of full actuality is precisely made possible through the structures that the cognitive schemas provide; the object needs to heave thresholds of functioning that are known, measured, normalized in order for it to be able to be divided into permanent parts and parts that are voluntarily fragile and subjected to replacement. The object is not only *structure* but also *regime*. And the normalization of *thresholds of functioning* expresses itself in the difference between relatively separate subsets [of the whole]; the degree of solidarity is precisely the measure (in the Greek sense of 'metrion') of the relation between the permanent parts and the parts subject to replacement. This measure is what defines the optimum of the regime in the relation of thresholds of functioning.

In conclusion, one can say that the technical mentality is developing, but that this formation has a relation of causality that recurs with the very appearance of postindustrial technical realities; it makes explicit the nature of these realities and tends to furnish them with norms to ensure their development. Such a mentality can only develop if the affective antinomy of the *opposition* between the artisanal modality and the industrial one is replaced by the firm orientation of a voluntary push towards the development of technical networks, which are post-industrial and thus recover a continuous level [of operation].

If one seeks the sign of the perfection of the technical mentality, one can unite in a single criterion the manifestation of cognitive schemas, affective modalities and norms of action: that of the *opening*. Technical reality lends itself remarkably well to being continued, completed, perfected, extended. In this sense, an extension of the technical mentality is possible, and begins to manifest itself in the domain of the fine arts in particular. To construct a building according to the norms of the technical mentality means to conceive of it as being able to be enlarged, continued, amplified without disfiguration or erasure. The 'Le Corbusier monastery' at Eveux-l'Arbresle is a beautiful example of the contribution of the technical mentality in architecture; it includes within its plan its proper line of extension, for a further enlargement. And this is possible not only because of the architectural conception of the whole, but also because of the spirit of paring down that manifests itself in the choice of forms and the use of materials; it will be possible, without any break between the old and the new, still to use concrete, shuttering, iron, cables and the tubulature of long corridors. The non-dissimulation of means, this politeness of architecture towards its materials which translates itself by a constant technophany, amounts to a refusal of obsolescence and to the discovery amongst sensible species of the permanent availability of the industrial material as the foundation for the productive continuity of the work.

NOTES

1. This unpublished text by Simondon was given to us by his son Michel, to whose memory this publication is dedicated. – J.-H. Barthélémy and Vincent Bontems.
2. TN: This text initially appeared in: Jean-Hugues Barthélémy and Vincent Bontems (eds), *Gilbert Simondon. Revue philosophique*, 3 (2006), pp. 343–57. The editors would like to thank Nathalie Simondon and the Simondon family for giving them the authorization to publish this translation.
3. [W]hich has been rich in schemes of plasticity and of phase changes, reversible or irreversible. These come without a doubt from the artisanal techniques of preparation, the shaping and baking of the clay. These schemes of ontogenesis, coming from an operation entirely possessed by the human being, an operation that is continuous, progressive, and that conforms with the human being's scale, have encountered other schemes, themselves also ontogenetic, but including the encounter of opposed and qualitatively antagonistic principles that are spatially and geographically distinct, and of a dimension that renders them *transcendent* in relation to the human being: the earth and the heavens, the hot and the cold, the dry and the humid. In order for these two realities to encounter each other, they have to be at the same scale. The nature philosophy of Antiquity comes from the encounter of the artisanal and the magical schemes of genesis (*ta eph'èmin* and *ta ouk eph'èmin*), of the schemes of continuity and the schemes of discontinuity. Agriculture and nursery are indeed industries and craftsmanships, when the human being does not hold the possession of their means in hand: ISLAM.
4. When the Boeings started exploding in flight, it was a gross mistake to judge them as 'bad planes'; a more precise approach has consisted in studying the behaviour of cells subject to vibrations and constraints of internal suppression, so as to determine the zones of 'fatigue' of metal. A jurist, De Greef, says in *Notre destinée et nos instincts* [Our Destiny and Our Instincts] that a criminal would never be condemned if he were judged in his 'nursery' [in English in the original]; this is undoubtedly because, starting from this initial phase of his life, one would

consider him as *constructed*, as composed of different layers in relative solidarity to one another. The condemnation generally sacrifices something by considering the individual as a homogenous whole. This is how racism and xenophobia are produced.

5. In a certain sense, agriculture, nursing and navigation with sails are more industrial than artisanal, to the extent that they appeal to forces that *do not depend on the human being*, and that come from a reality of which the scale surpasses the scale of that which can be manipulated. These operations introduce the *discontinuous* to the same extent; they are, eventually, *alienating*, and can give rise to a *magico-religious exercise of thought*. Indeed, they *commodulate the human operation of preparation and the cosmological action*. Human work remains without results, after the seeds have been sown or the ship has been constructed, if the cosmic act (rain, wind, overflowing of the river) does not come in to receive and amplify the human effort. The human effort must be in accordance with the cosmic act, and be '*en kairo*'. In the nursing of cattle, the prosperity of the herd depends not only on the growth of vegetables and of the regime of waters, but also on the epizooties.

6. Industry isolates the human being from nature because it takes charge of the relation human being–nature; it *is*, indeed, through the relation to the human being, which replaces the reality of the cosmic order (the wind, the rain, the overflowing of the river, the epizooty) while diminishing to a certain extent its independence in relation to the human being, but conserving the transcendence of the dimension and the character of discontinuity, of irreversibility.

Explications

Chapter 2

'Technical Mentality' Revisited: Brian Massumi on Gilbert Simondon

With Arne De Boever, Alex Murray and Jon Roffe

Question (Q): Several years ago, you tried to get Simondon translated – and to no avail. We thought we could start with the question: why Simondon today? One can see why it would be important, historically, that Simondon is finally translated into English. But is there any reason why his thought strikes you as particularly relevant – philosophically, politically, culturally – today?

Answer (A): I did make strenuous efforts over a number of years, starting almost twenty years ago, to have Simondon translated for a book series I was co-editing. The director of the press flatly refused to consider it, saying there was no interest in Simondon and no audience for the work. At the time, he was probably right. Now the translations are under way, and are impatiently awaited in many quarters, with a sense that they are long overdue. So what changed? Why today?

It might help to start by talking about, why not then? The early 1990s was a very particular moment in English-speaking academics and cultural thought. The intellectual movements of the preceding three decades had succeeded in chipping significant cracks into the walls separating the academic disciplines, which had undergone a process of increasing specialization in the postwar period that many experienced as a Balkanization of knowledge. It wasn't just a question of the much-discussed 'two cultures' divide between science on the one hand and the humanities and social sciences on the other. It was just as strong between the humanities and the social sciences, and even internal to each. An interdisciplinary field of thought had emerged that asserted the right to draw syncretically on wide arrays of disciplines. Although the diversity of this interdisciplinary field was great, it had come to be known in the singular: 'Theory'. That infamous term (used mainly by its detractors) was unfortunate for many reasons, not the least of them being that a major stake for 'Theory' had always been not only renegotiating the divide between branches of knowledge, but also placing the resulting interdisciplinary field of thought back into immediate connection with cultural practice (Cultural Studies' interest in contestatory reappropriations of popular culture being the most obvious example). All of this coincided with an increasing preoccupation with what was already perceived to be an epochal shift toward a world integrally reshaped – culturally, socially, and economically – by digital technologies. The issue of technological change brought a reflux of interest in scientific modes of knowledge and the associated practices constituting them as a cultural force (as seen in the rise of Science and Technology Studies, and more generally in the concern with 'power-knowledge' formations). This wasn't a return of the 'two cultures' question, although rear-guard attempts were made to rewrap it in that old packaging, most symptomatically in the Sokal affair. In fact, what was happening was that the intellectual terrain had shifted to the extent that the imbrication of the 'two cultures' was taken as a given.

The question was where this latest phase of their imbrication was leading. For many, it was toward the dawn of a posthuman age. Others scoffed at the millennarian tone. But where the opposing camps met was in the assumption that what was playing out potentially concerned the very nature of the human, and the conditions under which it changes – basically, how we *become*. Technology had come to be seen to be a constitutive factor in human life – and with biotechnology, in life itself. The question of technology was now directly a question of the constitution of being – in a word, ontology. Or more precisely: because, given the juncture, the question of being had to be approached from the angle of becoming; it was a question of *ontogenesis*. The ontogenesis at issue was constitutively entangled with modes of knowledge and their associated practices, so the problem was as directly epistemological as it was ontological.

What makes all this relevant to the question of Simondon is that his work was already there. His key concept of 'individuation' asserts the primacy of ontogenesis, a primacy of processes of becoming over the states of being through which they pass. Further, Simondon approached the question of epistemology as a function of ontogenesis. There is an individuation of thought, he said, by the same token by which there is an individuation of matter, on the physical plane and from there on to the plane of life, and following – or prolonging – the same constitutive principles. He recognized technological innovation as a key theatre of thought materializing in matter becoming, in ways imbricated with life transformations. Technology was a fundamental concern for him throughout. So Simondon was already there. The problem was that the terrain of 'Theory', or whatever less loaded appellation the interdisciplinary landscape of that period might be called by, was not. It was, in fact, unequal to the question of ontogenesis that it was called upon to take up by virtue of the juncture at which it found itself.

The problem was that the dominant currents of thought were hobbled by the very moves that had enabled them to reach that juncture, and in ways that excluded Simondon's approach from gaining any purchase. Speaking very generally, the overall orientation was constructivist. Constructivism does connote becoming. Its posture is that things can't be taken as givens, rather they come to be. Up to that point at least, the constructivism of this period was not incompatible with Simondon. But the constructivism of the period played out in ways that radically diverge from the direction he indicates. What was considered to come into being was less things than new social or cultural takes on them. What is constructed are fundamentally perspectives or paradigms, and the corresponding subject positions. Within the 1990s constructivist model these were understood in terms of signifying structures or coding, typically applying models derived from linguistics and rhetoric. This telescoped becoming on to the human plane. At the same time, it reduced the constitution of the human plane to the question of the human subject (if not its effective construction, then the impossibility of it, or if not exactly that, its subversion). A vicious circle results. The only conceptual tools available are prehumanized by virtue of the models they derive from. But becoming-human only makes sense in relation to a non-human phase-shifting into it. And becoming-posthuman only makes sense in terms of the human phase-shifting out of itself, back into a non-human. If the non-human phases in and phases out, it is conceivable that it phases *through* – which raises the issue of the immanence of the non-human to all of the vicissitudes of the human. Constructivism does not have the resources even to articulate effectively the issue of the non-human necessarily raised by ontogenesis, let alone begin to resolve it. All the less so in that the figure of the non-human is ultimately that of matter, and the question of matter that of nature – which is radically bracketed by constructivism for fear of falling into a 'naive realism'. In other words, for fear of attributing an ontological status to what lies 'outside' of social and cultural constructs. Ontology, several generations of theorists were taught, was the enemy. Epistemology, which always carries ontological presuppositions of one kind or another, was at best a false friend. Finding a path to ontogenesis by unabashedly bringing the two together again, albeit in a new way, was simply inconceivable.

Had it been conceivable, bringing them together on a level with matter, as part of what, as a result, could only be considered a nature philosophy, would be scandalous. To do that while purporting to make the resulting nature philosophy coextensive with a theory of information, would be downright absurd. Information, on a level with matter, would be a-signifying, making signification . . . what? 'An invention', Simondon would not hesitate to answer. And not just in the technical sense. Already in relation to the non-human, with the individuations of the physical and biological planes. For Simondon's thought to resonate, constructivism has to make room for an integral inventivism (if such a word exists). An inventivism that is not afraid of nature and *its* creativity.

This is all to say that I think the conditions are right today for Simondon to have a major impact, for it to make sense to consider an inventivist conversion of the kind of constructivism whose portrait I just painted, in far too brutal strokes. Much has changed in the intervening years. Modes of thought more comprehensibly and suggestively in dialogue with Simondon's have left their mark. Deleuze and Guattari, Bergson, Spinoza, and now Whitehead have garnered significant interest. Linguistics-based models have been reconsidered in light of models privileging affect (or affectivity, as Simondon would say). New forms of constructivism privileging the notion of invention are being developed: for example, by Isabelle Stengers. The conditions are right. The one thing that worries me is that there seems to be a tendency to concentrate on Simondon's theory of the technical object to the exclusion of the other aspects of this thought – physical individuation, vital individuation and psychic individuation (synonymous for him with collective individuation). The force of *Du mode d'existence des objets techniques* [On the Mode of Existence of Technical Objects][1] cannot be fully understood in isolation from the overall theory of qualitative change – what he calls 'allagmatics' – which is dedicated to understanding these modes of individuation in their relation to each other. Even within the book on technology, a major stake is the distinction between the technical object and the aesthetic object. In the context of Simondon's overall philosophy, the study of the one necessarily invokes the other. The appearance of his works in translation will hopefully do much to encourage an understanding of his thinking about technology in their 'natural' Simondonian habitat.

Q: You say that Simondon's thought on technical objects cannot be understood outside of the context of his theory of individuation. Could you explain this a little bit further, perhaps by drawing from the essay 'Technical Mentality' that is published in this volume?

A: The essay on 'Technical Mentality' is a fascinating case in point and might very well occupy us for the rest of the conversation. On the one hand, it is startlingly contemporary in its concerns, linking as it does the question of the nature of the technical object to the evolution of the network, long before the developments we have all experienced since his time – most notably, the rise of the internet – had created a general awareness of the necessity of that move. His evocation of the technical object evolving through the network into a postindustrial 'open object' frames the discussion in a way that is of the utmost relevance to today's situation. On the other hand, the essay employs a good deal of vocabulary which, read in isolation from the rest of his work, can come across as terribly anachronistic, if not downright off-putting. He speaks of a technical mentality 'harnessing nature' through increasingly norm-based functioning structurally embodying the proper 'cognitive schema' so as to eliminate the 'proliferation of the inessential' that comes when consumer choice interferes with design. This comes after a discussion of the difference between the Cartesian mechanism, with its structured hierarchy ordered by an ideal of stability, and the cybernetic model of the continuously self-adapting system regulating itself through feedback mechanisms horizontally linking recurrent operations as a condition of possibility for any functional hierarchy. Simondon falls, of course, more to the cybernetic side, which he praises for its kinship with a 'true realist idealism'. A rapid reading might well be forgiven for mistaking Simondon's 'technical mentality' for a scarily normative vision of ultra-rationalized technocratic cyber-control. It would be just that, though – a mistake. While Simondon is unarguably closer to cybernetics than to Descartes, his theories diverge from cybernetics in fundamental ways, and his ethics also turn out to be anything but normative and technocratic.

It's complicated to untangle what he's getting at from a single essay addressing a specific question concerning the technical object, particularly one as thorny as its 'mentality', in isolation from the larger theoretical context he develops in his books. For example, in this essay Simondon mentions a water turbine invented by Jean Guimbal, which managed to miniaturize key components while ingeniously solving the associated problem of overheating. He refers in this connection to the 'schema of concretization which brings the invention into existence'. It would be natural to identify the schema of concretization with the cognitive schema he mentions far more frequently in the essay, and to understand the cognitive schema as an abstract model in the mind of the engineer that comes before the object and guides its construction. By that understanding, the origin of the technical object is purely cognitive, and entirely internal to the human thinking subject. Human thought precognizes a solution, then externalizes it by finding a way to mould matter to the form of its prethought solution. The practical finding of that way would be the technical process: the set of mediating actions shepherding the abstractly thought object into concrete embodiment. Invention would move from the past of a thought, cognitively fully formed, toward the future of an embodiment materially repeating the original thought's abstract form. The relation of the technical object to its cognitive origin would be one of resemblance: conformity to a formal model.

This is clearly *not* what Simondon means by concretization. If this were all there were to the story, Simondon would be trafficking in 'hylomorphism'. Hylomorphism, or the idea that the generation of form is reducible to the imposition upon inert matter of a pregiven abstract form, is the philosophical enemy which Simondon endeavours to undo throughout his work. There may indeed be an abstract model in the mind of a human engineer that, as Simondon says, 'presupposes that the problem is resolved'. But that is not what interests Simondon. He sees something else that takes him in a very different direction.

Q: Could you explain this a bit more, perhaps again by means of an example?

A: Just how far away his own thinking moves from any conventional cognitive model that might be applied to invention is signalled by the fact that he scrambles the causal order it assumes. In the section of *Du mode d'existence des objets techniques* following his discussion in that book of the Guimbal turbine, he links invention to an *action of the future on the present*. What can this mean? The veritable moment of invention, he says, is when a circular causality kicks in. In the case of the Guimbal turbine, it has to do with the potential for the oil in the turbine and the water around it each to play multiple roles. The water brings energy to the turbine, but it can also carry heat away from it. The oil carries the heat of the generator to the housing where it can be dissipated by the water, but it also insulates and lubricates the generator, and thanks to the pressure differential between it and the water, prevents infiltration. There are two sets of multifunctional potentials, one in the water and the other in the oil. The moment of invention is when the two sets of potentials click together, coupling into a single continuous system. A synergy clicks in. A new 'regime of functioning' has suddenly leapt into existence. A 'threshold' has been crossed, like a quantum leap to a qualitatively new plane of operation. The operation of the turbine is now 'self-maintaining'. It has achieved a certain operational autonomy, because the potentials in the water and in the oil have interlinked in such a way as to regulate the transfer of energy into the turbine and of heat out of it automatically, allowing the turbine to continue functioning independently without the intervention of an outside operator to run or repair it.

Before the passing of the threshold, there were two discontinuous energetic fields. The oil and the water were separated by differentials of temperature, pressure, viscosity and pattern of movement. The respective energetic fields of the oil and the water were in a state of what Simondon calls 'disparity'. When the synergy kicked in, the disparity rolled over into an emergent continuity. The differentials between the two fields are still there. But there is also something else, which has leapt into existence. There is a circularity between them, a recurrent feedback that has crossed a threshold to bring another plane of operation into existence. That plane of operation – of self-maintenance – is continuous. But its continuity moves *across* the difference. It comes into itself across the difference, from which it simultaneously separates itself to claim an operative autonomy as a qualitatively new regime of functioning. The new quality of operation arises as an 'effect' of the disparity. This is not the same as saying that the disparity is the cause. What brings the new quality of operation into existence is the circling into each other of the multifunctionalities of the energetic fields of the oil and the water: their entering into a dynamic relation.

What matters for Simondon is the paradox that, before the oil and the water entered into relation, the respective multifunctionalities were not in effect. They were nowhere. They are not to be found in the past. It is when the relation kicked in that they were determined, by that very event, to *have been* the potential for what has come. If the potential was not effectively there in the past, there is only one place it could have come from: the future. The respective multifunctional potentials of the oil and the water came into existence at the very instant their disparate fields clicked together into automatic relation. The potentials in the oil and the water for the turbine have been *invented* by the relation's energetic kicking in. Invention is the bringing into present operation of *future* functions that potentialize the present for an energetic leap into the new. The effect is a product of a recursive causality: an action of the future on the present. This is why Simondon insists that the technical object is not the product of a hylomorphic causality moving from past to future. A technical invention, he says, does not have a historical cause. It has an 'absolute origin': an autonomous taking-effect of a futurity, an effective coming into existence that conditions its own potential to be as it comes. Invention is less about cause than it is about self-conditioning emergence.

This completely changes how we must think about the 'mentality' of the technical object. The fact that there was an abstract model of the turbine in the mind of the designer is, in a way, secondary. The idea for the technical object is finally dependent for its effectiveness on the autonomous taking-effect of the relation. Either it clicks in or it doesn't. The designer can bring the two disparate fields of the water and the oil to the brink of relation, but the passing of the threshold belongs absolutely to *their* potential. The designer is a helpmate to emergence. He can put the pieces in place, moving through a linear series of steps progressing from the past of abstract conception to a present on the brink. But the passing of that threshold to invention depends on the potentialization of the elements presently in place as a function of their future. The new-found potential expresses itself as 'operative solidarity' between the elements, across the disparity of their fields. That solidarity is not the result of a simple step-by-step accumulation, or of piecemeal adding together of elements. It is non-decomposable. It is holistic. It's not a structure, he says. It does not add elements together to form a structural unity. Rather, it is a holism-effect that adds a whole new dimension of existence to the elements' diversity.

I should pause here for a moment to say something about why I am using the words 'holistic' and 'non-decomposable' in spite of Simondon's bitter criticism of holism in the essay, and his listing of the decomposability of the elements as the first postulate for a thinking of technical mentality. Simondon insists at the same time that the elements remain decomposable *and* that they give rise to an 'effect' that consists of a 'mode of functioning' characterized by an 'operational solidarity' – and thus an effective continuity. These two propositions must not be seen to be in contradiction. As Deleuze liked to say, the whole is not *of* the parts, but *alongside* them and *in addition to* them. Whitehead also has a formula for this: 'the many become one, and are increased by one.' What I am calling a holism-effect is just that: an *effect*. The word 'effect' is taken in a sense akin to the optical 'effect'. Deleuze, under Simondon's influence, also speaks of scientific effects attached to the proper names of the scientists who invented them. He takes the optical effect as a model. An optical effect is an excess effect of a visual whole that detaches itself from the diversity of the elements conditioning its appearance, without in any way annulling that diversity. An example is an optical illusion that suddenly 'snaps to', carrying the perceiver in one non-decomposable go across a threshold to a new unitary appearance. Simondon's bitter critique of 'holism' in the 'Technical Mentality' essay applies to philosophies which replace the diversity of conditions from which an effect arises with the non-decomposability of the arising whole, annulling their diversity and attributing a foundational ontological priority to the whole rather than rightly placing it on the level of emergent effect. This is one example of one of the most original aspects of Simondon's thought: his endeavouring always to think discontinuity and continuity *together* (an orientation he shares with William James's radical empiricism). This endeavour is encapsulated in his emphasis on the *quantum*, a notion that he is borrowing from physics. A quantum leap in physics is non-decomposable as a movement across a threshold. But its non-decomposability takes off from one set of diverse and decomposable conditions (a collection of particles in a particular configuration) and leads to another (a collection of particles in a changed configuration). The dynamic wholeness of the quantum event (the all-or-nothingness of its occurrence) interposes itself between two diversities, whose discontinuity it marks by a change in level accompanied by a qualitative change in the defining properties of the system (a passage, for example, from one element of the periodic table to another). For Simondon, all transition, all change, all becoming, is quantum.

Now to return to the role of the cognitive schema as pre-existing abstract form, in relation to the absolute origin as quantum event of emergence. Following intermediary steps suggested by the cognitive schema, the designer organizes diverse elements, moving through a process of past conditioning, to the brink of the present. At that 'critical point', the future effect takes over. It takes care of itself, making the automatic leap to being a self-maintaining system. That moment at which the system makes the leap into operative self-solidarity is the true moment of invention. The past-conditioning by the designer is boosted into a new dimension of existence by the sudden taking-effect of a future-conditioning. Potentialities snap into place, enabling a new regime of functioning, anticipatorily useful for the future, from whose own back-action they effectively came into being.

It is crucial to understand that the 'schema of concretization' is the snapping-to of the emergent operative solidarity. That is why

Simondon says in 'Technical Mentality' that the schema of concretization *is* the multifunctionality of the oil. He means it literally. The oil, in its potential coupling with the water, in operative solidarity with it toward future uses, *is* the schema of concretization. The schema of concretization is the effective entering-into-relation of the oil with the water. It does not conform to the cognitive schema that was in the mind of the designer, according to a principle of resemblance, as copy to model. It effectively takes off from it into a new dimension of existence – which is that of the technical object's relation to its own autonomy. The snapping into operative solidarity of the coupled multifunctionalities of the formerly disparate energetic fields of the oil and the water *is* the schema of concretization. The instant of the schema of concretization's entering holistically into effect *is* the absolute origin of the technical object. It is not a cognitive form imposed from outside. It is flush with matter. It's the taking-effect of a new order of relation *of* matter. The taking-effect re-energizes matter, across the diversity of present elements and the disparity of their fields, propelling it on to a new emergent plane of operational solidarity, a new level of material existence. The schema of concretization is *immanent to matter's becoming*.

All of this has a major impact on how we understand the term of Simondon's that has been taken up the most widely and enthusiastically – that of the *associated milieu*. The associated milieu is often wrongly understood to be synonymous with 'environment'. It is interpreted as referring to the space surrounding the boundary of a technical object (or the membrane of an organism), considered from the point of view of the elements contained in that space that are liable to fuel the technical object's functioning. In fact, the associated milieu is not fundamentally a spatial concept. Simondon defines it as the '*regime*' of energy transfer *between* the technical object and its environment, *across* the boundary, by virtue of which the techical object takes on the autonomy of self-conditioning operative solidarity we were just discussing. The associated milieu is the *pattern* of energetic exchange that kicks in when the schema of concretization snaps to.[2] But its definition is not exclusively energetic either. Simondon ties it to the absolute origin. A being that has an associated milieu, he says, is also one that has an absolute origin (Simondon 1989: 57). This is because the regime of self-conditioning that makes the technical object functionally autonomous involves a circular causality, like that between the oil and the water in the Guimbal turbine, which cannot be mounted piece by piece. It comes of a piece, as a holism-effect, in a quantum leap through which the object's future potentials for functioning non-decomposably present themselves. The concept of the associated milieu is a philosophically loaded one, spiked with references to time, recursive causality, coming potential, and the immanence of the technical object's schema of concretization to matter's becoming. If it is simplified into a synonym for the environment, the force of its Simondonian complexity is lost.

Q: So how does Simondon's thought on technology depend on his theory of individuation? It seems that we still haven't quite addressed this point, which you insisted on at the beginning of our conversation.

A: Although Simondon never defines the term technical mentality in *Du mode d'existence des objets techniques*, and in fact doesn't use it in any of his published books, it is not hard to give it a meaning in keeping with his overall philosophical system – which is to say, a definition that is fundamentally *non-cognitive*, flush with matter and immanent to its becoming. The implications are far-reaching. Rather than modelling technical mentality on how we conventionally think about human cognition, Simondon's work challenges us to rethink human mentality in terms of a non-cognitive model, of which both human and technical mentality would be special cases. Given the lack of explicit development of the concept in Simondon's own work, it is perhaps not out of order to turn to another thinker to lend a hand. For Whitehead, each taking-form involves 'the swing over from reenaction to anticipation' due to an 'intervening touch of mentality'. He speaks of the re-enaction in terms very similar to Simondon, as an 'energizing' of a given set of conditions inherited from the past. The swing-over to anticipation introduces novelty into the world. A taking-form 'arises as an effect facing its past', no sooner to turn away from its past to become 'a cause facing its future': a future cause.[3] The snapping-to exemplified in the taking-effect of the operational solidarity (the 'subjective form' in Whitehead's vocabulary) of this new existence *is* the 'touch of mentality'. Whitehead also talks about this in terms of the passing of a quantum threshold consisting of the becoming of a qualitatively new existence. Saying that the becoming ends as a future cause does not mean that the invention, once it arises, takes its place in a linear chain of causality, as the historical origin of a reproductive series. The causation is always indirect, passing through an interval of immanence: a moment of concretization whose schema is immanent to active matter. Each subsequent exemplification of the mode of existence must return to the 'absolute origin', to come back to Simondon's vocabulary.

Technically speaking, it is this return event of formation – and not the form – that repeats itself. It is less that a form is reproduced, than that an invention repeats itself. If the repeat inventions fall into a strict pattern of conformity with each other, it is necessary to explain the serial production of this resemblance-effect. The collective conformity of a population of serially produced technical objects to the cognitive schema in the mind of the designer does not explain anything. It skips over all the 'intermediaries' – the chain of past actions bringing the elements to the threshold where they holistically take effect facing their future. It skips over the diversity of the elements. It skips over the disparity of their resident fields. It skips over the quantum leap of becoming that crosses the disparity, in the coming to effective existence of a new level. It skips over the touch of mentality immanent to matter. It forgets the action of the future. It forgets just about everything that is effectively ingredient of the event of invention. Far from explaining anything, the reproduction of resembling forms exemplifying an invention is precisely what is in need of explanation. The inheritance of the past conditions must have built-in constraints similarly limiting the degree of novelty of each retaking effect of the invention. Simondon accounts for these limiting conditions that serially restrict exemplifications of an invention to a formal resemblance to each other in terms of *standardization*. The technical object is an individuation – an event of taking-form – whose past conditioning precontains the coming potential of its functional autonomy within certain standardized parameters. The parameters are homeostatic, or equilibrium-tending. The technical object has only the margin of functional autonomy allowing it to maintain itself homeostatically. The key point is that the moment of technical mentality – the *technicity* of the technical object – is always immanent to a material event of taking-form. This event occurs at a critical point where the past effectively swings over into a futurity of functioning. The event of self-futurizing serially repeats itself. The potentialization of which it consists repeats, with a past-conditioned latitude of becoming. The difference between the technical object and the living thing is a question of how great a latitude of becoming their past conditioning will permit. There is life when taking-form maintains itself at the brink. Life lives on a moving threshold of metastability, of fragile, provisional equilibrium that is subject to constant perturbation, from whose jaws it must repeatedly snatch its homeostasis. The living thing is an individuation that has no choice but to *continue* its invention, or face dissolution. Its homeostatic equilibrium is not a simple self-maintenance, but an ever-renewed achievement.

Q: Do you see a connection here with Simondon's theory of physical, vital and psychic (and collective) individuation?

A: Psychic individuation is a further continuation of the achievement of vital individuation that widens its latitude of becoming. Psychic individuation is when vital individuation continues across a quantum leap that brings into existence a new level of operation on which homeostasis does not necessarily have to be maintained, or even renewed. Of course, a homeostatic equilibrium must continue to be renewed on the vital level, to which psychic individuation remains coupled as a necessary condition of its taking effect. Its quantum leaping to its own level moves with life's moving equilibrium. But it takes effect with a qualitative difference. It has the latitude to continue its invention across changes in operational parameters. It can continue inventing itself in such a way as to continue becoming *different.* Maturation is the lowest degree of the psychic individuation of life. The invention of cognitive schemas exemplifies a higher degree. The invention of axiomatics – schemas for the translation of cognitive schemas into and out of each other – is a still higher degree. Allagmatics, the metaschematizing of axiomatics, is the highest degree, corresponding to what Deleuze and Guattari call conceptual creation, and Guattari in his solo work 'meta-modelization'.

The crucial point is that all of these are *individuations* in their own right. There is an individuation of modes of thought, by the same token by which there is an individuation of modes of physical, technical and vital individuation. There is no linear causality between any of them. Each is an effective invention bringing into existence an autonomous level of operational solidarity. None can be adequately explainable without reference to an absolute origin. Each must return in its own way, at every iteration, to the absolute origin: an interval of immanence where taking-effect is flush with a self-formative activity of matter as immanent cause. Their coming to existence cannot be explained without eventfully factoring in this immanent cause.

All of the key terms of Simondon's philosophy revolve around the moment of inventive, eventive taking-effect, and taking *new* effect. In *L'Individu et sa genèse physico-biologique,* Simondon calls the holism-effect which clicks in at this point a *resonance.* Then he defines *matter* as this very resonance. Matter is thus defined in terms of a *form-taking activity* immanent to the event of taking-form. Nothing could be further from the form-receiving passivity of matter assumed by the hylomorphic model. *Nature* is then the universality of this immanent form-taking activity that is matter: that is, its immanence to each event of taking-form, as the principle of individuation animating every coming into existence. The disparity between energetic fields, from the point of view of the potential that their synergistic taking-effect brings into the present from the future, Simondon names the *pre-individual*. The disparity itself is *information*. Then there is a specific term for the clinching into synergistic relation of a diversity of elements, across the disparity of information and toward the emergence of a new level of functioning realizing the potential of the pre-individual. That term is *mediation*.

The definitions could go on indefinitely to cover the entire Simondonian repertory, all revolving around the same critical point of absolute origination. All of the familiar words that come back around that point take on startlingly new meanings which it is crucial to hang on to if one is to follow Simondon's thinking. Simondon's 'mediation', for example, has nothing to do with the meaning of that term in Communication Studies, Media Studies, or Cultural Studies. In Simondon, the term carries ontogenetic force, referring to a snapping into relation effecting a self-inventive passing to a new level of existence. Information, for its part, pertains to the 'pre-individual' preparatory to that passage. Information – Simondon is unambiguous about this – has no content, no structure and no meaning. In itself, it is nothing but disparity. Its *meaning* is the coming into existence of the new level that effectively takes off from the disparity and resolves the discontinuity it exhibits into a continuity of operation. Information is redefined in terms of this *event*. As for Gregory Bateson, information is a 'difference that makes a difference': a disparity that actively yields a new quantum of effect, and whose meaning is the novelty value of that effect. What differentiates Simondon in general from the cybernetic and information-theory traditions out of which Bateson was working (in particular, what differentiates him from Wiener and Shannon / Weaver) is that, for Simondon, this differencing process can in no way be understood in quantitative terms, and is not susceptible to any kind of stable formalization. The differencing process is not describable in quantitative terms because, although a quantum leap does coincide with the discharge of a measurable amount of energy, it also coincides with a passing of a threshold to a qualitatively new level of existence. That qualitative crossing is the crucial point for Simondon. It requires for its understanding the mobilization of a whole stable of concepts beyond the pale of quantitative method. The process is not susceptible to any stable formalization because it is continually giving rise to new operational solidarities that did not exist before, and therefore exceed all prior formalization. The 'mentality' of the process always avails itself of a *potential energy* of invention, in relation to which quantification and formalization are constantly playing a perpetual game of catch-up. Neither ever catches up. Quantification is always labouring under a deficit of potential, and formalization under an energy deficit. Even working together, they can only get so far as the possible – according to Bergson, nothing more than an anaemic, back-cast shadow of potential.

Q: Could you talk a bit more about the significance of 'potential energy' in Simondon's thought?

A: It is Simondon's insistence on the centrality of the concept of potential energy that makes his philosophy a 'realist idealism'. It is what he himself points to as differentiating his thought from information theory and cybernetics. The potential of the energetic taking-form that is Simondon's individuation is *real* in the sense that it always comes to pass in the material clinching of an effective event. It is *ideal* in the sense that it comes into the effective present of that energetic event as the action of its future. The real and ideal are two facets of the same event. Together they make the event of individuation more resonantly material than any mere formalization, and give it more of a mental 'touch' than any set of quantities could ever have. What differentiates Simondon from Bateson himself is that Simondon never lets the touch of mentality hypostasize into a 'Mind' that is one with Nature. There is no 'Mind' immanent to Simondon's Nature – only form-taking informational *activity* (with as yet – that is to say, until its own future occurs to it – no content, no structure, no meaning). There is no 'one' but always a one *moreness*: a 'more-than-one', everywhere energetically in potential.

Returning to the question of technical mentality in Simondon's article, the relation between the cognitive schema and the schema of concretization can now be better understood. The cognitive schema resembles the schema of concretization that is the effective invention of the technical object not because it effectively moulds it, but in the sense that it underwent an individuation that is *operatively analogous* to it. It also took emergent effect, from a pre-individual field of thought (consisting of an unresolved disparity between perceptions, some present, some appearing only possible). It also passed a quantum threshold across which its operational solidarity came newly into existence (inventing the emergent meaning – the cognitive schema itself – capable of resolving the pre-individual perceptual disparity into a well-formed anticipation energetically facing its own effective future). Thus effectively formed, the cognitive schema was able to follow the recursive traces of its anticipatory emergence back to the future from which it came, strategically guiding the setting in place of elements piece by piece, progressing step by step to the very brink of invention. But not beyond. At that point, it can do no more. It has prepared the pre-individual field. But it cannot take the ultimate step. Because that step involves the arising from the pre-individual of a new autonomy: the coming into self-maintaining existence of a brand new mode of functioning. Only the technical object can clinch that for itself. The cognitive schema must pass on the baton of invention to the schema of concretization, and step back. For the next step is the point of absolute origination at which the technical object, formatively touched by its own mentality, emerges on to its own level of reality. It is the point at which the technicity of the object takes effect. It taking-effect takes a whole new form, through which it effectively declares its ontogenetic independence from the cognitive schema. It snaps to its own effect, immanent cause of its technical future.

The cognitive schema and the schema of concretization are in operative analogy with one another in the sense that it is this form-taking *process* that is repeated between them. It is not, strictly speaking, a form, or even a structure, that is reproduced by one for the other. A thought does not resemble a turbine. A disparity between perceptions present and possible is not structured like a disparity between water and oil. But the taking-effect of the operational solidarity of the cognitive schema in thought, and the taking-effect of the operational solidarity of a schema of concretization in turbine-technicity do 'resemble' each other in the sense that they exemplify the same ontogenetic process. Their comings-to-be follow the same principle of individuation. In addition, one coming-to-be ends up passing the processual baton to the next, ending as future-facing as it began at the point of its own absolute origin. The two individuations are not only in operative analogy. They form between themselves a *transductive* series (a forwarding of futurity down the processual line of absolute originations relaying each other, in operatively analogous takings-form).

When this transductive process is taken into account, what Simondon means by the cognitive schema 'harnessing nature' takes on a completely new meaning. It carries an inventive connotation that distances 'technical mentality' from any technocratic vision of rationality. The 'recognized, measured, normalized' thresholds of functioning he invokes at the end refer specifically to the standardization that past-conditions the serial emergence of the technical object. His point is that, when the technical object under consideration takes the form of the postindustrial *network*, the standarization is actually the past-condition for an *opening* of the technical process to an unheard-of future latitude of becoming. Through network standardization the technical object in fact accedes to some of the same natural potentials 'harnessed' by psychic individuation. It 'maintains itself' not in a homeostatic equilibrium, but in a 'perpetual actuality', wherein its inventive individuation is 'eminently apt to be continued'. More and more, it comes to 'carry its own line of prolongation on its own plane' of operational solidarity, in operative analogy with psychic individuation. The 'touch of mentality' that constitutes its technicity intensifies and expands. Technical mentality ideally-realizes itself more fully. It is 'augmented, continued, amplified'.

As this happens, technical individuation and psychic individuation come to the very brink of each other. They enter into a relation of transduction. In concert, they rejoin Nature, without 'disfiguring' it the way that Simondon considers that the opposition between the 'affective modalities' of the artisanal and the industrial has done. These technicities were in affective disparity. They were antipathic. Which made their disparity ineffective. Instead of clinching forward over a threshold to a qualitatively new level of existence, they stubbornly clung to their antipathy for one another, prolonging their disparity. They remained in 'inessential' – that is to say, ontogenetically ineffectual, naturally uninventive – pre-individual tension. This locked out any resolution of their disparity through a quantum leap of future-facing potential snapping-to, to newly individuating effect. The lock-in was to a relative level of collective ontogenetic stupidity.

If the stubborn disparity between artisanal and industrial technicity can be said to have defined post-Enlightenment humanity, it was as its own perpetual crisis. The period was locked in an ineffectual dialectic between nostalgia for the simpler, more bucolic 'humanness' of artisanal production and the 'progress' of the human bought at the price of its own fragmentation at the mercy of the manic Taylorist drive for industrial efficiency. Does the 'amplified' technical mentality of the 'postindustrial' network presage a more intelligent taking-form *beyond* the human? Do technical individuation and psychic individuation not only brink upon each other, but transductively merge into a single lineage? In postindustrial technicity, will the cognitive schema and the schema of concretization finally converge? Simondon doesn't explicitly pose this question, much less answer it. But it is a measure of the effective potential of his own conceptual inventiveness that he came to *its* brink, so far ahead in anticipation, and in a way that furnishes us today with future-facing resources apt to assist us in coming to our own response, as an expression of an ethics of becoming.

Personally, I shy away from posthumanist discourse. For me, a Simondonian ethics of becoming is best to be found not in a next 'post-human' phase, but in the *non-human* at the 'dephased' heart of every individuation, human and otherwise. What I mean by the non-human is the ontogenetic clinching of the pre-individual that catapults it over the threshold of becoming. I mean the individual – that non-decomposable solidarity of occurrent existence – at the brink. Just coming eventfully to be what it will always have been, at a level where it has, as yet, no content, no meaning, no structure, only past-conditioning future-facing. The really ideal 'absolute origin', as a function of which every quantum of individuation effectively ends where it causally begins, so as to inter-link emergently all individuations in that vast network of transductive more-than-oneness that is the process of Nature.

Q: Thank you very much for this interview.

NOTES

1. Gilbert Simondon, *Du mode d'existence des objets techniques* (Paris: Aubier, 1989).
2. Ibid., p. 57; Gilbert Simondon, *L'Individuation à la lumière des notions de forme et d'information* (Grenoble: Jérôme Millon, 2005), p. 62.
3. A. N. Whitehead, *Adventures of Ideas* (New York: Free Press, 1967), pp. 192–4.

Chapter 3

Identity and Individuation: Some Feminist Reflections

Elizabeth Grosz

There are, for Gilbert Simondon, many kinds of individualities, many kinds of subject, many kinds of object, but all share the processes of individuation, which may serve equally to explain the coming into being and the existence of beings of all kinds, material, organic, human, cosmic. Individuations are the processes that distinguish between inorganic and organic existences, between cultural and technological orders, between objects and subjects, as well as what enables these terms to be linked. His understanding of the processes of genesis of individualities of all kinds has surprising implications not only for philosophies of technology,[1] but also for forms of feminist, anti-racist and radical political thought. In providing models for understanding how things, including living beings, are brought into existence as cohesive individuals, Simondon opens up new ways of understanding identity, transformation and creation – all central ingredients in a radical reconceptualization of thought.

I want to discuss here how physical and biological individuals come to be, and what processes of becoming are involved in their genesis. What orders and materials – conceptual, natural, technological – are involved in the generation of individuality? What forces are at work forming, deforming and transforming individuality such that we can understand the forms of power, and the forces of resistance, that both enable and limit individuals? Can Simondon provide feminist and other modes of radical political thought with a different model by which to understand the concept of identity, not through a notion of the self-same, but through what is radically disparate and continually changing? Can we explain individuality through that which is itself not individualized, through processes of individuation?

INDIVIDUATIONS

The question of how to think the coming into existence of individuals without presupposing the identity on which such individuality is based is one of a number of preoccupations that dominate Simondon's work. He aims to avoid the usual processes of reverse engineering, in which a given object's process of production is deduced from the identity of the constituted object in the present. Such a process can only move from identity to identity, from one individual to all those that precede it. Instead, Simondon is interested in understanding how pre-individual forces, the forces that constitute the condition for both natural and technological existence, not yet individuated, produce individuals of various kinds.[2] Instead of beginning with already existing individualities, it is pre-individual forces and processes that occupy much of the process of the becoming of individuals:

> [T]he individual is to be understood as having a relative reality, occupying only a certain phase of the whole being in question – a phase that therefore carries the implication of a preceding pre-individual state, and that, even the single act of its appearance all the potentials embedded in the pre-individual state. Individuation, moreover, not only brings the individual to light but also the individual-milieu dyad. (300)

Pre-individual forces pre-exist and make possible the emergence of individuality, those forces which are actualized in the individual. They not only predate the individual, but also they constitute both the individual and the potentialities that the individual contains that sustain and transform it. The individual is always more than itself, for it is an individual with the ongoing potential to undergo further changes after it is constituted as such. These pre-individual forces also constitute the milieu within which the individual is located, which provide the ongoing virtualities with which the individual must engage. The individual is merely one phase in the process of individuation, which is surrounded both before and after its emergence by pre-individual forces, potentialities. Being is at once pre-individual, individuating and individuated; it becomes something, something emerges or erupts, but it leaves in its context or milieu a residue or excess that is the condition for future becomings.

The pre-individual state is the resource by which beings emerge from becoming. Individuation is the process by which this occurs. The pre-individual contains a wide range of disparate forces – virtual resources, potentialities, conjunctions, disjunctions which a being may, in its own way, actualize. Becoming is the mode of being of beings that are not self-contained, that function through a kind of disconnection or syncopation, that function as out of phase; it is the creation of a process of disparity that resolves itself and uses up some of the pre-individual resources in the constitution of an individual (whether an individual object, an individual technological object or a biological individual). Being results from a kind of solution to the disparities of becoming. Individuality is one kind of solution to emergent disparities:

> becoming exists as one of the dimensions of being . . . it corresponds to a capacity beings possess of falling out of step with themselves, of resolving themselves by the very act of falling out of step. *The pre-individual being is the being in which there are no steps.* The being in which individuation comes to fruition is that in which a resolution appears by its division into stages, which implies becoming: becoming is not a framework in which the being exists; it is one of the dimensions of the being, a mode of resolving an initial incompatibility that was rife with potentials. (300–1)

In a paragraph that is itself rife with potential, it is worth clarifying Simondon's claims here: the pre-individual is not static or inert but fundamentally dynamic. It generates forces which act upon each other, which generate tensions, points of excess, the development of a tipping point or form of emergence, forms of becoming that coexist at best uneasily. These points of instability are the sites around which individuality may emerge. These sites may be understood as problems, questions, which do not seek a solution so much as address an emergent force. Being, individuality, cohesion, a provisional ability to work amidst and to bring together certain forces, erupts from the pre-individual to bring together these otherwise ever more tense relations in a unity, whether organic or inorganic. It is not a solution to the problem but a response, a new kind of order and organization that provisionally integrates what was formerly a source of tension. Individuality is not given but engendered, prompted by instability, and is itself a reordering at a different level and in a different manner of instability.

The individual resolves this tension or instability by operating at a different level; but also, the individual is marked and shaped by the particular forces or tensions that enable its emergence. The individual is a mode of management of instability or excess rather than its overcoming. Individuality is thus not one type of being, but one *phase* of being, a period, a movement, neither an origin nor an end. It becomes, once it exists, a phase (or many) in what would otherwise have no phases, stages or steps; the pre-individual is 'supersaturated', filled with potentialities, forces, becomings that come to fruition in a level of organization that can harness, but not exhaust, some of these forces. This process for the elaboration and emergence of individuality or being from becoming or the pre-individual is an ontogenesis: that is, 'the becoming of the being insofar as it doubles itself and falls out of step with itself in the process of individuating' (301).

Such a being must be considered, not as a stable phenomenon, one at rest or equilibrium, where all a system's virtualities have been actualized. Simondon insists that the pre-individual is *metastable*, form-taking, oriented to certain types of organization, and that it generates provisional resolutions that maintain the ongoing genesis of ever-new and commonly unactualized virtualities. Both material *and* ideal, the pre-individual cannot adequately distinguish between terms that only apply to what has identity; it is supersaturated, always rife with potential. Its virtualities engender many actuals – individuals, processes, actions and events – but these virtualities are incapable of exhaustion; they always renew and transform themselves through the actualizations they engender and the energetic potentials they produce This real is full of potential energy, energy never able to be drained to form an exhausted or stable point, and always able to generate more becomings.

Individuation doubles the pre-individual; it is this doubling, the duplication of the forces of the real within the emergent individual at a different level or order, that both produces new levels and orders within the real and enables the individual produced to intervene in and transform the pre-individual as its milieu. The pre-individual is both individual and collective, both wave and corpuscle, both matter and energy, both form and matter, both space and time, both conceptual and material. It can be expressed equally through either term, though each then entails the other as its necessary milieu. Like the doubling of the image that constitutes stereoscopic vision, each image is the image of the other; but each is slightly different, askew, and it is their non-coincidence that produces the possibility of three-dimensional vision, of depth.

This is a process of disparation. It is only when two series, two events, two processes or images double each other with a slight difference that the possibility for the eruption of a new level, the production of a new order of metastability, opens up. The individual doubles some of the processes within the pre-individual, in its own unity, bringing into being a new order that resolves at a higher level the disparation of the lower. Concepts are themselves the disparation of the matter they address. They address and express only individuated beings, only the pre-individual reinscribed in a different order. Thus the concept and matter, space and time, individual and collective are each expressions of what is individuated and not what is individuating.[3] The disparity between the processes of individuation and the individual they generate is the condition for an ongoing becoming of the being. This disparity generates the being of becoming.

This disparity, the differential between principles organizing various forms and levels of the real, requires a mediation. Individuation is that process of mediation which requires both the existence of a tension or duality of terms, levels or orders of magnitude, and an initial 'absence of interactive communication' (304) between these two. The generation of individuals of various types invents a way of communicating or interaction between these two orders that enables a provisional stabilization of their tensions and the forces that orient them in two or more pre-individual directions. Individuation mediates between two incompatible orders, inventing a way of bringing them together piecemeal, actualizing contrary forces in the pre-individual by making them complementary, two elements or features of one and the same real. An individual emerges, a metastable being, which carries within itself the pre-individual forces from which it was produced, which remain the potential for ongoing individuations even within this constituted individual. The virtual forces of the pre-individual, in not being entirely used up by processes of actualization, remain an ongoing source of transformation, the generation of new virtualities and new paths of actualization. These constitute a kind of 'memory', an inherence of the past in the present and of the virtual in the actual, an inherence within the individual of the pre-individual resources whose disparity brought it into existence and which remain to regulate its ongoing individualizations.[4]

Individuality is thus the establishment of a mode of resonance among disparate forces that otherwise coexist only with tension. It is the constitution of an internal resonance that brings together its elements, as well as being part of a larger order within which the individual is itself a fragment within other individuations. The disparation between two orders, two forces or energies, induces a process, an individuation, that produces from these forces a system or an order that magnifies their force without exacerbating their tensions. The system formed, whether the unity or identity of a tool or machine, of a material object or process, or of a living being, draws on these disparities, forms itself through them and is marked by their particular forces, and thus preserves many of their qualities while transforming them into a cohesive individual:

> What one assumes to be a *relation* or a *duality of principles* is in fact the
> unfolding of being, which is more than a unity and more than an identity;
> becoming is a dimension of the being, not something that happens to it
> following a succession of events that affect a being already and originally
> given and substantial. (311)

The being is more than a unity, more than an identity, for it is also the
possibility for the transformation and even the undoing of unity and
identity, as well as the milieu within and against which any unity or
identity establishes itself. The being engendered by pre-individual forces
continues to be engendered and continues various becomings in its own
ways. In reducing being to an identity or unity, not only are the forces
of becoming reduced to forms of equilibrium, but also the milieu is
regarded as background instead of as constitutive, a part of the being,
represented not only as its exterior but also that with which it must
internally resonate.

TRANSDUCTION

This movement of individuation, the ontogenesis of the individual,
is generated by a movement that Simondon calls 'transduction'.
Transduction is a process in which an activity generates itself, elaborating and structuring a region in its vicinity as its domain. It is a movement
through different forces that transforms them through the elaboration
of dimensions, magnitudes, vectors, by enabling a being to exist amidst
their contrary and competing forces. Transduction crosses through the
pre-individual to structure it so that some thing can emerge, can create
itself from the resources and forces of the pre-individual.[5]

Transduction is the process by which the various pre-individual forces
move out of step with each other, generate a disparation, a problem,
which individuation addresses through the creation or discovery of a
process, event, dimension or object that enables a new order to emerge
at another level; it is the generation of relations that individuate. The
movement of individuation is transductive, in so far as it cuts across
many forces, strata, dimensions to generate momentary or longer
alignments that temporarily structure the chaos of the pre-individual.

The processes of transduction not only generate the coming together
of heterogeneous forces into a provisional unity, but they also explain
the structuring of that which surrounds the being or entity, its milieu,
thus producing a mode of territorialization or spatialization, a mode of
production of a field or terrain that surrounds and enables the being and

its transformations. Transduction generates the creative leap from the past and present of the pre-individual to the unknown future, as well as fields, regions, regimes which surround and enable the being in and as its milieu. It thus generates its own kinds of temporizations and spatializations (perhaps even colonizations). It is a kind of problem-solving force, just as induction and deduction attempt to solve certain kinds of problems (problems linked to already individuated terms rather than terms in the process of their production). It is a movement through the specifics of a real, like Bergsonian intuition, that discerns the natural contours of the real rather than its logical or abstract forms and uses these natural contours to develop a being that directly expresses them.

Transduction addresses singularity and particularity, the forces of the real in its nuanced specificity, rather than general rules as do deduction and induction. It is a 'logic' for the emergence of objects, things, processes rather than a mode of generating conclusions. It is the 'logic' of eruption, the coming into being of beings where before there were forces. Simondon claims that in some respects it functions like the dialectic, conserving and reconciling contradictory forces; but unlike the dialectic, there is no residue abandoned and left behind in superseding the opposing terms. Further, as Simondon notes, the dialectic presumes an already existing history and temporality, where transduction explains without assuming the genesis of time: *'time comes from the pre-individual just like the other dimensions that determine individuation'* (315, emphasis in the original). It thus articulates a logic of invention, of creativity, a mode of bringing into being something that sustains its own internal resonances while functioning within a milieu. This is not the logic of an inventor or a creator, but the logic of the invention of processes, objects and practices that produce themselves.

Transduction must take into account the form-producing qualities of various types of matter, the tendency within material systems for emergent order and the cascading effects of new modes of emergence on further forms and higher degrees of emergence. Simondon has articulated the mode of coming into being of all kinds of objects, not simply through humans who invent them (though he does address this too), but what it is that human inventors must capitalize on in order to invent – natural forces, laws, principles, materials, and their potential modes of mutation and transformation. But it must also take into account the mind-forming activities in which matter is also implicated, the ways in which the coagulating and transforming relations of matter generate problems to which the creation of mind, mentality, conceptuality is a kind of solution or mode of address. It is thus not a knowledge of individuation that Simondon seeks but a knowledge as individuation, a knowledge that is itself the transductive effect of processes preceding and exceeding knowledge.[6]

Transductive or transforming forces transmit energy even as they transform it from one type to another; and they inform matter, make matter meaningful, capable of new energies and resources that move them into another movement or order. Transductions generate metastable positions, those which individuals occupy. These individuals may be 'physical, biological, mental or social' (313), but what they share is the bringing together of disparate orders and forces to generate a particular being, which is contingent on the order and organization of lower-level beings. The biological individual requires, in order for it to exist, physical individuals; and mental individuals, concepts, ideas, thoughts, images require that biological individuals pre-exist them, just as social individuals – neighbourhoods, factories, workshops, cities, nations, and collectives of all kinds, whether human or animal – require a certain conceptual and perception cohesiveness of biological and conceptual individuals.

Each is, as it were, conditioned on the emergence of an order which it elaborates and intensifies. And each is directed by the maximal reharnessing of pre-individual forces in ever more inclusive ways, in ways that internally direct the emergent individual. Individuality is an ongoing and changing consequence of the ever more intense and close integration and transformation of 'elements' of the pre-individual into the inner operations of the constituted individual. This provides something like an open-ended entelechy for the being, a direction or orientation, not toward an end, but toward the maximization of the forces and processes which gave rise to the being. Beings are under an imperative to evolve, to harness and put to work ever more efficiently resources that are not resources until they find a way of being channelled. This is their becoming – to include what is outside and before into what is inside and becomes with the being.

MATTER / INFORMATION

What Simondon describes as individuation is a process of materialization that is not exclusively material. Materiality in its pre-individual state neither is distinct from conceptuality, nor is it to be identified with material objects – that is, with material individuals. If the pre-individual is material, it is the material without discernment, without the operation of a distinction between matter and its others, mind, spirit, soul; it is a materiality that includes ideality, conceptuality, mentality. Matter has a positive property immanent in any of its particular characteristics – it is capable of being modelled, formed. Matter has what Simondon understands as plasticity, the capacity to become something other than what it is now, as its positivity, its openness, its orientation to transformation.

The pre-individual is material only in this sense – that its resources, its contents, have not yet distinguished between terms that, when they become terms or entities, will be opposed. It is, in short, metastable. It is marked by singularities, specificities, particular forces, specific locations, singular potentialities. It is the order of pure difference, of difference without distinction, of disparity, a 'mobile overlapping of incompatible wholes, almost similar, and yet disparate'.[7] This pre-individual is the real, the world, the universe in its unordered givenness. What is given are singularities, specificities, tendencies, forces but not yet modes of ordering and organizing them into systems, levels, dimensions or orders. Chaos. A plethora of events but without outline, distinction, discernibility. Such matter is precisely not formless, pure unformed matter waiting for the Idea to take on form. Rather, matter is multiformed, for it has the potential or virtuality, the capacity, to take on a number of forms, not an unlimited capacity, but a capacity by virtue of, and limited to, its singularities.

Simondon's rejection of hylomorphism is by now quite well known. He rejects both terms in the hylomorphic schema, both the notion of matter as unformed indetermination and the notion of form as what actively imprints a model on the inert passivity of matter, a schema that has long been invested in the active / passive and masculine / feminine oppositions that have marked Greek philosophy and its heirs. His claim is not that matter is formless, but that it contains the potential for many different kinds of forms, many different kinds of individual. It is only by taking into account the particular configurations of informed matter and their potentials that new kinds of being are generated through new orders of becoming. These potentials are the possibilities precisely for disparate forms, for disparate modes of organization to erupt from materiality in this broad sense.

Simondon is interested in the capacity for emergence or evolution that this pre-individual real holds, its form-taking positivity. This is the self-organizing capacity of metastable states. Matter is the capacity to be organized in various limited but not contained forms. It is an openness to reordering, to transformation in its relations with other forces and forms in its vicinity. The processes of individuation can only begin when there is a provisional resolution of the disparity or tension between forces in relative proximity, not through logic but through the creation of a mode of interaction, a form of communication, created by actualizing some of the potential energy of the pre-individual. Disparation is the problem for which individuation is an attempt to provide a solution: how to draw the disparities together in some kind of higher-order resolution that maximizes and proliferates the potentialities from which they result? This is the 'experimental' task of the various orders and forms of matter, a task provided without a controlling consciousness and without any external mediation. It is the task internal to matter itself, its entelechy, its forms of orientation.

Individuation is the process initiated by the disparation of 'material' forces; it is a mode of resolution of the disparity through the constitution of a relation which draws together these differences, this misalignment. Individuation has two complementary effects: it generates an internal resonance between forces, the condition under which an individual as such might emerge; and it generates information, a relation of communication or exchange between the two disparate orders, in which one order brings in the forces of the outside, while the other provides from within itself a form. Individuation thus materializes new orders of information, where matter and information cannot be understood as separable (unlike in cybernetic models), but where each order marks the other and is in turn enhanced by it. Individuation takes place *between* matter and form in this new sense. Matter is not in-formed. Rather, its forms evolve, change, and contest the boundaries of its potential through its encounters with what resists, what itself forms and is formed.

LIFE

Life is not a special kind of substance, a vital force that must be definitively distinguished from matter. Rather, for Simondon as for Bergson, life is a deviation of matter, one of the forms that matter generates. In other words, life too, as much as matter, is a consequence of the same forces of individuation. Physical and vital individuations not only share the same pre-individual resources, but also the nuances by which life elaborates itself are to some extent already contained in physical individuations. The vital is an order of elaboration of the physical, which is itself the expression of the resolution of 'material' or pre-individual tensions or disparities.

What is so fascinating and relevant about Simondon's work for us now is his insistence that the modes of organization that characterize life are not all that different to the modes of organization that characterize physical systems. Physical and vital systems both retain a relation of constructive deformation and transformation between forms of matter and systems of information. Each retains its own relations of internal resonance and external force. Each is linked to the dual modes of elaboration that matter retains in materializing life itself. Life is a mode of matter's actualization. It therefore carries within it the laws of matter, along with the capacity to attenuate these laws (as the second law of thermodynamics affirms, life only returns to entropy at its termination).

Life is not a difference in kind from matter (as Bergson suggests) but a difference in degree; the living never attain the cohesion and unity of the material individual that 'crystallizes' all it needs of its pre-individual forces at once. There is no moment of attaining an individual, self-identical or stable state which dramatically transforms pre-individual forces, the disparities in potential energy between incommensurable and non-communicating forces, into fixed individuals, as occurs chemically in quantum-type leaps of molecular reorganization. In life, the processes of individuation never cease; they coexist with the duration of the living organism itself – the organism never fully coincides with itself, or attains an identity in which it is what it is. The living organism is more a singularity than an individual; and ironically, it is material individuals that attain the self-identity for which we assume a subject strives.

For Simondon, life is differentiated from the non-living by three principal differences. First, the living being's individuality is coextensive with a permanent process of individuation, whereas in the case of a physical object individuation may be effected through a single encounter, and through the reiteration of an initial encounter between two incompatible forces or orders of energy. In the case of the living being,

> individuation is no longer produced, as in the physical domain, in an instantaneous fashion, quantum-like, abrupt and definitive, leaving in its wake the duality of milieu and individual [as in the case of the movements of individuation that form a crystal from a super-saturated liquid] – the milieu having been deprived of the individual it no longer is, and the individual no longer possessing the wider dimensions of the milieu. It is no doubt true that such a view of individuation is valid for the living being when it is considered as an absolute origin, but it is matched by a perpetual individuation, like the crystal or molecule, but is a veritable theater of individuation. (304–5)

Second, the living being produces individuations from an internal resonance, and not simply through the disparity between internal and external forces, a disparity between its internal qualities and its external milieu – it thus grows not only at its extremities, the points of surface contact with its outside, but from within, through an internal organization. Unlike the crystal which elaborates itself at its surface, the border between it and its milieu, the living being elaborates itself from within, through the forces of its internal resonances:

> the entire activity of the living being is not, like that of the physical individual, concentrated at its boundary with the outside world. There exists within the being a more complete regime of *internal resonance* requiring permanent communication and maintaining a metastability that is the precondition of life. (305)

And third, the living individual engenders continuous individuations from within itself. It directs itself to problems, provocations not only through adaptation, but also through the potential to reconsider its own internal organization, through its own individuating interiority, the condition for the eruption of conceptuality itself:

> The living being resolves its problems not only by adapting itself – which is to say by modifying its relations with its milieu (something a machine is equally able to do) – but by modifying itself through the invention of new internal structures and its complete self-insertion into the axiomatic of organic problems. *The living individual is a system of individuation, an individuating system and also a system that individuates.* (305)

Life modifies itself, where the physical individual is modified by its milieu. Life exists within itself and not only at the borders of its engagement with its milieu. Life elaborates itself through the ways in which its engagements with its milieu reconstitute or reframe its internal resonances. Life resonates, as it translates information. It exchanges energy and information, in the same manner as matter but at a different level or dimension, and directed at different problems.

The crystal, a favourite image for the individuating process for Simondon but one that privileges the formation of the physical individual, is produced at the boundary between itself and its milieu. It accrues through iteration rather than transformation; it grows outward, but only at its surface; its inner resonances are its outer forces at work. Whatever internal resonance it has is established through the direct impact of its pre-individual forces. It solves the problems it addresses – the problems of the differential potential energies within the pre-individual forces from which it emerges – once and for all, in one action. The physical individual is, for Simondon, 'perpetually ex-centric, perpetually peripheral in relation to itself, active at the limits of its own terrain' (305), while the living individual, by contrast, is fundamentally a kind of attunement between its modes of internal resonances and the forces that make up its environment or context. Each 'element' of its interior is in contact with all of its interiority.

Life becomes self-organizing through the prolongation and resonance of an internal disparity, an out-of-phase-ness[8] with itself that it shares with matter. Life remains indebted to the pre-individual to the extent that the resources for all its becomings, all its future individuations, self-actualizations, must be drawn from these singularities which its own must incorporate. The 'phases' of life, from fertilized egg to corpse, are internally structured, organized through the forces that enable life to elaborate itself; they are part of the permanent processes of individuation that occur even when an individual has already been produced. Life does not emerge as a self-driven force; rather, it is possible only to the extent that it perpetuates but also finds a further form of elaboration and development of the pre-individual and of physical individuality.

The emergence of life from the self-organizing properties of matter provides the conditions for a series of ongoing becomings, becomings that elaborate and experiment with the forms of life and their immanent conditions for transformation and for the emergence of new self-organizing states and properties. The eruption of the psychic individual from the living individual is one such emergence. The concept, conceptuality, mind, consciousness and the unconscious are themselves the emergent properties of particular affective modes of organizing living beings.

They are the properties or capacities of a being that is unable to resolve or adequately address problems of the living being, problems carried within life and within materiality already, in other ways. The psychical is the elaboration of a problematic, a context that raises questions, which a living being is able to address through the constitution of itself as a subject. A psychical order, an order of interiority in which the living being is the subject, is the consequence of a form of internal resonance that elaborates itself at a higher order than that from which it emerged:

> The living being, which is simultaneously more and less than a unity, possesses an internal problematic that is capable of being an element in a problematic that has wider scope than itself. As far as the individual is concerned, participation here means *being an element in a much larger process of individuation* by means of the inheritance of *pre-individual reality that the individual contains* – that is, due to the potentials it has retained. (306)

The living being elaborates the conditions for the emergence of a psychical individual. Such an individual is only possible when the living being can think itself as a unity and can represent its activities to itself. The living being elaborates both perception and affect entwined, not as separate dimensions, but now brought together in a new dimension. Thought, conceptuality, modes of addressing the problematic by representing one's own inner states and practices coincide with the emergence of a new order, not itself singular or directed by logic but rather by practical imagination, another doubling of the pre-individual but this time through the concept, through ideality.

It is the generation of another order of problems, again a residue of unspent or unactualized forces from the pre-individual, that also constitutes the possibility of collective individuation, the coming into being of an entity that is larger than but inclusive of the individual – the possibility of ensembles, groups, collectives, the eruption of transindividual relations. Transindividual or collective relations are themselves the consequence of a transduction, the transformation at a higher level of a problem encountered in the relation between informed matter and transmitted information. Transindividual collectives address problems that psychic individuals are unable to – they create a mode of higher-order resolution and utilization of the tensions that remain unresolved from the pre-individual.

Collective relations are largely mediated by technical objects which elaborate and contribute to psychical cohesion.[9] Psychical and collective individuations are modes of emergence, forms of quantum-like leaps, that are each conditioned on prior individuations that have themselves not exhausted either their own potential for transformation or those of the pre-individual from which they have come. The transindividual, whether in the form of thought itself, or in the form of supraindividual collectives, both exceeds and extends the individual. It is both part of the individual and beyond it. Psychical and collective life each have metastable states capable of actualizing previously unelaborated potentials or resources; each is a surprising but conditioned outcome of the production of further metastabilities, each a kind of resolution to the problem of the relations between material form and information.

This is, for Simondon, a kind of ethics of actualization, an ethics of the transformation of information and materiality: '*Ethics* exists to the extent that there is information, in other words, signification overcoming a disparation of the elements of being, such that what is interior is also exterior.'[10] Ethics is the movement that includes and incorporates more and more of the pre-individual, not in its pre-individual states of tension and potential, but through forms of actualization. Such an ethics reverses the movement of the dialectic; instead of superseding and leaving behind that which it cannot incorporate or resolve, it aims eventually, through the opening up of the future, to aspire to the maximization of actualization, the maximum incorporation of pre-individual potentials, disparations, into the individuals and supraindividuals that emerge.

SIMONDON TODAY

Simondon's work is remarkably prescient in light of many of the technical and particularly informational elaborations that have occurred since his texts were originally written. He has not only anticipated how we are to understand the developments that have occurred in genetics, the human genome project and evolutionary biology more generally, he has also provided a remarkable anticipation of the unfolding of computer networks that constitute the worldwide web and have provided communication networks that are themselves gigantic networked collectives, traversing the globe. He has become something of a visionary figure within the philosophy of technology and in the philosophy of science, but his relevance for social and political thought, for theories of subjectivity, identity, sexuality and sociality, has been less clear.[11] I would like to address this question at least briefly.

I am not the first to ask the question of Simondon's relevance to feminist and anti-racist theory.[12] In looking at how his work may inform feminist and other radical political projects, I am not suggesting that his work in any way anticipates the emergence of second-wave feminism or feminist theory; clearly it does not. And moreover, one must understand feminist theory as itself the unexpected emergence of a trajectory that may have had some force in earlier theoretical positions but was elaborated in entirely new and unpredictable ways only after many of Simondon's texts were written. Nevertheless, for readers of Simondon's work today, his work may provide some new concepts and ways of thinking that may enhance how we understand individuality, both in the material sense of the individuality of things, and in the biological sense of the individuality of living beings. This concept has long been the centre of various political and social struggles, and Simondon's work promises to revitalize our understanding of its openness.

Feminism itself has long been based on the assumption of something like a theory of the social or representational construction of identity, the constitution of identity as a form of ideology, or a historical construct that represents the interests of dominant social forces and not always the individual constituted. Theories of the constitutive or performative power of representations (whether psychical systems or cultural systems of representations) have framed much of feminist thought over the last three decades or more. Poststructuralist feminism has emphasized the power of images and representations in constructing the real, in producing nature as the retroactive condition of culture, created only by culture, and in establishing the lived body as a cultural rather than a biological body.

While these claims were perhaps a necessary corrective to the assumption of a masculine and feminine nature or essence, they rendered impossible the notion of a pre- or non-representational real, seeing in biology only fixation and resistance to change, and regarding what is creative as what is consciously created by human intentionality. In affirming many of these broad principles, feminist, anti-racist and postcolonial discourses become more remote from and disinterested in conceptualizing the real, in understanding forces that run below or beneath consciousness, before or beyond culture. They lose the ability to explain the development of cultural and representational systems and to see the limits of representation, that which representation is unable to order or understand. Feminism's commitment to structuralist and poststructuralist accounts of the integral relation between language and human culture, and the constitutive relation that language has in the constitution of subjectivity has meant that many other questions about materiality and ideality, about the ways in which language and culture develop in the prehuman and from the precultural, about the reality of the body and its various processes, about natural and material forces, are all pre-empted.

Simondon's work may serve as a corrective to this corrective! By returning to the work he developed in the 1950s, precisely at that moment when poststructuralism was elaborating itself through its meandering trajectory through developments in cybernetics and general systems theory, phenomenology and Marxism, psychoanalysis and structural semiotics, through Lacan's linguistic interpretation of Freud to the birth of deconstruction, we can reorient some of the central questions of feminist thought. Perhaps feminist theory, instead of orienting itself so thoroughly to the elaboration of these models of representation, could now elaborate itself in different terms that may capitalize on Simondon's insights regarding the processes of individuation. Instead of the prevailing conception, emerging (in its most recent incarnation – for it is, in fact, a reborn form of Platonism) in nascent form in the 1950s, that matter is unformed, non-meaningful, without orientation, purpose or direction and in need of meaning, form, purpose and value which must be brought to it from the outside, through human intervention, through the intervention of impersonal systems of meaning or signification, Simondon has demonstrated that matter, the pre-individual in its non-oppositional states of differences or singularities, is always already formed, oriented, laden with its own forces of emergence, its own instabilities and potentialities which enable it to unfold and elaborate itself without external intervention. It does not require representation in order for its processes of self-organization to begin because they are always at work. Moreover, representation itself is an emergent phenomenon or capacity, something that is conditioned on thousands of prior orders of individuation, that can only be actualized to the extent that material, biological and psychic individuality frames and enables it. This is not the intervention of a system, an order of meaning, a structure on unformed matter; rather it is the inner elaboration of informational forms that come from the disparity of forces or potentials. It is the operation of a myriad of microforces of self-organization and orientation without the need of an inventor, an animator, a purpose-giver, forces that are prehuman (and will continue long after the human).

What Simondon offers feminist and other forms of radical thought is a new way of understanding a world that is not ultimately controlled or ordered through a central apparatus or system, that has no inherent or necessary hierarchies, that does not require animation or coordination by culture but instead enables and makes culture itself possible. He offers feminism a way of understanding subjectivity or personal identity, not as an attainment, a given, something of fixed value, a category that will enable one to be definitively identified as something, a member of a group, with certainty. Rather, subjectivity is nothing but the elaboration of a new order of object that is now able to take its own operations, its own forms of inner resonance as its object and mode of addressing problems. Subjectivity is not the centre of political life, not the conditions under which political struggles are waged, but the condition under which social and collective life is possible. Subjectivity can never be identified with a particular identity – a singularity – for singularities exist only at the level of the pre-individual. Subjectivity is instead the internal enfolding of a multiplicity of bodily and conceptual operations, never finished or finalized, never reducible to a thing, never identifiable with any of its stages, never complete, never determinate, always in the process of becoming-more and other. Subjective identity is not the stable and abiding identity that founds a politics, whether it be a politics of recognition or an egalitarian politics of formal similarity.

Simondon understood a world in which unities and stabilities are always capable of further elaboration and evolution; unities and stabilities were never unified or stabilized enough to remain unchanging universals. Only in their elaboration and enhancement can we understand the most fundamental qualities and forces that populate the pre-individual. And it is only through these processes, which are also the processes of increasingly elaborate and inclusive orders of individuation, well beyond the order of thought itself, that individuals, subjects and objects, natural entities and cultural artifacts, can emerge and complexify themselves.

The division of humanity into genders, races, classes, ethnicities and so on, the primary concern of many forms of social activism, can be explained in quite open and surprising ways, if we understand that these categories are neither structures nor forms, neither intersected nor singular and self-identical. They are social collectivities, transindividual groups, that cohere not only because they share a common milieu (the environment of various forms of oppression) but also because they share some kind of internal resonance, some form of informational coding that brings together their members, in various degrees of adhesion, to social / political collectives. These are systematic groupings of different orders; what is usually understood (or misunderstood) as gender is, in fact, the overcoding and transformation of relations of sexual difference that result from sexual selection (as I have argued in other work[13]) that take on and elaborate what is an emergent condition for vital individuation.

Cultural 'gender' is the transcription, at another level, of the tensions and sources of upheaval posed by sexual selection at the level of animal or vital existence. In this sense, it functions in different terms from all other forms of social collectives; it is a problem, an irresolvable tension of animal life that is animated and transformed, negotiated, in socially variable ways. Race, class and ethnicity, while each involves various forms of transduction and individuation from vital or animal existence, nevertheless address and produce modes of differentiation, quasi-stable forms of collective identity that can operate only *beyond* the level of biological existence. They have few animal antecedents and cannot be understood as an inheritance or a given. These collectivities are culturally produced, the effects of various complex relations between technologies, proximities / geographies, forces and modes of regulation. They are not stable products but are themselves metastable, prone to forms of becoming and transformation, open in their ongoing forms.

Simondon may not provide solutions to the ongoing problems facing feminist theory and practice. This may require a different kind of inventiveness. Instead, his works may be regarded as provocations to feminist and other forms of radical thought to continue to question the dominant assumptions that structure thought at a particular moment in time, to question the assumption that individuals, whether biological, social or collective, are given and that their characteristics are static rather than evolving, self-transforming and milieu-transforming elaborations. Simondon provokes us to rethink the most basic assumptions about what it is to be a subject in a world of pregiven objects, and in doing so, he stimulates us to think in new terms about unresolved problems, problems about the real, about forces, about forms of power, and to open up these problems to new modes of address.

NOTES

1. See, for example, Bernard Stiegler, *Technics and Time, 1: The Fault of Epimetheus*, trans. Richard Beardsworth and Gregory Collins (Stanford: Stanford University Press, 1998).
2. Simondon describes his goal as 'to grasp the entire unfolding of ontogenesis in all its variety, and *to understand the individual from the perspective of the process of individuation rather than the process of individuation by means of the individual*' (Gilbert Simondon, 'The Genesis of the Individual', in J. Crary and S. Kwinter (eds), *Incorporations* (New York: Zone, 1993), pp. 297–317; p. 300). All further references to this essay will be left in-text and are the only in-text references in this essay.
3. Brian Massumi suggests that the distinction between thought and matter, fundamentally Platonic, is itself an effect of individuation:

   > [Simondon's] key concept of 'individuation' asserts the primacy of ontogenesis, a primacy of the processes of becoming over the states of being through which they pass. Further, Simondon approached the question of epistemology as a function of ontogenesis. There is an individuation of thought, he said, by the same token by which there is an individuation of matter, on the physical plane and from there on to the plane of life, and following – or prolonging – the same constitutive principles. (Brian Massumi, ' "Technical Mentality" Revisited: Brian Massumi on Gilbert Simondon', with Arne De Boever, Alex Murray and Jon Roffe, *Parrhesia*, 7 (2009), pp. 36–45: 37)

4. [T]he process of individuation does not exhaust everything that came before (the pre-individual), and . . . a metastable regime is not only maintained by the individual, but is actually borne by it, to such an extent that the finally constituted individual carries within it a certain inheritance associated with its pre-individual reality, one animated by all the potentials that characterize it. Individuation, then, is a relative phenomenon . . . There is a certain level of potential that remains, meaning that further individuations are still possible. The pre-individual nature, which remains associated with the individual, is a source of future metastable states from which new individuations could eventuate. (306)

5. Transduction occurs when there is activity, both structural and functional, which begins at a center of the being and extends itself in various directions from this center, as if multiple dimensions of the being were expanding around this central point. It is the correlative appearance of dimensions and structures in a being in a state of pre-individual tension, which is to say, in a

being that is more than a unity and more than an identity, and which has not yet passed out of step with itself into other multiple dimensions. (313)

6. Massumi argues that Simondon understands epistemology in the same terms as he understands being. Knowing is only possible because it too undergoes an ontogenesis, it too is individuated and organized along principles that are not self-produced but the effects of its pre-individual precursors. See Massumi, ' "Technical Mentality" Revisited'.

7. Gilbert Simondon, *L'Individuation à la lumière des notions de forme et d'information* (Grenoble: Jérôme Millon, 2005), p. 233.

8.   In the living being, . . . the interior plays a constitutive role, whereas the frontier plays this role in the physical individual; and in the latter case, whatever is located on the inside in topographical terms must also be thought of as genetically prior. The living individual is its own contemporary with regard to each one of its elements; this is not the case with the physical individual, which contains a past that is radically "past", even when it is in the throes of growth. The living being can be considered to be a node of information that is being transmitted inside itself – it is a system within a system, containing within itself a mediation between two different orders of magnitude. (305–6)

9.   The technical object taken according to its essence, that is, the technical object insofar as it was invented, thought and willed, assumed by a human subject, becomes the support and the symbol of this relation that we would call *transindividual* . . . Through the intermediary of the technical object an interhuman relation that is the model of *transindividuality* is created. (*Du mode d'existence des objets techniques*, pp. 247–8, quoted in Jean-Hughes Barthélémy, ' "*Du mort qui saisit le vif*": Simondonian Ontology Today', *Parrhesia*, 7 (2009), pp. 28–35: 30.)

10. Simondon, quoted in Gilles Deleuze, 'On Gilbert Simondon', *Desert Islands and Other Texts 1953–1974*, trans. Michael Taormina (Los Angeles: Semiotext(e) Foreign Agents Series, 2004), p. 89.

11. There have been many texts, however, that have at least attempted to indicate the potential relevance of Simondon for the humanities rather than the sciences. These include Miguel de Beistegui, 'Science and Ontology. From Merleau-Ponty's "Reduction" to Simondon's "Transduction" ' (included in this volume); Mark Hansen, 'Internal Resonance, or Three Steps Towards a Non-Viral Becoming', *Culture Machine*', 3 (2001); Brian Massumi, ' "Technical Mentality" Revisited'; and Olivia Harvey, Tamara Popowski and Carol Sullivan, 'Individuation and Feminism. A Commentary on Gilbert Simondon's "The Genesis of the Individual" ', *Australian Feminist Studies*, 23:55 (2008), pp. 101–11.

12. See Harvey, Popowski and Sullivan, 'Individuation and Feminism'; they have also addressed Simondon's possible relevance for feminist thought, though in terms that seem fundamentally to misunderstand Simondon's account of individuation. For example, they critique what they argue is an opposition in Simondon between material and living beings without recognizing the crucial role that relative levels, dimensions or orders of magnitude play in Simondon's writings. Living being emerges from material being; there is not the slightest suggestion in Simondon that their relation is oppositional. This problematizes their claims about Simondon's relevance to feminism; it is no longer clear, if his account of the emergence or evolution of the living being is problematic, why it should be of interest to feminist thought.

13. Most particularly in the final sections of *Becoming Undone* (Durham, NC: Duke University Press, 2011).

Chapter 4

Crystals and Membranes: Individuation and Temporality

Anne Sauvagnargues, translated by Jon Roffe[1]

In order to escape from what he calls the hylomorphic schema, which has oriented occidental metaphysics towards a substantialism which forecloses becoming, Simondon transforms the philosophy of individuation. Every doctrine according to which individuation results from the impression of an exterior principle, like a mould, on to the material individual, such that form remains external to matter, invokes the this schema. By presupposing the hierarchical subordination of matter to a transcendent form, the constituted individual is considered to be explicable on the basis of a principle of individuation anterior to it. However, the presupposition of a preformed principle of individuation that transcends the operation of individuation renders the becoming of the individual as a real process impossible to explain. Simondon therefore challenges the notion that the process of individuation can be considered in a unitary manner, and refuses to presuppose that the principle of this individuation can be conceived as a formal cause exterior to the real process. Purely nominal, abstract and explicative, the principle of individuation must become the genetic principle contemporary with real individuation.

What is in question is thus no longer individuated being, being come into being, but rather the real genetic process of its transformation. Simondon's work thus opens on to a new conception of time as ontogenesis, such that becoming is no longer conceived as the becoming of individuated being, but rather as the becoming of the individuation of being.

THE CRYSTAL AND INDIVIDUATION

A Logic of Metastable Becoming

Simondon thus engages in a project of immense scope: the reformulation of metaphysics on the basis of a critique of the hylomorphic schema. It is this project that allows him to critique in the same gesture the Aristotelian separation of matter and form in nature and sensation, the Kantian separation between matter and form, or sensibility and understanding, along with every separation between matter and form that conceives of form as an eminent, transcendent and explanatory principle, rather than conceiving of it at the level of forces. Simondon judges that the Ancients had to privilege a conception of stable being on the basis of their cosmology, itself put into play by their epistemology. To the extent that they only conceived of being in a state of equilibrium, they were led to privilege a formal conception of individuation by taking form and matter separately, leaving the operation of individuation itself in the dark, a darkness Simondon proposes to illuminate. For this, we must pass from an ontology of being to an ontology of becoming, an ontogenesis, made possible by the objective knowledge that contemporary science proposes of becoming through the study of the conditions of metastable systems.

This epistemological transformation provides for the conceptualization of a being in becoming, on the condition of understanding a 'metastable' genesis, which is to say a type of equilibrium which is no longer situated at the lowest level of potential energy – that of stability, all the Ancients were capable of thinking – but which theorizes the transformations operating in a system which has not yet exhausted its potential difference, with the augmentation of order or information (negentropy) which can result from it. The concept of metastability intertwines the theory of information and the physics of phase shifts in matter, which Simondon gives a metaphysical extension by applying it to every field of individuation; metastability thus qualifies the conditions of every actualization. Metastable being, in disequilibrium, involves this state of asymmetrical disequilibrium which accounts for tension and the production of the new.

Metastability thus becomes the key concept of a philosophy of becoming. Simondon applies this new conception to philosophy, freeing metaphysics from hylomorphism, and producing a new theory of culture which extends material and vital individuation into the processes of psychic and collective individuation. Metastability, a transgeneric concept, allows for an ethics of differentiation, and engages with natural formations and political affects on the same terrain. Simondon applies it to theories of matter in the study of crystallization, and shows that it applies as well to theories of life, in the analysis of the interior milieu or the membrane, as it does to the social formations of culture. This Bergsonian or even Spinozist continuism, which treats matter, organism and both psychic and collective individuation on the same plane, allows for a new conception of time; becoming integrates the accident and contingency, or rather makes of determinism and indetermination two limit cases, in order to think the emergence of singularities. Metastability, or the theory of the phases of being, thus opens on to a theory of transductive time.

Crystallization and Transductive Time

Crystallization, the Simondonian example *par excellence*, allows for a definition of individuation that combats with a polemical vigour the hylomorphic schema by accounting for individuation as a transductive modulation. The crystal provides the simplest image of transduction; beginning with a very small seed, it grows in every direction within its pre-individual milieu, each already formed layer serving as the structuring basis of the next molecular stratum in the process of being constituted through an amplifying reticulation.[2] Transduction consists of this individuation in progress, whose elements are as follows: a pre-individual milieu of individuation, here a mother-liquor, a supersaturated solution rich in potential and in metastable equilibrium, that the second agent of crystallization, the seed, makes 'take' in an aggressive fashion. Individuation operates with this first heterogenous couple: the pre-individual milieu and the catalytic singularity. The crystalline seed figures this eruption of singularity, which brings the metastable milieu to the point of disparation. The crystal thus emerges as a result, an individuation which creatively resolves the tension between the disparate reals of the mother-liquor and the seed. As Simondon explains,

> the extreme terms attained by the transductive operation do not preexist this operation; its dynamism provides the primitive tension in the system of heterogenous being that dephases and develops the dimensions through which it is structured; it does not arise from a tension between the terms which will be attained and discarded at the extreme limits of transduction. (IGPB 31)

Becoming is therefore not produced between terms given in advance, but consists of this transductive tension, which produces the terms in the course of its process, such that the ontological monism of a being subject to the occurrence of accidents must be replaced with a pluralism of phases; as such, individuation will no longer concern individuating being, but rather the becoming of individuation.

In order to be made concrete, the individuation of the crystal reclaims the encounter between a metastable milieu and the singularity that emerges. It is this encounter, throw of the dice, or aleatory chance which gives rise to its own necessity, that Simondon subsumes under the term 'problematic disparation', and which allows for the theorization of this mixture of the aleatory and dependent which changes the conception of necessity, which relies upon a transductive theory of time.

If the catalytic encounter is aleatory, the processes that it induces are constrained, since nothing necessitates this encounter. Or rather, it itself depends on the conditions required by the system in the process of being constituted, in which the conditions for crystallization are not pre-existent. In order for the encounter to come about, it is again necessary that the singularity emerges as information for this nascent system. And for this, different conditions are required.

The first condition is the irruption of a singularity. The seed – which is to say, an impurity, intentionally introduced in the case of artificial crystallization – must intervene in order to be able to play the role of catalytic singularity bearing information. It is this that Simondon calls a problematic disparation: an emergent tension of problematic hetero-geneous elements, which requires the production of a new dimension in order to resolve the disparity, such as the constructive production of a third dimension or volume in the case of binocular vision, which emerges in order to resolve the parallax difference of two incompatible retinas. But in order for the disparation to work, it is, second, necessary for the singularity to emerge in a pre-individual milieu, whose metast-ability promotes disparation with the introduced singularity (here, the seed). Not every milieu can play this role. A compatibility must therefore exist between the milieu and the seed, a compatibility which is above all not of the order of identity, but rather of difference.

It is this conflictual emergence, which determines the problematic encounter between pre-individual milieu and singularity, that Simondon defines as disparation. In order for the latter to arise, a supplemen-tary condition is required, which Simondon describes as the internal resonance between milieu and singularity: which is to say, an objective problematic which allows for the emergence of the singularity as infor-mation in the system. The crystalline solution, a pre-individual milieu in a metastable state, can only begin to emerge, begin to crystallize, on this condition: that a seed, which must 'resonate' with the milieu in order to produce disparation, be introduced, to which the individual responds as a resolution of the problem.

The individual must therefore be conceived of as an operation, putting the disparation of the pre-individual milieu to work in order to resolve progressively the disparation of the system. One can thus speak of a veritable interiority of the crystal, to the extent that it incorporates a primitively amorphous matter, rich in potential, into the milieu in which it is developed, progressively structuring it according to its specific prescriptive disposition. The crystalline seed resolves the disparative problematic of the metastable solution and guides crystallization through iteration. In radiating out from its point of introduction, the crystalline structure spreads a fraction at a time. An individual crystal is thus formed, whose regularity, transparency and organization explain the fascination that it has, from the Renaissance to Romanticism, given rise to – a physico-chemical structure whose growth can be observed.

The crystal, in being individuated, is temporalized. This is why Simondon defines transduction as a tension of heterogenous being that changes phase and develops new dimensions through which it is structured. The development of the crystal takes place on the basis of the initial insertion of the seed, and crystallization spreads in every direction, each crystallized molecular layer serving as the structuring basis for the layer that forms next. The seed must be conceived of as an effective singularity in this tense hylomorphic state, in order for the polarization of amorphous substance by the crystalline seed to be possible. Under these conditions, it acts as an instance of structuring information that crystallizes the milieu and which takes hold around this initial point; the first layer of crystallized molecules thus polarizes step by step the other layers around their edges (IGPB 85–6).

Crystallization manifests the appearance of dimensions and structures in the process of becoming. At issue is a shift between phases and not states. Simondon compels us to conceive of individuation as a series of dynamic transformations, marshalling our capacity to theorize change. First, a crystalline solution at the point of supersaturation, then the introduction of a crystalline seed capable of producing this problematic tension, then the disparation which precipitates the formation of the crystalline individual, before, finally, the emergence of the crystal, as a creative response to the disparation of the system. There is here a succession of transductive phase-changes, since each rearrangement of the system provides the starting-point for a new transformation.

Transduction, Disparation, Modulation

The relations between transduction and disparation must now be accounted for more precisely. Transduction qualifies not only the individuation of the crystal in process, but also the operation of thought capable of theorizing these phase-changes and the thought of becoming. It therefore involves the operation of creative structuration through which each structured region provides the principle of constitution for the following region, according to the step-by-step propagation that we have seen in the growth of the crystal. Since it is defined by this succession of dephasings and restructurations which form concatenating cascades, the discovery of a solution marks the point of crystallization which sets in motion a new structuration of the field and entirely modifies it at each stage of the process.

Transduction thus implies a new conception of temporality conceived as creation and differentiation: structuration by heterogenous disparation that leads into a complete reconfiguration of the field, starting from a new, differentiating restructuration. Here, disparation qualifies the type of transductive structuration that operates by engaging two disparate realities in a problematic tension – here the seed and the crystal, the pre-individual milieu and the singularity bearing transformation. It therefore consists in a problematic tension, which is resolved through the appearance of a new dimension, the formation of the individual crystal. Individuation is thus revealed at the same time as 'the solution of a conflict, the discovery of an incompatibility, the invention of a form'.[3]

With this analysis of the formation of systems, Simondon proposes a conception of the relations between form and matter which completely transforms the hylomorphic schema. The first result of this analysis consists in this new conception of form which requires the constitution of the individual and its milieu, an emergent individuation responding to a metastable situation that resolves and thus transforms an objective disparation within the pre-individual milieu, and thus the transformation of the milieu, to be thought together. Since there is, first of all, no aparation of a constituted individual in an amorphous milieu, but only one which already has form, modulation by disparation between the milieu and the seed acts like an accident, a catalytic event. For Simondon, 'the individual is not only the result but the *milieu* of individuation' (IGPB 115). It is never first, nor even contemporary with its own individuation, since what characterizes the conditions of its aparation is the existence of a problematic disparation which brings the supersaturated mother-liquor into resonance with the crystalline seed. The condition of individuation is therefore the metastable disparation of the milieu: which is to say, the dephasing of a reality into disparate orders. This in turn implies a fundamental difference, a state of dissymmetry which produces a new individuation – for example, the crystal.

Second, the example of the crystal casts light on the necessarily associated character of the milieu and the individual. The individual comes into being as that which is distinguished, as the result of creative disparation between its milieu and the singularity introduced by the structural seed. Its introduction as event, as singularity, determines pre-individual substance – 'amorphous', writes Simondon, which is to say lacking order rather than form – to 'take form'. Simondon therefore proposes a new theory of form, transductive and material, which arises through the resolution of a problematic in the state of disparation and is no longer conceived as an active principle imposed on matter. In reality, it engages in a modulation with its associated milieu. This taking-form is brought about through the modulation between milieu and individual.

Individuation is the result of an encounter between a structural condition and an energetic condition, an encounter which must also be actualized in order for individuation to take place. From this steadfast solidarity between the individual and its milieu of constitution follows an indifferentiation of the individual and its milieu in individuation, since the individual which results – for example, the crystal – emerges along with its milieu.

Individuation is therefore conceived as a relation in becoming – that is, in a synthetic, plural and passive fashion rather than in terms of a completed unity. The individual is never dissociable from its process of individuation, which literally coproduces the individual and its associated milieu together. As such, the individual must be defined as an encounter, a result, but also as the milieu of individuation, through a succession of configuring phases. The individual is the result of a process of individuation that brings about the formed individual and the milieu of individuation together. From the point of view of this ecological vision, the associated milieu becomes as morphogenetic as an organ. Individuation and the transformation that it renders in its milieu cannot be dissociated; in reality, the formation of the individual and the transformation through which it takes place must always be theorized together, in terms of a disparative becoming.

The concept of the individual completely changes; neither unified nor identical, it becomes relative, phased, perpetually putting into play a process of individuation and an associated milieu. The individual is thus never relative to a *single* order of reality but is always transductive, implying a disparation between different dimensions, arising as the resolution of a problematic, a tension between disparates. It appears as a response, as genetic as it is dynamic. In reality, the unitary individual does not exist; there are only multiple processes of individuation. Furthermore, the individual invokes neither unity nor identity, since it reclaims the heterogeneity of the phases from which it emerges through differentiation.

Internal Resonance

The various elements of this extraordinary analysis can be recapitulated as follows: first, relation is primary, being is relation, and relations are external to their terms. Second, properties are always relational, and only come into play in the service of what Simondon calls, in a fine phrase, 'the interruption of becoming', the introduction of a singularity. It follows, third, that time is not external to the individual, but intervenes as a fundamental asymmetry and relation of differentiation, at the limit of the individual, a striking consequence that will only be explicable once we consider the individuation of the living, and the analysis of the membrane. Fourth, transduction, or the genesis of a structure in a milieu in a state of pre-individual tension, requires what Simondon calls internal resonance – that is, a disparative point of entry, or a problematic coupling between the different realities that it engages in communication.

Simondon thus entirely renovates the conception of form, proposing an intensive and material theory of formation and emergent information. Far from being external to the matter which it transforms, form acts at the level of forces and functions as a signal: that is, as an instance of information capable of catalysing a process through the irruption of an emergent singularity in a system, engaging disparates in a system of correspondence.

Internal resonance is thus defined as the situation of a system-in-tension that makes possible individuation. It is an instance of information, in the sense Simondon gives to this term: not a defined, quantifiable and stable magnitude, but a relation, and even a moment of individuation. The emergence of form presupposes the presence of information and serves as the transductive basis for information, such that information is the transition of being which is dephased and which becomes: it is 'the seed around which a new individuation will be able to be achieved', and constitutes the transductivity of different phases of individuation (IGPB 241). It thus functions on the near side of a certain threshold. This is because, as Simondon specifies, 'there is only information when what emits signals and what receives them form a system. Information is *between* the two halves of a system engaged in a relation of disparation' (IGPB 221, n30).

The greater the disparation, the more information grows, but only up to a certain point, beyond which it is quickly nullified. Simondon explains with recourse to the example of stereoscopic photographs, which present two images and force the brain to induce between them a disparative resonance in order to create a single unified image: the further the photographs are separated, the better the effect, but only up to a certain distance, beyond which the effect is no longer produced.

Information is thus a notion at once plural, relational and phased; it can never be relative to an homogenous being but requires of necessity two orders in a state of disparation. Disparation no longer only demands the condition of a difference or disparity, but equally involves an internal resonance, which allows the system to communicate; information is thus never given or pre-existent. It is, as Simondon brilliantly puts it, 'the signification that suddenly emerges' – grammatically marking the nature of its creation through this leap into the future – 'when an operation of individuation will discover the dimension in which two disparate reals can become a system' (IGPB 31). In the exemplary case of binocular vision, disparation takes place between two retinal images, on the condition that the tension between them, a gap necessary in order for the image in depth to arise and which intervenes as the signification of the duality of the two images, is maintained.

Thus information is tension and not term; it relies upon a minimally disparative problematic and engages the future in order to resolve emergent states. It always implies a change of phase, a heterogeneity which is able to appear as decisive. For Simondon, information is 'the sense [*sens*] according to which a system individuates': 'information is therefore a primer of individuation, a *demand of individuation*, it is never something given' (IGPB 221). Tension and not term, it presupposes a system in a disparative state, and requires a problematic. Simondon thus calls a signal that which is transmitted in the process of disparation; form, that in relation to which the signal is received; and information, that which is integrated into the functioning of the receptor after the test of disparation between extrinsic signal (seed) and intrinsic form (mother-liquor) (IGPB 222).

THE MEMBRANE, AND LIFE IN THE FOLDS

If the analyses that Simondon presents of the crystal, of individuation and disparation, transform the conception of becoming, his analysis of life is even more remarkable. Two spatiotemporal conditions are required in order to define life: a spatial or topological determination, folding [*plissement*], and its chronogenetic consequence, the instantiation of a temporality that hems in its wake the outskirts of the living, and bifurcates through the differentiation of relative interiorities and exteriorities. This difference between interior and exterior is temporalized within lived temporality and within an emergent exteriority, and actualizes the threshold of the living by unfolding in the real the difference between matter and memory, past and future. Life emerges as a fold in the tissue of matter and brings about a bifurcation in the transductive logic of crystalline individuation.

At work here is an inspired reprise of the Bergsonian theme of the image as a fold in matter, later taken up by Deleuze, equally for whom life must be able to be defined on the plane of immanence of material forces. It is in just this way that Simondon proceeds; life does not depend on specific chemical constituants, but only on the differential disposition of matters which is not perceptible on the physico-chemical plane. Vital subjectivity is never anything more than a topological arrangement: a spatial enfolding translated by a chronogenesis. It does not emerge in the form of a sudden rupture, in the form of special structural or energetic conditions, but due to a simple torsion of materiality. It proceeds on the basis of an entirely spatial individuation, the apparition of a specific tissue equipped with the chemical property of functioning as a limit endowed by a selective permeability: a membrane. This allows for the emergence of a new property of time, at the level of vital individuation; from this point on, dissociation or differentiation of a multiple temporality is added to transductive becoming, distinguishing at the level of present actuality the irruptive streams of the past and the future.

The membrane is defined with reference to two properties implied in this spatiotemporal differentiation: a selective porosity, which allows only certain elements to pass, and which animates the surface by endowing it with a functional metastable property. In addition, second, it is also characterized by an even more remarkable property: this porosity is polar. It animates this selective porosity or differential selection in both centripetal and centrifugal directions, allowing some bodies to pass through in selective opposition to the passage of other such bodies (IGPB 223). To define the living is to describe, as Michaux said, life in the folds, this arrangement of matter which proceeds from the functional characteristics of the membrane, allowing certain substances and not others to pass, and organizing space according to the characteristic asymmetry of the living. In doing so, it promotes the emergence of an entirely new property. Inducing a sense of circulation, the membrane literally constitutes interiority; it creates it.

This is why the membrane must not be understood as an inert limit, the border of the interiority of the living. In polarizing, it defines a milieu of interiority. It in no way presupposes a constituted interiority, but is, to the contrary, what differentiates the interior from the exterior, and which produces this differentiation in the polar and simultaneously beneficent and detrimental mode. The polarity of the membrane distinguishes the favourable (which it integrates and retains) from the unfavourable (which it avoids and rejects) in a Spinozist manner. The functional and active polarity of the membrane configures the external milieu as much as it constitutes its internal milieu.

The membrane thus defines the leap from the chemical to the living, and promotes the emergence of this new property: the difference between exterior and interior, the result of its differentiating action. The fold simultaneously produces interiority and exteriority, inside and outside, such that the inside is formed as 'the outside of the outside', to adapt Deleuze's beautiful formula. The polarized membrane therefore folds its organic pellicule and curves around itself in order to rediscover, at the terminus of this torsion, its own milieu of interiority. Some, but not all, external bodies can pass into the interior, and an identical selection comes to bear on bodies of the internal milieu, some of whose elements migrate towards the exterior. The selective membrane is thus productive of its own interiority.

Now, this interiority and exteriority are not absolute but metastable, dynamic, relative to each other, and their interfacing surface is itself in becoming, in relation. The membrane thus brings about this polarity of milieus, in which interiority and exteriority remain entirely relative, and even dephase themselves, since the living is characterized as that which engenders a proliferation of interior and exterior milieus in the organism, without ever being content to oppose in a static way corporeal interior and an exterior world. The human body is thus characterized by the diversity of its interior spaces, the digestive cavities remaining exterior to the blood, which itself turns out to be relatively external to the glands that discharge their secretions into its flux, and so on. Exteriority and interiority are not therefore given as states but are entirely relational.

Thus, if the living substance contained in the membrane regenerates it, it is none the less necessary to define the living by this membrane, solely capable of producing the mobile distinction between interiority and exteriority since it polarizes and distinguishes substances that it admits or rejects, in one direction or another. The membrane defines the living, in accordance with the Simondonian formula, 'the living lives at the limit, on the borders', that Deleuze cites with admiration in *The Logic of Sense*; it is on the side of the limit, of the exteriority of the skin, that the characteristic polarity of life emerges as an aspect of the dynamic topology that itself fosters its own metastability.

The skin thus commands a properly superficial vital potential energy. It is in this non-metaphorical sense that Valery's celebrated formula, 'there's nothing more profound than the skin', attains its proper validity – not in terms of a facile inversion of surface and depth, but, because depth is literally produced, secreted by the skin. Only the characteristic polarity of the living membrane, the skin, determines this differentiation between interior and exterior that characterizes life. Without a doubt, this one-way permeability exists on the chemical level, but it characterizes life as a continued transduction. The crystal polarizes once and for all, but the membrane is continually repolarized. The individual is defined, in any case, as a system of transduction but, if this transduction becomes indirect and hierarchized in complex biological systems, it remains direct and belongs to a single level in physical systems. The crystal is only transductive on the margins, where it undergoes crystallization, its exteriority comes to bear only on its external layer. But even here, then, 'interiority and exteriority are everywhere in living being' (IGPB 159).

A second, equally strong consequence also follows. In separating interiority from exteriority, the polarized membrane differentiates the fluxes of temporality and creates the interiority of lived time. If the polarization of the membrane characterizes the living, it is not only topological and spatial, but chronogenetic, productive of time. The polarized pellicule, in distinguishing interiority and exteriority, separates the facets of the temporality of the living into two streams. The present emerges on the exterior of the membrane; it catalyses action and intervenes on the reality to come [*à venir*], however beneficent or detrimental this reality may be. What appears on the exterior may or may not be assimilated, may or may not do damage to the living individual; exteriority induces tendencies of assimilation or rejection, and provokes the imminent material encounter, the encounter to come. The future [*avenir*] depends on action, and is split between favourable and unfavourable, useful and harmful. Correlatively, what remains within the grasp of interiority is the organic memory of the living, its vital identity, its formula of repetition, the past – whence Simondon's remarkable formula, often cited by Deleuze: 'at the level of the polarised membrane, the interior past and the exterior future face one another' (IGPB 226).[4]

The future and the past, topologically speaking, form the two sides of the membrane, which distinguishes the one side from the other. At the level of the skin interior and exterior are topologically distinguished, a border that also operates chronogenetically, the creator of time as much as it is of space. Kant wrongfully accounted for space and time in terms of internal and external sense, *a priori* forms of transcendental subjectivity, since, if the effectuation of forms is at issue, they are materially produced through the sensible metastability of the membrane, the polarity of living tissue.

By defining interiority as topological, relative and differential, Simondon allows for the taking into account of the temporal differentiation at the heart of becoming. The same analysis that carries weight for the production of interiority and exteriority also does so for the plurality of time, which is split between the actuality of the present, its relative past, and its tension towards the future. The individual is no longer, Simondon says, a 'way of being', but rather a 'moment of being', in so far as the logic of becoming leads into a differentiation of the phases of time. 'After individuation, being *has a past*': it is individuation that thus divides and dephases temporality (IGPB 232).

The purely functional difference between past and future is only inscribed in the living at its margins, in its folds. The temporality of the living is in no way continuous, unitary or durable but traverses in the movement of time the different phased temporalities of the interior past and the current exterior present. Living tissue produces time, supports this bundle of divergent temporal lines: past and future distinguished by virtue of a pure localization.

The future is concentrated in this relative exterior, while the past subsists in the relatively durable interiority of the organism. With this analysis, Simondon marks the point at which the spatial and temporal character of vital individuation must be understood in a strong sense. In separating a relative exterior milieu of action to come from a relative subsistent milieu of affection, the living produces a plurality, a differentiation of temporalities. While the borders of the skin, sensible contact, turn out to be the creator of temporality, organic depth condenses memory; interiority, harnessing duration, becomes a temporal condenser, a time trap.

This creative topological separation of interiority and exteriority takes account of the complex treatment to which Simondon subjects time, defined as metastable becoming and phases of being, and which opens on to a conception of the event that is decisive for contemporary philosophy, in particular that of Deleuze, who can write, following Simondon: 'Events are like crystals, they become and grow only out of the edges, or on the edge.'[5] This edge of the event, a surface of demarcation between the actual of transductive individuation and the tension that is played out between the future and the past in vital individuation, receives a new function in this analysis, where it accounts for a border that no longer passes between the interior and physical exterior of the membrane, but rather between psychic interiority and corporeal and perceptible exteriority. The Simondonian membrane can thus be appropriated by Deleuze in order to account for sense as that which produces difference between the exteriority of the states of bodies and the interiority of the incorporeal event. Just as the membrane produces the topological difference between the imminent exterior and the past interiority in Simondon, sense, for Deleuze, determines the difference between the exteriority of bodies and the incorporeal interiority of the pure event. As event, sense has the property of both broaching and separating actual corporeality from virtual thought.

For Simondon, as for Bergson or Deleuze, to be present would be to be – that is to say, to stop, to arrest becoming. This is why Simondon supplements his transductive logic of individuation, of the time of the present, of the density of bodies and of actualization, with becoming, the double streams of the past and the present, chronogenetic trails opened up by the membrane. The present is action; the real traverses the edges of the membrane, and fractures around the metaphysical selvage of the surface, differentiating itself into a temporality of the past and to come, which are never actual. From the transductive logic of individuation, we are led to a complex and phased temporality, producer of its own past and its own capacity for the future.

NOTES

1. TN: The translator would like to thank Arne De Boever for his comments on an earlier draft of this translation.
2. Gilbert Simondon, *L'Individu et sa genèse physico-biologique. L'Individuation à la lumière des notions de forme et d'information* (Grenoble: Jérôme Millon, 1995 [1964]), p. 31. This text will be cited hereafter as IGPB.
3. Gilbert Simondon, *L'Individuation psychique et collective: à la lumière des notions de forme, information, potentiel et métastatique* (Paris: Aubier, 1989), p. 77.
4. See also Gilles Deleuze, *The Logic of Sense*, trans. Mark Lester with Charles Stivale, ed. Constantin V. Boundas (London: Athlone, 1990), p. 104.
5. Ibid., p. 9.

Implications

Chapter 5

The Question of Anxiety in Gilbert Simondon

Igor Krtolica, translated by Jon Roffe[1]

The question of anxiety occupies a singular position in the process of psycho-collective individuation in three regards.[2] It marks, first of all, the threshold of this process, designating the problematic moment at which the subject feels the necessity to pursue its individuation without yet becoming its operator. Anxiety constitutes here a state of blockage for the individual, who is invaded by the charge of pre-individual nature but who is rendered incapable of being individuated in the collective; conscious of being more than an individual, the anxious being has none the less not yet become a transindividual personality. As is the case with every threshold phenomenon, anxiety provides a particularly incisive point of view on the two aspects that it separates and articulates – the psychic subject and the transindividual dimension – and simultaneously casts light on the logic of psychic and collective individuation. For the same reasons, the question of anxiety signals, second, the constitutive ambiguity of the concept of the transindividual in Simondon.[3] Indeed, the transindividual is at once immanent and transcendent to the individual, the condition of the individuation of the subject and the accomplishment of a spirituality, both a given and a result. The decisive concept of the second part of Simondon's main thesis (*L'Individuation psychique et collective*) – the transindividual – is confronted there with certain major difficulties: far from being a contradiction or an incoherence in Simondon's thought, we will see that this ambiguity is in fact of central interest. Finally, the question of anxiety leads us to take stock of the limits and stakes of the theory of emotion in the logic of psychic and collective individuation, where it constitutes, in a certain way, the heart of the theory. A sign that all is not given, emotion implies a seemingly teleological vocabulary with respect to the relation between the subject and the collective in Simondon's work: '*incomplete* and *unachieved* insofar as it is not accomplished in the individuation of the collective', '*initiation* of a new structure', 'it manifests in the individuated being the continued presence of the pre-individual; it is this real potential that, at the heart of what is naturally indeterminate, incites in the subject the relation at the heart of the collective that it institutes; there is a collective to the extent that an emotion is structured; . . . it *prefigures* the discovery of the collective.'[4] The examination of the question of anxiety demonstrates, as we will see, that, in the final instance, Simondon's thought (concerning psycho-collective individuation, the transindividual and emotion) is heterogeneous to every teleological perspective, a thought in which teleology is only the inversed reflection of the constitutive paradox of the transindividual.

ANXIETY AND THE PROBLEM OF ITS GENESIS

Anxiety as the Impossible Attempt to Resolve the Problem of Subjectivity

What does Simondon claim about anxiety? In anxiety, he writes, 'the subject feels existence as a problem posed to itself, i.e. to the subject' (ILFI 255); taking account of the definition according to which the subject is the being who 'bears within itself, more than individuated reality, an unindividuated aspect, pre-individual but also natural' (ILFI 310), we must say that

> the problem of the subject is that of the heterogeneity between the perceptible and affective worlds, between the individual and the pre-individual; this problem is the problem of the subject *qua* subject: the subject is individual and other than individual; it is incompatible with itself. (ILFI 253)

The problem of the subject – which is to say, the incompatibility between the constituted individual and the pre-individual – is, however, insufficient to define anxiety. This problematic connection not only is between the individual and the pre-individual, but also concerns the subject *as it searches in vain for resolution within itself*. This is why, in itself, the subjective experience of the pre-individual does not lead to anxiety; on the other hand, when the subject fails to resolve *within itself* the tension between the constituted part of the individual itself and the pre-individual part which must give way to a new individuation, when the problem does not find the adequate dimension for its resolution, then – and only then – is there anxiety.

Anxiety therefore does not reside in the problematic insistence of the pre-individual within us, but in the experience presented by the impossibility of actualizing this pre-individual *in us*. Certainly, the individual 'does not feel itself to be limited as an individual to a reality entirely its own' (ILFI 304), 'the individual is not only an individual, but also the reserve of being that remains neutral, available, in waiting' (ILFI 303). And yet, it is in this individuality that the anxious individual searches for a means of effectuating this pre-individual reality. The apparent contradiction lies precisely in the fact that the constituted individual must be able to be undone [*destitué*] in order for the unindividuated to emerge in the individual. In other words, it would be necessary for the individual to disappear in order for it to arrive. It is therefore insufficient to say that anxiety is the problem of the *subject*, since the contradiction resides in the impossible attempt to make the subject of individuation the pre-individual in its individual being. In anxiety, the subject is engaged in a relation with itself as if to an individual[5]: *anxiety is an experience of the subject, but the subject as an individual.*

Intending to individuate the entire pre-individual that affects it internally, the anxious being is submitted to an intense expansion, whose description occupies half of the paragraph on anxiety. Anxious subjectivity, grasped in a movement of unlimited expansion, attempts to coincide with the dimensions of the universe: 'The anxious being dissolves into the universe in order to find another subjectivity; it is exchanged for the universe, submerged in its dimensions' (ILFI 256). Now such an expansion, the fusion of the individual being and the charge of nature associated with it, provokes a decline in the structures and functions of the individual. 'The individual is invaded by the pre-individual: all of its structures are attacked, its functions animated by a new force which renders them incoherent' (ILFI 256). The expansion of subjectivity in anxiety envelops, as a result, two profoundly contradictory perspectives, to the extent that the 'new birth' of the individual can only come about at the price of its annihilation. The subject is carried to a point of self-contradiction or auto-abolition: 'Anxiety is the renunciation of the individuated being and that being agrees to traverse the destruction of individuality in order to pass to another unknown individuation' (ILFI 257). In a sense, the anxious being desires its own dissolution, its own death, but in order to arise better from its ashes:

> anxiety already bears the presentiment of this new birth of the individuated being on the basis of the chaos with which it is in accord; . . . but in order for this new birth to be possible, the dissolution of the previous structures and their reduction in potential must be complete, in an acquiescence to the annihilation of the individuated being. (ILFI 256)

In anxiety, the redeployment of the potential of individual structures and functions operates in a contrary fashion to ontogenesis, moving along the inverse path. Thus, with respect to anxiety as the expansion of the subject – the invasion of the individuated by the pre-individual, the impossible attempt to make room for a wholly other subjectivity – Simondon can affirm without contradiction that it is at once the greatest accomplishment of a *solitary* subject and a tragic attempt on the part of this subject to the extent that, deprived of the collective, it fails to produce a new individuation:

> Anxiety translates the condition of the solitary subject; it goes as far as this solitary being; it is a kind of attempt to replace transindividual individuation with the individual non-being that the absence of other subjects renders impossible. Anxiety realises the highest accomplishment of what the solitary being is capable of as a subject; but this realisation appears in fact to only remain a state, not leading to a new individuation, because it is deprived of the collective. (ILFI 256)

In sum, if we attempt to reconstruct the logic which belongs to the phenomenon of anxiety, we obtain the following series: vital individuation is not achieved, but bears a charge of the pre-individual reality associated with the individual; the connection between this pre-individual part and the constituted part of the individual poses a problem to the subject that calls for resolution; anxiety occurs when the isolated subject engages in a contradictory attempt to resolve this problem *in itself* and to live this impossibility. According to a tragic logic, the subjective problem cannot find its creative solution in the dimension of individuated being alone:

> psychism cannot be resolved solely at the level of the individuated being; it is the foundation of the participation in a much vaster, collective individuation; the solitary individual being, putting itself in question, cannot go beyond the limits of anxiety – an operation without action, a permanent emotion that cannot resolve affectivity, proof that the experience through which the individuated being explores the dimensions of its being is without the capacity to exceed them. (ILFI 31)

The Paradox of the Transindividual

That such a route appears catastrophic to Simondon, that it is unavoidably bound to fail, is rendered comprehensible by the situation of the anxious and isolated being, deprived of this greater context to which the problem of the subject must lead. This object that the anxious being lacks, or rather the dimension which is lacking, is the collective. We have seen that, for Simondon, if the anxious being is anxious, it is due to the tension between the pre-individual and the part of the constituted individual whose field of resolution is limited to that of the individual. The subject 'lacks' something; it is 'deprived' of a supplementary dimension. On many occasions, Simondon employs this vocabulary of deprivation and lack, of *the negative* or *the incomplete*. In what sense, though, can the subject be said to *lack* the collective? It seems to us that this vocabulary of the negative is provisory or partial, and that it reveals only one aspect of Simondon's thought, which is so foreign to the negative.[6] In a general fashion, we know that the use of the vocabulary of the negative returns us to Simondon's pre-Socratic inspiration, according to which Nature is defined as unlimited totality, the infinite-indefinite (*apeiron*); however, it seems here that such terminology reveals a *prima facie* difficulty in Simondon's thought. A difficulty, to be more precise, which is not an incoherence but rather an objective paradox – not a difficulty in affirming, but a difficult affirmation.

The paradox is due to the fact that if the subject lacks the collective, if it is deprived of it, this is only the case from the point of view of the collective, that of the transindividual dimension. The paradox can thus be summarily posed by asking: *why does the collective appear simultaneously as that which precedes the anxious subject and that which the subject lacks, both as the condition and the horizon of anxiety?* This paradox requires elaboration. On the one hand, when Simondon adopts the vocabulary of privation, he occupies the point of view of a subject who will have already conquered the collective and would be in a position to prescribe the path to follow in order to resolve the subjective problem. And yet a problem, in the strict sense, can never be posed under the mode of privation; it is positively determined. In virtue of the ontogenetic perspective advocated in the Simondonian project, it seems that the question would be posed less in terms of knowing what the anxious subject *lacks* than what carries it in a positive mode towards trying to resolve in itself the problem posed to it. If the subject 'lacks' the collective, would this not be the case if it does not perceive its existence, or rather if it perceives something entirely different? And yet, if we maintain this, we would be faced less with paradox than with incoherence. It is therefore the case that, on the other hand, the collective precedes the subject in a certain sense, while *at the same time failing it* – but in what sense?

To understand this paradox, it is necessary first of all to explain one of the reasons why Simondon seems at times to employ a negative or retrospective point of view (though we will see that there is another more profound reason, which bears on the constitutive ambiguity of the transindividual); the statement of the general thesis of his work is inscribed in the first instance in the form of a refutation. As the first lines of the Introduction to *L'Individu à la lumiere des notions de forme et d'information* already show, Simondon positions himself in an explicitly critical position, distancing himself at the outset from two apparently opposed and concurrent approaches, substantialism and hylomorphism. These approaches are, in fact, tributaries of a common presupposition. Certainly, 'the monism centred on itself found in substantialist thought is opposed to the bipolarity of the hylomorphic scheme' (ILFI 23). However, these two paths proceed from a single postulate: 'that a principle of individuation exists, anterior to individuation itself, which is susceptible to being explained, produced and guided' (ILFI 23), and that this principle is named *human being, psychic individual* or *social group*. To anthropology as a metaphysical mode of thinking, Simondon objects that it presupposes through abstraction an essence of human being, whether individual or social, which is at the root of two difficulties: it separates the unity of the Human Being from the vital, becoming incapable of thinking the connection between the two, and it renders incomprehensible the relational zone between the individual and the social, a zone undermined and obscured through its operation of abstraction.[7] Now, psychology and sociology both adopt an anthropological point of view on the human being.[8] Simondon opposes to both a formally identical objection: if psychology presents the individual as a primitive fact and the fact of the group as the result of their association, sociology presents in a symmetrical fashion the existence of the group as a brute fact from which individuals are derived. In short, their common error for Simondon concerns the fact that in each case they evacuate the problem of the *operation* of individuation of the group, which is relegated to an 'obscure zone' – in psychology by treating this operation as prior to the individuation of the group, and by sociology as consequent, but neither the fact of the already constituted individual nor that of the existence of the group is able to account for the *simultaneous genesis* of the psychic and the collective.[9]

The perspective of a critique of the presuppositions of the human sciences[10] and the promotion of the transindividual dimension misrecognized by them does not limit the envisioning of the subjective problem to the point of view of this dimension. From this, there follows a torsion in Simondon's argument, to the extent that the transindividual appears to precede the subject itself, while at the same time dissimulating the *positivity of the process* which brings about anxiety. Thus, the critical approach would tend to obscure an underlying ontogenetic logic, which alone is able to retrace the advent of anxiety and its effective resolution. In short, in place of the process that leads to anxiety (which the subject lives while looking within itself for a solution to the subjective problem), Simondon provides a negative point of view on this process (that which the subject lacks in order to succeed; the fault which explains its failure). But in reality the transindividual is also the *condition* of the individuation of the subject in psychic life – and not only its *accomplishment* – and it is in this sense that what is paradoxical is not incoherent. It must be affirmed that this paradox is not a contradiction; *the anxious subject is deprived of the collective precisely because it is not entirely deprived of it.* Such would be another way of expressing the ambiguity of the transindividual, simultaneously immanent and transcendent to the subject.

To say that there is an ambiguity here is to say that there are two paradoxically coexisting aspects of the subjective problem: the absence and the presence of the collective, even in anxiety. This is why it can be conceived as positively (in itself) and negatively (with respect to the collective) at the same time. We have seen the second aspect of this – namely that the anxious being is deprived of the collective – but what is its first aspect? What process leads to anxiety (which drives the individual to be able to resolve in itself the subjective problem) and what event (which drives it to actualize this tension in a domain which is no longer individual but rather transindividual) arouses it?

THE DISCOVERY OF THE TRANSINDIVIDUAL: ZARATHUSTRA AND THE TIGHT-ROPE WALKER

Interindividual Connections and Transindividual Relations

By virtue of Simondon's pre-Socratic inspiration, the ensemble of the vocabulary of the negative (incompleteness, hollow, reserve, delay, lack, privation, and so on) has only a functional meaning, and does not imply a teleological understanding of the constitution of the transindividual, but rather insists on the *a fortiori* vital excess that is manifested at the heart of all individuation. The negative is nothing other than the irreducible power [*puissance*] of the unlimited (*apeiron*) of the charge of pre-individual nature that insists within all individual and social structures, and that prevents these structures from finding their proper end within themselves. These social structures are what Simondon names interindividual reality, a reality that would certainly merit an equally central place in the analysis, alongside the entry into the collective (*qua* transindividual objective) with which it is concurrently achieved. We find a differential analysis of the interindividual connections and transindividual relations in the passage entitled 'The Problematic of Reflexivity in Individuation', in which Simondon confronts the problem of the consistency of the psychological world in relation to the physical and biological domains. In this text, he affirms the non-autonomy of the psychological world, the non-independence of psychological individualization in relation to vital individuation. He motivates this thesis with reference to the dialectical character of psychological individualization; psychology is not a separate order but a mediation between the physical and the biological, between the world and the self, which instantiates a dialectic between the exterior and the interior that, although it is not independent, possesses an ontological value, that of transduction. By virtue of the dialectical nature of psychological individualization, Simondon consequently refuses to grant the domain of psychological individuality its 'own space':

> The domain of psychological individuality is at the limit of physical reality and biological reality, between the natural and nature, as an ambivalent relation having the value of being. Thus the domain of psychological individuality does not have its own space; it exists as a superimposition in relation to the physical and biological domains; it is not properly speaking inserted between the two, but reunites and partially comprehends them, by being situated in them ... The psychological detour does not abandon life, but is an act through which psychological reality is excentred with respect to biological reality, in order to be able to grasp the relation between the self and the world, the physical and the vital, according to its own problematic; psychological reality is deployed as a transductive relation to the world and the self [*moi*]. (ILFI 278)

For Simondon, the importance of such a thesis is threefold. In the first instance, it founds the critique of substantialism by rendering impossible the idealist operation consisting in the abstraction of the psychological world from its physical and biological underpinnings – according to which substantialism takes the form of a substantialist dualism (Descartes) or that of an idealist monism (Bergson), which is for Simondon in reality an asymmetrical dualism. The latter accounts for the relation between vital individuation and psychological individualization by placing the model of the living (individuation) on the side of psychosomatic unity. In the former, the relation is asserted between body and soul, as the result of a continued division (individualization) at the heart of which the psychic and the somatic appear not as real entities but as limited cases 'never present in a pure state' (ILFI 271). Finally, it none the less permits us to confer upon psychology an ontological tenor, which is not that of substance but of the transductive relation:

> the dialectical relation of the individual to the world is transductive, because it deploys an homogenous and heterogeneous world, consistent and continuous but diversified, a world which belongs to neither physical nature nor life, but to this universe in the process of constitution that we can call mind. (ILFI 278)

It is certainly the case that the psychological world is not substantially separate, but an *operation* of transduction between the vital and the physical; likewise, there is certainly no purely psychological world but only the *process* of psychologization. And yet, the regime of the psychological is objectified in a certain sense, precipitated into a world, since it is effectuated in things, in habitual comportment, mental schemata and works. Simondon calls this objective mind *culture*, the concrete existence of the psychological in the world:

> The psychological world exists to the extent that each individual finds before them a series of mental schemata and modes of conduct already incorporated in a culture, and which incites them to pose their particular problems according to a normativity already elaborated by other individuals. (ILFI 279)

To the precise extent that the connections between individuals at the heart of the world of culture come about on the basis of these values, schemata and modes of conduct, Simondon qualifies these as inter-individual connections, thereby designating a specific mode of social linkage which is effectuated at the level of constituted individuals and not that of their pre-individual zone. In interindividual connection, the individual enters into relations with others through their individuated self [*moi*] and appears to itself as the sum of social images which issue from 'a pre-valorisation of the self [*moi*] grasped as a personality through the functional representation made of it by others' (ILFI 279–80). Interindividual connections mark the utilitarian aspect of social relations, *qua* the simple functional mediation between individuals. It is these connections that the descriptions of psychology and sociology concern themselves with, thereby limiting their perspectives to the constituted individual or social group.

In reality, the interindividual connections are defined less by the constituted individuals (their formed selves, their social functions) or by the socially instituted group (the ensemble of exchanges between individuals) than by *the element of pre-individual nature which persists, not yet effectuated in them*. Interindividual connections are the sediment in social objectivity of transindividual nature that constitutes its ground. Just as we must refer the substantialist perspectives of the human sciences back to the operations of individuation that underlie them, we must also return the interindividual to the transindividual domain that is its condition. Thus, in the final instance, interindividual connections and culture derive their sense from the transindividual reality that they bring about, a reality which none the less exceeds and neutralizes them.

> The psychological individual has a choice to operate amidst the values and modes of conduct present to it as examples: but *not everything is given* in culture; we must distinguish between culture and transindividual reality; culture is in a certain sense neutral; it needs to be polarised by the subject putting itself into question; on the contrary, there is in the transindividual relation an imperative for the subject to put itself in question, because this putting in question of the subject has already been begun by the other. The decentralisation of the subject in relation to itself is effectuated in part by the other [*autrui*] in the interindividual relation. Nonetheless, we must note that the interindividual relation can mask the transindividual relation, to the extent that a purely functional mediation appears as a means to avoid the true position of the problem of the individual by the individual itself. The interindividual relation can remain a simple connection and avoid reflexivity. (ILFI 279)11

That not everything is given[12] is the index of the necessary excess of the transindividual over the interindividual, of a pre-individual nature always swarming beneath individuals and constituted groups; this charge of pre-individual reality possesses a potential of individuation capable of carrying individuals and groups towards new becomings. It is fundamental to perceive the asymmetry of the distinction between transindividual relations and interindividual connections, the latter being only the objective sediment of the former, their stabilization in a culture. Culture *qua* the mundane objective existence of the psychological, and interindividual connection *qua* functional sociality have an entirely relative existence. Just as Simondon brings out the operation of individuation from beneath the constituted individual, he also reveals the transindividual reality beneath culture, which conceals more than it reveals.

None the less, the primacy of the transindividual domain with respect to the interindividual given does not efface the consistency proper to interindividual connections. That the distinction is asymmetrical does not mean that we can do without the subordinate term. On the contrary, it is necessary to maintain two theses simultaneously (the primacy of the transindividual over the interindividual and the coexistence of the two) in order to be able to comprehend the *genesis* of the transindividual relation and the dislocating effect it produces. The question of knowing what it is that the individual perceives as constraining its attempt to resolve the subjective problem (anxiety) in itself, rather than engaging the dimension of the collective, can now receive a precise response: the individual evolves through interindividual connections with personalities (constituted individuals), grasped with respect to their functional distributions (the utilitarian division of society), that lead it to misrecognize the dimension of the transindividual. Now misrecognition is not ignorance, but rather not knowing how to know [*ne pas savoir connaître*], not knowing that one knows. As a result, we would have been wrong to say that interindividual connections are the first stage in the experience of the transindividual, that they are merely a prelude, destined to self-destruction for the good of the collective. And this is so for two reasons: because they produce an effect of *blockage* in the transindividual – they mask it and make its discovery difficult (as the previous citation stated, 'the interindividual relation can mask the transindividual relation, to the extent that a purely functional mediation appears as a means to avoid the true position of the problem of the individual by the individual itself'); and, because even if the transindividual persists beneath these connections, its effective constitution depends on an event likely to suspend them, unravel their fabric and reveal their relativity.

The reference to Nietzsche, and more specifically to the Prologue of *Thus Spoke Zarathustra*, occurs at this crucial moment of Simondon's argument, in which he describes the effective constitution of the transindividual (this time as the accomplishment of psychic life rather than as its condition) on the basis of interindividual relations, in favour of an 'exceptional event'. 'A first encounter between the individual and transindividual reality is required, and this encounter is perhaps only an exceptional situation which presents in an external fashion the aspects of a revelation' (ILFI 280). This event will be constituted by the encounter between Zarathustra and the dying tight-rope walker, an encounter which will provoke a destitution of the functional relation and will bring about in Zarathustra a painful disindividuation. Such a disindividuation is, however, profoundly different from that of anxiety – that is, with respect to the expansion to which the anxiety subject is submitted. Anxiety tends towards an annihilation of all the structures and functions of the individual without permitting a new individuation, due to the solitude of the subject.[13] On the contrary, rather than being solely concerned with the annihilation of the individual, the disindividuation implicated in the encounter with the transindividual is only provisional and constitutes the condition of a new individuation in the collective.[14]

The Rent Veil

We have seen that the interindividual connections function as a veil that blocks the discovery and effectuation of a pre-individual reality in the transindividual: the interindividual as a function of misrecognition. Now, only the event of an *encounter* can tear this veil by suspending 'the functional modality of the relation with the other [*autrui*], and in which an other subject, deprived of its social function, can appear to us in its more-than-individuality'.[15] Simondon sees such an event in the accidental death of the tight-rope walker at Zarathustra's feet in the Prologue of *Thus Spoke Zarathustra*. *Contingent*, in so far as it is unpredictable and impossible to guarantee, this encounter none the less constitutes the *necessary* condition for the discovery of the dimension adequate to collective individuation. The realization of the reality of the transindividual thus rests on the contingency of an event, of which we can determine three principal characteristics: it is involuntary, disindividuating and isolating.

In so far as it is contingent, it can never be the object of a subjective decision, will or choice, but it is always an encounter, an external constraint, a violence exercised from the outside on the subject. The event is necessarily *involuntary*. Involuntary, it is at once contingent and necessary. Contingent-necessary: this double aspect of the event refers in reality to the exteriority of the forces that are manifest in the encounter and which take hold of the subject. In so far as it is involuntary, it seems that the transindividual is transcendent rather than immanent to the subject, and, as the forces external to it, overcomes it. (We will see none the less that the self-constitutive character of the transindividual will provoke a more detailed assessment of this idea.) Zarathustra left his mountain and decided to descend towards the people in order to speak to them of the overman. After holding forth, affirming that man – a rope tied between animal and overman – must be overcome, he is forced to admit his incapacity to address the people as a being understood by them.[16] Incapable of being alone, having left his mountain to teach of the overman, he yet proves incapable of addressing his peers. It is in this way that the scene with the rope-walker begins: 'But then something happened that silenced every mouth and fixed every eye. In the meantime, of course, the tight-rope walker had begun his work.'[17] Dancing on a rope stretched between two towers, he suddenly falls to earth, suffering at Zarathustra's feet while the crowd scatters and turns away.[18]

Faced with the suffering of the tight-rope walker, Zarathustra discovers a relation to an other profoundly different from that which bound him to the people, and which bears on a movement of *disindividuation*. Moribund, the rope walker is dispossessed of his social character; Zarathustra can now befriend this man lying at death's door, since the interindividual relations in which they were previously held have disappeared.[19] The suffering tight-rope walker no longer appears according to his social function, but belongs to another order.

> The transindividual relation is that of Zarathustra and his disciples, or that of Zarathustra and the tight-rope walker who is broken on the earth before him and abandoned by the crowd; the crowd only considered the rope walker with respect to his function; they abandon him when, dead, he ceases to exercise this function; in contrast, Zarathustra feels this man to be his brother, and carries his body to burial; it is with solitude, in Zarathustra's presence to this dead friend abandoned by the crowd, that the experience of transindividuality commences. (ILFI 280)

The second determination of the event is related to the first; the encounter can only be voluntary because it is a break from the link instituted between the individual and others. The event occurs as an event in so far as it breaks with the interindividual mode of existence, a break that the disindividuation of anxiety fails to accomplish; in so far as the disindividuation of anxiety is catastrophic, what takes place thanks to the event of the encounter permits the pursuit of individuation. None the less, if disindividuation is the necessary condition for a new psycho-collective individuation, it is not yet a sufficient one. New individuation is never guaranteed by disindividuation, even if it necessarily passes through it; in order not to degenerate into anxiety but rather consist in a positive emotion which assures the passage to the transindividual, disindividuation must only be *provisional*. Zarathustra is not yet sheltered from the catastrophe of anxiety.

The *solitude* that Zarathustra is necessarily subject to must be traversed in order for the dimension of the collective to be entered into. Beyond the interindividual, solitude; beyond solitude, the collective. And yet the transindividual as task is never constituted, it is never entirely given, but remains to be done; this is why Zarathustra has need of neither other individuals nor the people in their entirety (neither believers nor herds), but of co-creators, those capable of producing a new individuation called forth by solitude. In other words, the solution to the problem of the subject resides in neither the individual nor the social dimension, but rather in the collective dimension.

> The creator seeks companions, not corpses or herds or believers. The creator seeks fellow-creators, those who inscribe new values on new tables. The creator seeks companions and fellow harvesters: for with him everything is ripe for harvesting . . . Zarathustra seeks fellow creators.[20]

The Ambiguity of the Transindividual and Emotion

The need to make the discovery of the transindividual depend upon the event of an encounter, to relate the possibility of psychic and collective individuation to the requirement of any necessary condition, however contingent in its appearance, underlines another difficulty. Simondon insists less on the necessity of such an encounter for collective individuation than on the *self-constitutive* character of the transindividual. In so far as the idea of encounter could allow us to think that the transindividual is a dimension which comes to supplement the vital individual in favour of the event in question, Simondon, to the contrary, puts the accent on what he calls the 'fundamental ambiguity' of the transindividual; this is not immanent to the individual, but neither is it transcendent, able to survive external to it. It is rather both at once, profoundly interior and more external than every exterior, sometimes conceived as the profound interiority of the self [*soi*] (that it will be a matter of rejoining), and sometimes as divine transcendent exteriority (from which revelation is awaited):

> If we admit that the transindividual is self-constitutive, we will see that the two schemata of transcendence and immanence only take account of this self-constitution from the point of view of their simultaneous and reciprocal positions: indeed, it is at each moment of this self-constitution that the connection between individual and transindividual is defined as that which *exceeds the individual in prolonging it*. The transindividual is not external to the individual, and yet it is detached to a certain degree from it; furthermore, this transcendence which takes root in interiority, or rather at the limit between the exterior and the interior, does not belong to an exteriority, but to the movement which exceeds the dimension of the individual. (IFLI 281)

Consequently, a certain tension between the idea of the event and that of the self-constitution of the transindividual subsists. This paradox is in reality easily resolved, if the conception of the event as an encounter with the arrival of a pure transcendence, and the conception of self-constitution as the simple pursuit of vital individuation are rejected – in virtue of what Simondon calls a 'postulate of discontinuity' over the course of successive individuations (ILFI 317). The self-constitutive character of the transindividual is not opposed to the effect of discontinuity produced by its constitution, just as, symmetrically, the idea of the event does not exclude a certain immanence of the transindividual in the subject, since the transindividual is already present as pre-individual in the subject even before it is individuated in the collective. What, then, happens between the pre-individual and the transindividual? The pre-individual returns to being in so far as it is monophased, returns to its being prior to any individuation[21]; the concepts of pre-individual and transindividual are both certainly returned to the charge of nature, but to a monophased charge in the first case, and a polyphased charge in the second. Nevertheless, 'it is pre-individual reality which can be considered as the reality which grounds transindividuality' (ILFI 317).[22]

The event of the encounter is double (whence its paradoxical character): neither immanent nor transcendent, it occurs as a rupture while already being there as ground rather than structure. The transindividual never will be given, never is; it must provide, to the contrary, the object of a creative effectuation, a neotenic amplification of the pre-individual which is never achieved before being pursued, each time the object of a recommencement. The stakes of psycho-collective individuation and the risk of a fall into anxiety are to be found, concentrated, in the theory of emotion, which designates the link between the pre-individual with the transindividual (and which precedes the general conclusion of Simondon's principal thesis):

> The essential instant of emotion is the individuation of the collective; both before and after this instant, a true and complete emotion cannot be discovered. Emotive latency, the non-adequation of the subject to itself, the incompatibility between its charge of nature and its individuated reality, indicates to the subject that it is more than an individuated being, and that it conceals within itself the energy for an ulterior individuation; but this ulterior individuation can only take place in the being of the subject; it can only take place through this being of the subject, and through other beings in a transindividual collective. (ILFI 315)

The *beginning* of an other individuation, a *sign* that not everything is given, an incomplete and unachieved manifestation in so far as it is not structured in the collective, emotion opens on to a field without yet being equal to it. No teleology is at work here; emotion is an *opening of possibilities*. In order to give these possibilities to the body, instead of activating the catastrophe of anxiety, it is necessary to discover the transindividual collective anew each time – today for tomorrow, in order that these possibilities remain open.

NOTES

1. TN: The translator would like to thank Arne De Boever and Ashley Woodward for their comments on a draft of this translation.
2. TN: Throughout, the word 'anxiety' and its cognates translate the French *angoisse*. This word has a complex place in twentieth-century French thought, playing an important role in both psychoanalysis and existentialism. It bears an analogous range to the German *Angst*, which is at the root of both the Sartrean use of *angoisse* (whose ultimate heritage is Kierkegaard's *Angest*) and the Lacanian deployment of Freudian concepts. (To recall, the title of the 1926 'Hemmung, Symptom und Angst' is translated as 'Inhibitions, Symptoms and Anxiety'.) Unfortunately, as these examples illustrate, there is no single word in English to convey the full scope of the French. Furthermore, Simondon's interest in *angoisse* cannot be reduced to either of these perspectives, both of which he explicitly criticizes. The choice of 'anxiety' is meant to avoid the maudlin connotations of the English 'anguish' – at the very least, we should be wary of reducing 'anxiety' as it is treated here in terms of any superficial or secondary affect, a point amply attested to by the author – and to keep in line with the forthcoming translations of Simondon's work.
3. Cf. J.-H. Barthélémy, *Simondon ou l'encyclopédisme génétique* (Paris: PUF, 2008), 111–12; M. Combes, *Simondon. Individu et collectivité* (Paris: PUF, 1999), 84–5.
4. G. Simondon, *L'Individu à la lumière des notions de forme et d'information* (Grenoble: Jérôme Millon, 2005 [1964]), 314–15, emphasis added; hereafter this work will be cited in text as ILFI, followed by the relevant page number.
5. This is what Muriel Combes sees so well when she remarks in a note on Simondon's work that

    > 'It is true that anxiety, as an experience of a pre-individuality, is not an *individual* experience, but already *subjective*. And yet, in the measure to which the subject endeavours to resolve the whole of the preindividual submerged within it in its individuality, we cannot say that it accepts itself as a subject: anxiety is rather the experience in which a subject – *at the same time* as it discovers in itself a dimension irreducible to that of simple constituted individuality – endeavours to reabsorb it into the interiority of its individual being.' (Combes, *Simondon*, 67)

    On this point, see also M. Combes and B. Aspe, 'L'acte fou', *Multitudes*, 18, (September 2004).
6. Recall the celebrated passage found in the Introduction of his thesis where Simondon demarcates ontogenesis from every dialectic grounded in the substance of the negative:

    > the study of the operation of individuation does not seem to correspond to the manifestation of the negative as a second stage, but to an immanence of the negative in the first condition in the ambivalent form of tension *and* incompatibility; there is something more positive in the state of pre-individual

being, namely, the existence of potentials, which is also the cause of the incompatibility and non-stability of this state; the negative is in the first instance ontogenetic incompatibility, but it is the other face of a richness of potentials; it is not therefore a substantial negative; it is never a stage or phase, and individuation is not synthesis or a return to unity, but the dephasing of the being beginning with its pre-individual centre of potentialised incompatibility. (ILFI 34)

In place of the metaphysical vocabulary of the negative, Simondon proposes a physical-problematic conception of potentials and of metastability that he sees at work in pre-Socratic thought, but which finds its epistemological model in the Bachelardian interpretation of contemporary physics (cf. J.-H. Barthélémy, *Simondon*, Chapter 1: ' "Le Réalisme des relations": un préalable épistémologique').

7. Cf. ILFI 297:

Anthropological investigation would thereby presuppose a prior abstraction, such as a division between the individual and society, and a principle of prior abstractions. Anthropology cannot be the principle of the study of Humanity; to the contrary, it is human relational activities, such as that which constitutes work, which can be taken as primary for any anthropology to explain. It is this being as relation which is primary and must be taken as a principle; the human is social, psycho-social, psychic, somatic, without any one of these aspects being taken as fundamental, at the cost of rendering the others as mere accessories.

8. On anthropology, see ILFI IV, Chapter 1.4: 'The Insufficiency of the Notion of the Essence of Human Being and of Anthropology'.

9. Cf. ILFI 312–13:

By taking the reality of groups as a fact, in the manner of sociological objectivity, one situates them as prior to grounding the collective. Correlatively, if one begins with the postulates of an interpsychology, one locates the tendencies or social needs of the individual as prior to the group, and consequently accounts for this group in terms of the psychic dynamisms internal to individuals. Now, the true collective is a contemporary of the operation of individuation, and can only be known as a relation between the extreme terms of the purely social and the purely psychic. Being is deployed across the entire spectrum, in a movement from social exteriority to psychic interiority. The social and the psychic are only limit-cases and not the foundations of reality, the true terms in the relation. They only exist as extreme terms from the point of view of knowledge, because knowledge needs to apply a hylomorphic scheme, using two clear ideas to mask an obscure relation.

10. On this perspective, see the beginning of the text 'Forme, Information, Potentiels' (presented at the conference held at the Société Française de Philosophie on 27 February 1960), in ILFI 531–51. Simondon here regrets the absence of a general theory of the human sciences, which he sees as the index of a task for reflective thought, a task he explain in detail in this text:

The absence of a general theory of the human sciences and psychology incites reflexive thought to search for the conditions of a possible axiomatisation . . . We would be able to show that an outline of an axiomatics of the human sciences – or at least of psychology – is possible if we try to grasp the three notions of form, information and potential together, provided that we also consider the definition, required to link them together and internally organize them, of a type of operation that appears whenever we find form, information and potential: the transductive relation.

Cf. J.-H. Barthélémy, 95–101.

11. Simondon illustrates this distinction and the effect of the dissimulation produced by interindividual connections through reference to the Pascalian antagonism between distraction and reflexive consciousness: if we assess this according to the conceptual influence of distraction in Pascal – that is, if we take seriously the role of this mask-effect in the constitution of the transindividual – we will see it is of extreme importance. Recourse to the Prologue of Nietzsche's *Thus Spoke Zarathustra* will confirm this.

12. 'Everything is given' is a recurrent Bergsonian formulation in *Creative Evolution* (it appears seven times), serving to qualify the monist position criticized by Bergson.

13. Let us recall the strange reservation that Simondon appends to this thesis: 'Nevertheless, there is no absolute certainty to be had on this point: this transformation of the subject-being towards which anxiety tends is perhaps only possible in very rare cases' (ILFI 256). Is he thinking of the triad of specific figures that he will mention later as effectuations of the transindividual: the sage, the hero and the saint (ILFI 282)?

14. On this point, Barthélémy clearly demonstrates the difference between anxiety as failure and emotion as the success of the passage to the transindividual, due not to the disindividuating effect (present in both cases) but rather to 'the provisory character of the disindividuation provoked by positive emotion' (J.-H. Barthélémy, *Simondon*, 88–90).

15. M. Combes, *Simondon*, 66.

16.   They do not understand me, I am not the mouth for these ears . . . Unmoved is my soul and bright as the mountains in the morning. But they think me cold and a mocker with fearful jokes. And now they look at me and laugh: and laughing, they still hate me. There is ice in their laughter. (Friedrich Nietzsche, *Thus Spoke Zarathustra*, trans. R. J. Hollingdale (London: Penguin, 1986): 'Zarathustra's Prologue' §5, 47)

TN: The author refers throughout to the French translation by G. Bianquis, *Ainsi parlait Zarathoustra* (Paris: Aubier, 1969).

17. Nietzsche, *Zarathustra*, §6, 47.

18. Nietzsche, *Zarathustra*, §6, 48: the tight-rope walker

lost his head and the rope; he threw away his pole and fell, faster even than it, like a vortex of legs and arms. The market square and the people were like a sea in a storm: they flew apart in disorder, especially where the body would come crashing down. But Zarathustra remained still and the body fell quite close to him, badly injured and broken but not yet dead.

19. On anguish as the revelation of singularities, cf. Gilles Deleuze, 'Immanence: a life', trans. Anne Boyman, in *Pure Immanence: Essays on a Life* (New York: Zone, 2001), pp. 25–33:

Between his life and his death, there is a moment that is only that of *a* life playing with death. The life of the individual gives way to an impersonal and yet singular life that releases a pure event freed from the accidents of internal and external life, that is, from the subjectivity and objectivity of what happens. (28)

20. Nietzsche, *Zarathustra*, 'Zarathustra's Prologue', §9, 52.
21. Cf. ILFI 320:

only the pre-individual phase can be properly called monophased: at the level of the individuated being, being is necessarily already polyphased, since the pre-individual past survives alongside the existence of the individuated being and remains the germ of new amplifying operations.

22. In this sense, we can affirm that the connection between pre-individual and transindividual concentrates the problem of the self-constitution of the transindividual. On this connection between pre-individual and transindividual, and the constitutive ambiguity of the concept of the transindividual, cf. J.-H. Barthélémy, *Simondon*, Chapter 4, 'La Question du transindividuel'; see also M. Combes, *Simondon*, 84–5.

Chapter 6

Infra-Psychic Individualization: Transductive Connections and the Genesis of Living Techniques[1]

Marie-Pier Boucher

In the biotechnological age, life has taken a dramatic form; today's life is not only concerned with technology, it co-emerges with it. Contemporary biotechnological interventions create intelligent machines, responsive materials, hybrids, cyborgs, semi-living beings, partial life, chimeras: all categories referring to monstrous entities whose demonstrations orchestrate our evolutionary dis/continuities – all kinds of *biotechnical individuals*. By foregrounding the relationships between life, technique and the environment, I investigate here the potential for the integration of life's materials and processes into design practices that give rise to what I call living techniques or techniques of bringing to life (*techniques du faire vivant*). Living techniques amount to life's operational and creative identity by raising the question of the level of complexity at which life presents itself as an emerging property. Central to this question is these living techniques' political field of emergence: that is, living techniques' potential to discover new goals in the course of their becoming as well as to invent new forms of actions to achieve these goals. The complex relationships between perception and action are therefore at stake.

Gilbert Simondon's thought holds great potential to think – or rethink – the political relations entangled in the process of coupling life's materials and processes with technology. One could argue that contemporary debates about biotechnology combine the two principal themes of Simondon's work: (1) the modes of existence of technical objects and (2) the concept of individuation. A key aspect of his thought revolves around the application of the concept of the individual to that of the technical object. This peculiar contribution opens up a conceptual milieu for thinking about the onto-epistemology of the emergence of living techniques as biotechnical individuals.

Living techniques' ontology is irremediably dynamic. Their becoming follows a series of forceful relations whose operations give birth to *bios* and *tekhnē*. The way we foster the political but also the ontological implications of the emergence of this new class of beings is therefore at stake. In order to articulate a politics of dynamic becoming, a programme of individuation in cooperation – one which acknowledges the becoming of the object and the subject, of *bios* and *tekhnē* – certainly stands out as a point of departure for engaging with the monstrous unpublished works produced by sciences and technology. Simondon's theory of individuation notably asserts this mutual becoming of subjects and objects, of quasi-objects and/or partial subjects.[2] 'Objectivity and subjectivity', he says, 'arise between the living and its milieu, between man and the world, at a moment where the world does not have a complete object status, nor man a complete subject one.'[3]

Living techniques' individuation questions their potential to operate at the intersection of the born and the manufactured, between the natural and the artificial. It puts a demand on their capacity to respond creatively to the problematic tensions they encounter in the relationships they share with their environment (relationships from which they also emerge): that is to say, their capacity to individuate psychically. According to Simondon, there are five phases of individuation: vital, physical, psychic, collective and transindividual. These different phases do not follow one another in succession; rather they complement or supplement – they complexify – one another. They are not chronological but correlative. That is why one should not distinguish them substantially, but rather focus on the 'rhythm of their becoming': that is, on the 'differences of speed in the process of their formation'.[4] Simondon's theory of individuation cannot be thought outside the relationship between the individual's ontogenesis and its milieu (which in turn are also related to a generative field of emergence, or plane of immanence, what he calls pre-individual nature: namely, a reality charged with potentials, a reality to which I will come back later).

Psychic individua*liza*tion arises when biophysical individuals face 'environmental' conflicts – problematic or yet to be resolved relationships with their milieu. Psychic individualization is therefore synonymous with a creative response to 'ecological' tensions. These tensions may actuate a reactivation of biophysical individuals' potentialities and generate processes of individuation that reach new levels of magnitude. The reactivation of a biophysical individual's charge of potentialities is conditioned by this individual's coming into a collective. The emergence of collective individuation is that which conditions the actualization of these potentialities, potentialities that would otherwise not achieve full expression/signification. As we shall see, the coming into a collective introduces the possibility for an amplification of the potentials of the biophysical individual, for a coupling that reaches another level of magnitude and goes beyond the individual's already constituted individualities. Hence the couplings that result from the amplification of biophysical potentials, and unlock the likelihood for new actions to emerge. From this perspective, investigating the potential of biotechnical individuals to individualize psychically (and therefore collectively) becomes the key aspect of living techniques' political field of emergence: their capacity to individuate inventively and creatively within the relations they share with their environment.

In order to focus the discussion on the materiality (both corporeal and incorporeal) of living techniques, I will address the emergence of replicative life in the context of recent work on protocells. Protocell technology is conceptualized here in terms of an emerging biotechnical individual and it is asked whether they hold creative relationships with their environment. In doing so, I elicit the possibility for Simondon's thinking to offer operational tools of engagement with contemporary biotechnological development by exploring the possibilities of protocell technology to (1) individuate infra-psychically and (2) generate biotechnical, though non-human, collectives. For Simondon, however, psycho-collective individuation seems only to be enacted by and through a human subject. Consequently, his argument tends to negate the possibility for non-human living entities – for biotechnical individuals – to individuate psychically.

In order to engage creatively in such an anthropomorphic misreading of Simondon's individuation, I refer to some operational tools found in Alfred North Whitehead's speculative philosophy. Whitehead's notion of 'poles of mentality' (the intermixing of physicality and mentality) will be used to open up Simondon's conception of the subject. I will therefore investigate the ways in which Whitehead's physico-mental intermixing, when grasped from the ontogenetic becoming of protocells, generates new milieus of association that activate a protocell's infra-psychic individualization. Whitehead's application of the subject to non-humans amounts to a non-anthropomorphic understanding of the subject and offers productive tools for the analysis of the transformative processes immanent to non-human entities.

By offering a critical analysis of the anthropomorphism associated with Simondon's notion of individuation, I evoke the potential for non-human life (here protocell technology) to individuate psychically, meaning, their capacity to reconnect with their potentials in ways that activate their power of amplification: that is to say, their capacity to achieve greater orders of magnitude by coming into collectives. Though some of Simondon's ideas will not appear as fundamentally new, a combined reading of the two themes that animate his thought has, in my opinion, not yet been fully expanded. The understanding of technical objects as activators of individuation has been addressed, although the application of the concept of the individual to that of technical objects has not been given adequate attention. Accordingly, I suggest that Simondon's contribution can activate a restaging of the relational frameworks within which contemporary technological interventions on biological systems are conceptualized.

INDIVIDUATION AS PROCESS OF RETICULATION

Before addressing the individuation process of protocell technology and its psycho-collective phase, let me first introduce Simondon's theory of individuation. Some preliminary ontological and epistemological considerations will lay the necessary foundations for a better understanding of its five phases. Simondon argues that the fundamental epistemological postulate of his theory is that 'the relation between two relations is itself a relation.'[5] For him, a relation does not relate two pre-existing terms; rather, it emerges through constituting the terms as relations. Hence, relations constitute Being's modalities and are simultaneous to the terms to which they provide existence. 'A relation', he says, 'does not arise between two individuated terms; it is rather an aspect of the internal resonance of a system of individuation.'[6] The notion of internal resonance amounts to the incompletion of the individual, to the individual's permanent becoming. It also insists on the fact that the evolutionary transformations of the individual are immanent to Being. Simondon asserts the primacy of Being over the individual. He considers the individual as a 'relative reality', as a 'phase of Being'. Accordingly, individuation insists on Beings' constitutive relations (Being-in-relation) rather than on constituted Beings (or Beings' existing conditions). When Being is understood as a 'Being-in-relation', it cannot be reduced to a constituted individual that would exhaust its potentialities. It is therefore the process of individuation, which shall be explained, rather than Being that allows the explanation to be found. *'Individuation is thus considered alone as ontogenetic, as the operation of the complete Being* [Simondon's emphasis].'[7] And so, ontogenesis accounts simultaneously for the genesis and the becoming of Being.

For Simondon, Being-in-relation is a multiplicity, a *'non-un'* (not-one), which can be seized by and through a reality that is both prior and simultaneous to individuation: the pre-individual nature. The pre-individual nature is a 'reality charged with potentials actually existing as potentials, as the energy of a metastable system'.[8] Nature is, for Simondon, a source of generation: a reality carried by the individual, a reality that is not 'man's opposite, but the first phase of Being, the second phase being the opposition between the individual and the environment'.[9] Here the act of carrying generates a confusion of sense. Carrying a charge of potentials does not mean that the individual contains the potential of his own becoming. This confusion can be solved by referring to the way in which Brian Massumi qualifies the virtual. 'The virtual [here the pre-individual nature] is not contained in any actual form assumed by things or states of things [here the individual]'; by contrast, it 'runs in the transitions from one form to another'.[10] Simondon's description of the pre-individual nature is analogical to Massumi's qualification of the virtual: the pre-individual runs in between the individual's different phases of individuation. Conceptualized as such, the pre-individual nature is a zone of indetermination charged with the individual's potentials, the reality of his becoming.

For Simondon, individuation is not attributable to the becoming of the individual and to its relation with the pre-individual nature alone. The individual is always coupled with an associated milieu, which acts as the individual's complement. Hence, the process of individuation is the complete system within which the genesis of the individual takes place. This system as a whole is concerned with the relations between three terms: the individual, the associated milieu, and the pre-individual nature that bridges the former two. The pre-individual nature is the primitive unity from which both the individual and the associated milieu are split (*dédoublés*). The individual is therefore in relation to the pre-individual nature by and through its associated milieu. The fact that Being is a multiplicity, a '*non-un*' becomes clearer; being is both the individual and its associated milieu, and that relationality is reticulated by and through the pre-individual nature.

This general framework enables one to understand individuation as a reticulation process of the relations between the individual and its associated milieu, a process made possible by connecting the individual and its milieu to their primitive unity, the pre-individual nature. Let me now encounter the connections that these processual and genetic relations share with the concretization process proper to technical objects. There are indeed some great resonances between individuation and technical concretization. According to Simondon, technical evolution occurs through the passage from an abstract object to a concrete one, where concretization is the name of the process that takes place in between both forms, a process that acknowledges the way in which they mutually in-form one another. Concretization as a process insists on the indeterminate, on the not yet fully concrete, and in so doing, it opens up a space of indeterminacy and reveals the creative difference of the biotechnical becoming. Indeed, the passage from the abstract to the concrete is determined by singular points that contain numerous variations; the concrete form is therefore not directly linked to the abstract one. The passage is one of creative difference. Such an understanding of technical becoming makes visible the field of emergence of technical objects that tends to vanish in the fully concretized objects that emerge from it. Here, as with individuation, concretization is an ontogentic process doubled with becoming.

Nevertheless, the 'form' generated, whether concretized or individuated, must not be understood in terms of a static form – that is, in terms of a constituted, complete and stable individual – but rather as a dynamic form: a metastable individual. For Simondon, equilibrium is always already metastable. The individual can achieve a structure, but as it is always coupled with an associated milieu and pre-individual nature, this structure is never stable. Through processes of internal development and progressive saturation – that is, by conservation of primary tensions – technical individuals produce structures. Thus a technical individual emerges through a process of 'resolution of primary tensions and a preservation of these tensions in the form of structure' but 'the discovery of a structure is indeed the resolution, at least provisory, of the incompatibilities, but it does not destroy the potentials; the system remains tense and able to modify itself.'[11] Technological lineages develop as stability plateaus emerge within the technical environment. Once they have reached a particular saturation point in their evolution – that is, after having accumulated various micro-changes saturating their technical environment – reconfigurations occur in order to allow new exploitations and new expansions into the environment itself. Concretization as a process operates within incompatibilities that force technical objects to perform compromises between requirements in conflict. In technical evolution, incompatibilities are means for realization rather than obstacles. As Simondon puts it, technical objects 'evolve through internal redistribution of functions between compatible units . . . specialization does not occur function by function but rather synergy by synergy'.[12]

CHRONO-TOPOLOGIES: LIFE AS MODE OF RELATION

The analogical relationships between technical concretization and individuation raise the question of the passage from physical to biological individuation. As Muriel Combes notes in her excellent book on Simondon, 'the difference that exists between the physical and the biological domains is the one which distinguishes a primary individuation of inert systems and a secondary individuation of living systems'.[13] She adds that it is necessary to 'conceive biological individuation not as something that adds determinations to an already individuated being, but rather as a process that slows down physical individuation'.[14] Biophysical individuation is therefore not a synthesis but a connection. Following this logic, Simondon qualifies the living as an interior 'theatre of individuation' coupled with a physical exteriority and he argues for the space of interiority to constitute the living's difference.

> The physical individual, perpetually de-centered, perpetually peripheral to itself, active at the limit of its domain, does not have a veritable interiority; the living individual, on the contrary, does have a veritable interiority because individuation carries itself out within the individual; the interior is constitutive in the living individual, whereas in the physical individual, only the limit is constitutive . . . Within itself, the living is a nexus of informative communication; it is a system within a system, containing *within itself* a mediation between two orders of magnitude.[15]

In this context, life's difference is that its topological configuration generates a space of interiority that allows it to perform its own limitation and its own organization when receiving in-formation. Conversely, inert matter does not have the capacity for structural ontogenesis.[16] Following this line of argument, Simondon claims that the membrane constitutes life's most important mediating element and insists on the fact that the polarized and asymmetrical character of cellular permeability is at the basis of every function. According to him, the membrane is a *sine qua non* condition of the living. In addition to being alive, it maintains the milieu of interiority in relation to the milieu of exteriority. It acts as a force of connection, as a link, as a nexus.

Simondon asserts that in order to approach the inherent duality between the living and the non-living, one should produce a topology of the living: namely, an analysis of the mediating relations between milieus of interiority and milieus of exteriority. However, such an analysis should not frontally differentiate spaces of interiority and exteriority, but amount to their coming together, to their common connective energy. Simondon adds that life not only is characterized by these mediating relations, but it is also a theatre of confrontation between an interior past and an exterior future. Every topological character, he says, has a chronological correlative, and vice versa. Chronology alone, however, implies a sort of linearity, whereas the relationship between the interior past and the exterior future is not linear. Topological individuals are also chronological because time breaks their spatial coherence. When the interior opens itself to the outside, it opens itself to the indeterminate, to a futurity, to a changing potential. From this perspective, life really exists in relationality by maintaining a chrono-topological structure. It would be correct to say here that life emerges from within, but is always in between.

According to Simondon life is a mode of relation. It is not the form of individuation, nor is it a vital substance opposed to a physical one. Life is a form only when considered a 'dynamic form' or a 'form of process': a form existing in relationality, a relational form. Life is a mode of relation conditioned by its capacity to maintain a topological structure. Life's milieu of interiority is active. It is a relational milieu *carried* by the individual, a space of reconfiguration of the membrane that holds the potential to activate a change in the relational system by passing again through the membrane to exteriorize itself another time. This exact passage is one of the central questions concerning protocells: namely, whether they have an active space of interiority that can exteriorize itself.

PROTOCELLS: CHEMISTRY'S CLOSE ENCOUNTER WITH BIOLOGY

The protocell is a technology currently developed in the field of synthetic biology, a field emerging at the intersection of the sciences and engineering that seeks to engineer biology and that claims to lay the foundations for the eventual invention / generation of a protocell proper. The core question regarding protocells concerns the initial transition from chemistry to Darwinian evolution; that is, it concerns how the evolution of life might have started on earth. Protocells are the object of an operational fiction. To date, they mainly operate on the level of science fiction; they fully perform on the discursive level but have yet to achieve concrete unity. They still exist in a dispersed abstract state, although have already begun an *in vitro* individuation process in the labs of synthetic biologists.

A protocell is an ordered structure, enclosed by a membrane that carries out some living activities, such as growth and division. According to Jack W. Szostak (Professor of Genetics at the Harvard Medical School), their basic elements can be grouped under two fundamental categories: (1) a membrane and (2) genetic information. Szostak does not include metabolism and replication, most likely because he associates (1) the membrane with the metabolism, as metabolic energy transfers are ensured by it, and (2) the capacity to replicate with both the membrane and genetic information. Szostak and his team use fatty acids, presumed to have been around when life first emerged on earth, to trigger the generation of the membrane. On the level of genetic information it is not clear whether they require RNA itself or a simpler progenitor material that might have been replaced later by RNA.[17] As Szostak and his colleague Alonso Ricardo have argued,

> recent experiments suggest it would have been possible for genetic molecules similar to DNA or to its close relative RNA to form spontaneously. And because these molecules can curl up in different shapes and act as rudimentary catalysts, they may have become able to copy themselves – to reproduce – without the need for proteins.[18]

The key point here is that they need to synthesize a system with (1) a membrane able to grow spontaneously, and (2) genetic information that also has the capacity to replicate spontaneously. Szostak's team, however, has not yet successfully achieved the replication of genetic information. So, on the one hand, the protocell is based on its capacity spontaneously to generate (1) a membrane (and to replicate it) and (2) chains of RNA. On the other, it is based on its capacity to assemble the membrane and the RNA chain together. The latter has been successfully achieved. As Szostak explained in his Noble Prize lecture, they use a common clay mineral that triggers the assemblage of chains of RNA and membranes. This common clay mineral catalyses the assembly of membranes and brings the two together (the RNA chain – or genetic material – and the membrane). The problem yet to be solved is the replication of the genetic material.[19] Protocells operate at the boundary between the physical and the biological, and the issue at stake is not whether they are alive, but that of the dynamic form that the relations between the physical and the biological take.

TRANSDUCTIVE CONNECTIONS: DYNAMIC FUTURE AS QUASI-CAUSE

Protocell technology is a form of design that triggers the emergence of connections between milieus of interiority and milieus of exteriority, but its incapacity to replicate cells that contain genetic material is a significant limit that questions the protocell membrane's real capacity to connect the interior with the exterior. That is how the space of interiority is actively presented to the exterior on the limit of the living. In the protocell case, the limit expressed in the concretization process questions the transductive connectivities of its individuation process. The connections between milieus of interiority and milieus of exteriority, between past and future, are transductive. However, the transductive power of relational connection is not contained within the interior or the exterior, within the past or the future; rather it acts as an incorporeal cause that triggers or activates the coming together of these heterogeneous planes of operation according to what Simondon calls a process of disparation.

Transduction is a mode of dynamic efficiency that generates the possibilities for emergence by opening a gap between the result and the conditions of a situation, between its causes and finalities. Transduction is a dynamic relation that breaks with linear causality, a mode of relation that effects modifications or modulations by virtue of how elements hold together or come together, and that bears on all the elements at once. Transduction is not a linear causality but a quasi-cause. According to Brian Massumi, a quasi-cause is a cause that acts as a 'formative participation of the future . . . because [it is] more like an attractor in chaos theory than an efficient material cause'.[20] From this perspective, in the realm of transductive operations, it is the future that causes a change in the present.[21] A future cause, however, 'is not actually a cause; it is a virtual cause, or quasi-cause'.[22]

Following this logic, the field of emergence of the protocell is not alive in itself; it is the futurity of the field, its potential to generate a living entity, that acts as the cause of the protocell's emergence. In fact, although the protocell has not yet expressed the necessary chrono-topological conditions for life to emerge (as it has not demonstrated its capacity to put its milieu of interiority in relation to its milieu of exteriority), its potential to emerge as a living technique resides in its transductive power of connection between an interior past and an exterior future.

Protocells are transductive in fiction and soon likely in fact. They break with linear causality and become according to a regime of associated causality and finality as their emergence necessitates specific conditionings and actions. Their becoming does not follow a linear logic because their emergence is the expression of a new dimension that breaks with linearity. Protocells are a mix between objective conditions and the action of a terminus, a mix of simultaneous impositions of constraints and new possibilities. These constraints or objective conditions are given to the situation without predetermining it since they are connected to the action of a terminus. Thus, protocells hold the potential to become living techniques according to their transductive or quasi-causal dynamism, according to 'a memory of the future, which is the quasicausal force of tendency, as governed recursively by the futurity of the terminus toward which it tends'.[23]

The difference between the physical and the biological, between the interior and the exterior, is not a substantial difference. It is rather a relative difference that distinguishes the living individual according to its potential to fold the exteriority inside, to exteriorize it again and to effect changes in the overall system of relations. These processes take place by and through the membrane that acts as the mediator – or connector – of both spaces according to a chrono-topological structure. In a physical system the interior is a past that cannot exteriorize, that cannot individuate again. It has become inert and cannot cross the membrane again. In his famous example of the crystal, Simondon explains that matter within the crystal is inert but that it holds the potential to individuate again once it is in contact with its solution. Here the solution has become the interior past but it is also exterior to the crystal's space of interiority; it presents itself as the crystal's futurity. A living individual operates with an oriented memory – a memory that combines past and futurity and that makes possible the emergence of new forms of actions. The interior is not defined spatially or substantially; it is a form of enveloping of potentialities. It is a structure that carries tendencies and tropisms that give orientation without, however, dictating a pre-given final form, as it carries only implicit forms.

SUBJECT-BEING: INFRA OR MINIMAL PSYCHIC

Even though protocells have not yet fully performed the exteriorization of their space of interiority, they beckon the question as to whether they hold the potential to trigger the emergence of a sensorimotor schema that does not depend on DNA's replicative machinery. DNA is known as the molecule that programs all aspects of the behaviour of living cells. However, as Szostak has argued, it is not certain that protocells necessarily require DNA to replicate. In other words, the question here is whether protocells can invent new dynamic structures by and through the relationships they share with their environment at a level situated below that of DNA. This is crucial, as research on the protocell focuses mainly on genetic information, replication and metabolism: meaning, on the possibility to preserve the protocell itself, its functional identity. In order to put protocells' functional identity back into their operational field of emergence, I will refer to other protocols that foreground protocells' sensorimotor through the investigation of their ability to move. The scientists working on these protocols recognize the importance of replication and metabolism but investigate movement as one of life's most basic conditions: its continuous avoidance of equilibrium – far from equilibrium or metastable protocells. Hence, what is at stake with living techniques is not only their capacity to maintain a chrono-topological structure but also their ability to invent novel and dynamic ones: transductive individuals.

Movement brings protocells back into relational dynamism, back into process. As a mode of operational investigation, it speaks to the way in which Gilles Deleuze, following Henri Bergson, has defined the living: 'one defines the living by the existence of an interval, a distance or a gap between the movement it receives and the one it gives, namely the movement it executes'.[24] The key notion is the one of the executed movement, the interval between received and given movements. The interval , however, to be understood not in terms of a spatial movement alone, but also in terms of a qualitative variation that emerges over time, a temporal saturation – temporal movement – that expresses itself in the form of a moving movement. That temporal saturation is here equalized with psychic individualization.

Scientists who investigate protocells' ability to move (for example, Martin Hanczyc from the University of Southern Denmark and Takashi Ikegami from the University of Kyoto) suggest that a protocell is a sensorimotor system. Their protocol consists of adding oil to a water phase. As oil has a greater density than water, it forms a 'spherical oil droplet that sinks into water'.[25] The oil–water interface is a boundary that interacts physically and chemically with the environment. They argue that the interface acts as the sensor of the system and that the motor system arises from the flow structure within the droplet. When the interface senses chemical gradients (pH), an 'imbalance in the tension surrounding the droplet results in flow structures.'[26] The observed flow structure (convection) triggers the motor of the system. Thus, movement in the system is a result of an 'intimate coupling between a chemical reaction and the physical structure of the droplet'.[27] In brief, their experiments suggest that convective flow and movement are responses to pH gradients. Convection is what keeps the droplet in an active state; it is that which regulates the equilibrium of the droplet – a metastable droplet. As Hanczyc explains, the convection flow can resolve the instability and the droplet will stop moving. However, it continues to move because convection mixes up the droplet, bringing more chemicals to the interface, which then sustains the instability. So convection is the key in providing feedback (in this case physical feedback) to the system.[28]

This feedback loop, between shifting chemicals near the interior surface of the cell wall and the pH of the chemicals exterior to the cell, allows the droplet to 'sense' gradients and to respond by moving in the environment. This process also speaks to the chrono-topological structure. As the convection flow is inside the droplet, the resulting movement can also account for the exteriorization of the protocell (at a level below that of DNA).

Research carried out by these scientists closely encounters Simondon's psychic phase of individuation, a phase which emerges when the structure between an individual and its environment is broken up, when a biophysical individual is shattered and calls upon the invention of a new structure.[29] Psychic individualization's deployment takes place on the preconscious level, and more precisely on what Simondon refers to as the subconscious: namely, the stratum found in between unconscious and conscious states.[30] That relational stratum is, for him, the centre of individuality and is essentially affectivity and emotivity. Affectivity and emotivity, he says, are the psyche's transductive forms *par excellence*. Together they link the individual to itself and to the world; they trigger both the individual's auto- and hetero-positions – a bipolar individual. The process emerges with the experience, the sensation of a gradient, whose correlative is the response to a tropism (in contrast to a reflex): the act of seizing a direction. In other words, sensation orients an individual in the world along a series of gradients that tend toward perception. When the act of orientation faces the experience of various gradients, the individual experiences a conflict between a plurality of tropistic orientations and calls upon perception in order to resolve a sensitive contradiction. Tropisms are never overcome; they are integrated in a complex system that exhibits emerging properties. Affection is the experience of the resolved contradiction experienced as a becoming, one that anticipates further action with respect to a bipolar frame of reference: namely, the one that links the relationship of the individual to itself and to the world. This bipolarity is both emotional and collective; emotion is what links the individual to itself whereas the collective relates it to the world. This mode of operationalization asserts that the coming into collective is ultimately found in collective action but that it is primarily conditioned at the level of affectivo-emotive themes.

Here the issue raised revolves around whether protocells' movement is an automatic response (a reflex) or a tropism (quasi-automatic). Hanczyc and Ikegami mainly work on changing the size of the protocell to increase its internal instability. By so doing, they suggest that protocells' ability to perceive is conditioned by both convection flow and shape. This is an extremely important combination, as it prevents a reductionist understanding of protocells that would reduce them to a geometrical substance. The droplet, they assert, can 'sense' a pH gradient 'because the internal flow pattern and movement of the droplet change accordingly'.[31] One could draw upon these conclusions and suggest that the flow pattern is what maintains protocells' metastability and that the resulting movement acts as a resolving action to the sensation of pH gradients, as an act of selection that compensates for a change in the velocity of the reaction. Here I can only speculate, as experiments that concern these modes of selection are yet to be published. I will nevertheless highlight two tendencies that resonate with Simondon's theory of individuation. First, Hanczyc and Ikegami report that in different experiments droplets climb to different gradients, which suggests that they are indeed capable of selecting. In addition, in a soon-to-be published paper, they investigate collective droplet behaviours and convey that droplets sometimes follow and sometimes avoid other droplets' behaviours. Their experiments perform protocells' incipient collective individuation as conditioned by shared affectivo-emotive themes.

Protocell technology still exists in a state of dispersal, though its concretization process is under way, and it has not yet fully exhausted itself. Nevertheless, the experiments upon which I draw for my analysis do understand protocells as individuals and highlight the relevance of Simondon's contribution. Individuation is a process in action. Epistemologically, it would be absurd to anticipate how protocells' psychic individualization gives rise to collective and transindividual phases of individuation. What protocells do not perform is Simondon's subject. For him,

> the problem of the subject is that of the heterogeneity between the perceptible and affective worlds, between the individual and the pre-individual; this problem is the problem of the subject *qua* subject: the subject is individual and other than individual; it is incompatible with itself.[32]

It can only coincide with itself in the collective. Protocell technology has not yet come into collective individuation. It would, however, be wrong not to consider them as subjects. Simondon's individuation might consider life as a mode of relation; it never asserts that non-biological individuals might achieve a subjective level. Expanding Simondon's approach to that of Whitehead's speculative philosophy is an operational deviation that opens Simondon's notion of subject to non-humans and even to non-biological individuals.

For Whitehead, all entities, alive or not, feel the world. Apart from the experience of subjects, he says 'there is nothing, nothing, nothing, bare nothingness'.[33] That which feels is, for him, a subject (or maybe more a subjectivity). All entities have a physical and a mental pole. The intermixing of mental and physical poles is a transductive reality based on affection (in opposition to cognition). Whitehead, here referring to psychologists, suggests 'emotions, hopes, fears, inhibitions sense-perceptions arise, which physiologists ascribe to bodily functionings'[34] and goes on to say that 'what we perceive as present, is the vivid fringe of memory tinged with anticipation'.[35] The physical pole is a past driven by the mental pole's force of tendency. This intermixing develops the possibility for new forms of determination, for new modes of actions. Physico-mentality is active; it is a mode of activity. Following Whitehead and James, Massumi relates activity to the event, and not to the opposition between subjects and objects:

> Neither potential nor activity is objectlike. They are more energetic than objectlike (provided that no presuppositions are made as to the physicality of 'energy' or the modes of causality involved in the energizing of events). For the basic category they suggest is just that: occurrence. Neither object nor subject: the event.[36]

An entity, or individuality of occasion, is the becoming between the poles; a subjective form is what happens in between. It is the reality of the in between, the event. *'There is no subject separate from the event ... the event itself is a subjective self-creation.'*[37] From this perspective, the protocell's capacity for selection is not a subjective choice; it is the active reality of an event. As is the case in Simondon, Whitehead's mentality is situated beyond stimuli reaction and below consciousness; mentality is for Whitehead active in all relationalities. Individuation, operating in this case analogically to mental and physical intertwining, ultimately makes no difference between living and non-living, between object and subject, and opens its subjective field to non-humans and non-biological entities. It is a subjectivity without subject.

TRANSDUCTIVE CONNECTIONS AS TECHNIQUES OF BRINGING TO LIFE

Simondon's conception of life incorporates exterior / interior dynamical flows that make no substantial difference between the living and the non-living. His contribution foregrounds life as dynamic relational structure. Protocell technology amounts to the understanding of living techniques in terms of chemical individuals rather than biotechnical ones. However, the conceptualization of their becoming in terms of Simondon's ontogenetic theory of the individuation process can shed light on the fact that living techniques do not lay claim for an essentialist or susbtantialist understanding of what life is. Whether living techniques are 'really' alive is not the point. The key issue is whether or not their becoming is analogical to that of living systems, whether they perform life's relational form of process, whether their becoming is that of a chrono-topological structure that extends itself into affectivo-emotive themes in such a way that new forms of action might emerge. As a dynamic system that connects the interior past with the exterior future, the chrono-topological structure acts as the bootstrap of living techniques. Chrono-topologies are dynamic structures that condition the emergence of a psychic phase, of an individualizing individual. It is a structure that connects physical and mental poles, and that opens the gap between causes and finalities by maintaining the individual in metastable relation, one that constantly links to its associated milieu and pre-individual nature.

Living techniques are inventive in the sense that their becoming is not predetermined or precoded; they are transductive becoming. They must be able to respond creatively to their environment, to invent new connective structures that link them to themselves and their environment in unexpected ways. They ought to perform new forms of relationalities. Living techniques are techniques of emergence whose process of becoming is ontogenetic. Living techniques are not necessarily biological in the literal sense. They are relational techniques whose processes ultimately bring to life. The process as a whole is not conditioned by peculiar forces. Living techniques' individuation is neither a vitalism, nor a substantialism. It is a dynamic form, a form of process, a mode of relation, a performative in-between – one that folds exteriority into a womb already pregnant with a past-futurity, an incipient process already present in the fringe of the indeterminacy of its driving force of tendency. Transductive connections are at play in the laboratories of protocells' midwives, and they are amplifying; they are techniques of bringing to life. 'Cut away the future, and the present collapses.'[38]

NOTES

1. I want to thank Brian Massumi and Tim Lenoir for their productive comments on this paper. I am also grateful to the Max Planck Institute for the History of Science for providing me with a stimulating milieu of exchange where I wrote the first draft. (I am particularly grateful to Hans Jörg Rheinberger, Didier Debaise, Henning Schmidgen and Julia Kursell.) Lastly, I want to thank Jamie L. Ferguson for her patience and language assistance.
2. Brian Massumi. *Parables for the Virtual: Movement, Affect, Sensation* (Durham, NC: Duke University Press, 2002), p. 71.
3. Gilbert Simondon, *Du mode d'existence des objets techniques* (Paris: Aubier, 2001), p. 168.
4. Muriel Combes, *Simondon: Individu et collectivité* (Paris: Presses Universitaires de France, 1999), p. 42.
5. Gilbert Simondon, *L'Individuation à la lumière des notions de forme et d'information* (Grenoble: Jérôme Millon, 2005), p. 83.
6. Simondon, *L'Individuation*, p. 29.
7. Simondon, *L'Individuation*, p. 25.
8. Simondon, *L'Individuation*, p. 313.
9. Simondon, *L'Individuation*, p. 305.
10. Brian Massumi, 'Sensing the Virtual, Building the Insensible', http://www.brianmassumi.com/textes/Sensing%20the%20Virtual.pdf.
11. Simondon, *Du mode*, p. 163.
12. Simondon, *Du mode*, p. 34.
13. Combes, *Simondon*, p. 41.
14. Combes, *Simondon*, p. 41.
15. Gilbert Simondon, 'The Position of the Problem of Ontogenesis', trans. Greg Flanders, *Parrhesia*, 7 (2009). http://www.parrhesiajournal.org/parrhesia07/parrhesia07_simondon1.pdf.
16. Simondon, *L'Individuation*, p. 131.
17. Jack W. Szostak, 'Noble Prize Lecture', http://nobelprize.org/mediaplayer/index.php?id=1218&view=1.
18. Alonso Ricardo and Jack. W. Szostak, 'Origins of Life on Earth', *Scientific American* (2009), p. 54.
19. Craig Venter and his team recently challenged this limitation in their own work on synthesis of an artificial cell complete with DNA. Their protocol included a bacterial cell with protoplasm, a cell wall and DNA. They removed the DNA and reinserted an artificially created genome into the bacterium. The chromosome is capable of replicating, and takes over the bacterium within a couple of generations. While the protoplasm of the bacterium was present before the insertion of the genome, the DNA machinery completely takes over after it begins replicating and replaces the original protoplasm with its own unique protoplasm (see J. Craig Venter et al., 'Creation of a Bacterial Cell Controlled by a Chemically Synthesized Genome', *Science*, 329: 5987 (2010), pp. 52–6). But as I have explained above, the synthesis of a protocell might not require DNA itself. In addition, the difference with the genome inserted into the bacterium is that it is not self-generating. It does not replicate spontaneously. Besides these limitations, I would add that Venter's team has not *created* a cell through synthetic processes. Rather, they have *mimicked* life. In fact, what Venter's team means by 'synthetic' is that the synthetic genome takes over the bacterium. Their meaning of synthetic is more a rhetorical trope than an actual fact. In the same line of argument, Jim Collins, a bioengineer at Boston University, has argued that 'what has been created is an organism with a synthesized natural

genome. But it doesn't represent the creation of life from scratch or the creation of a new life form', which is the goal of protocell technology (see Nicholas Wade, 'Researchers Say They Created a "Synthetic Cell"', *The New York Times*, 20 May [2010]).
20. Brian Massumi, 'Of Microperception and Micropolitics: Exploring Ethico-Aesthetics', *Inflexions* (2009). http://www.senselab.ca/inflexions/volume_4/n3_massumihtml.html.
21. Brian Massumi, 'Fear (The Spectrum Said)', *Positions*, 13:1 (2005), p. 35.
22. Ibid.
23. Massumi, 'Of Microperception'.
24. Gilles Deleuze, 'Cours Vincennes–St Denis: Bergson, *Matière et Mémoire* (1981)', http://www.webdeleuze.com/php/texte.php?cle=70&groupe=Image%20Mouvement%20Image%20Temps&langue=1.
25. Martin M. Hanczyc and Takashi Ikegami, 'Protocells as Smart Agents for Architectural Design', *Technoetic Arts*, 7 (2009), p. 118.
26. Martin M. Hanczyc and Takashi Ikegami, 'Chemical Basis for Minimal Cognition', *Artificial Life*, 16 (2010), p. 235.
27. Martin M. Hanczyc and Takashi Ikegami, 'Protocells as Smart Agents for Architectural Design', p. 118.
28. Quoted from the author's personal correspondence with Martin Hanczyc.
29. Note here that Simondon does not refer to psychic individuation but rather to psychic individua*liza*tion, as the psychic phase does not give rise to a new individual. Rather it complexifies an already existing individual; it is an individual in a process of individuation. While physical individuation and biological individuation give rise to an individual, psychic individualization is the individuation of an already individuated individual.
30. Simondon, *L'Individuation*, p. 248.
31. Hanczyc and Ikegami, 'Chemical Basis for Minimal Cognition', p. 235.
32. Simondon, *L'Individuation*, p. 253.
33. Alfred N. Whitehead, *Process and Reality* (New York: Free Press, 1978), p. 167.
34. Alfred N. Whitehead, *Adventure of Ideas* (New York: Free Press, 1967), p. 189.
35. Alfred N. Whitehead, *The Concept of Nature* (New York: Cosimo, 2007), p. 77.
36. Brian Massumi, *Semblance and Event: Arts of Experience, Politics of Expression* (Cambridge, MA: MIT Press, 2011).
37. Ibid.
38. Whitehead, *Adventure of Ideas*, p. 191.

Chapter 7

'Du mort qui saisit le vif': Simondonian Ontology Today[1]

Jean-Hugues Barthélémy, translated by Justin Clemens

INTRODUCTION: THE CHEMICAL, THE APOPTOTIC AND THE ARTEFACT; OR, THE HYPOTHESIS OF THREE TYPES OF 'NON-LIFE' THAT *CONDITION* LIFE AS EVOLUTION

As the title of this Introduction indicates, I will not ask myself about the as-it-were metaphysical distinction between the dead ['*le*' *mort*] and death ['*la*' *mort*]. What interests me is more generally the presence of 'non-life' in life, and as the very *condition* of life. I would like to suggest that different *stages* of life *qua* evolution correspond to different *types* of essential non-life. The 'non-living' can certainly designate the artefact, but it first of all signifies inert *naturalness* [*naturel*], therefore the physical. Simondon sees in the physical and the 'vital', as he says, two 'regimes of individuation'. But in choosing to treat of '*le mort qui saisit le vif*',[2] I propose in fact, as will appear, to cover the whole genetic ontology of *Individuation in the Light of Notions of Form and Information*[3] in so far as it derives from the living the third regime of individuation itself, called by Simondon the 'transindividual'. But the red thread of this traversal of genetic ontology is in another way what, to my mind, allows us at the same time to unify and exceed it, because this red thread is what I have elsewhere called the 'auto-transcendent sense'[4] of the Simondonian genetic ontology. Such are the stakes of my account, because the exegesis of the Simondonian *œuvre* from which my first two works emerged would already be polemical in its very fidelity, and concerned by this to locate in Simondon what might give him all his contemporaneity.

The expression '*du mort qui saisit le vif*' comes from Marx, who in fact wrote at the beginning of *Capital*: 'We suffer not only from the living, but from the dead. *Le mort saisit le vif!*'[5] Marx here concludes a remark about political and social consequences '*à contre-temps*',[6] which are engendered by certain past modes of production. For my part, I want to give another sense to this formula, broader and closer to the famous proposal of Auguste Comte regarding the historicity of humanity as the presence of the dead. My thesis will be more precisely the following: humanity is that form of *psycho-social* life which, *by means of the non-living artefacts* that support it and *found* its historicity, *extends bio-psychic* animal life of which the non-living *condition* is not yet the artefact but simple *apoptosis* ('cellular suicide'), and whose *origin* is a third form of 'non-life': the *chemical* non-living.

In order that there is no misunderstanding about this thesis, I will immediately specify, doing so in the order of its different points, that:

1. It is supposed here that the life of the living comes from what it is not. Simondon himself, while refusing mechanism as reductionism applied to life, accepts that vitalism is not any more defensible. His own way of refusing mechanism thus consists in thinking the physical and the vital as both coming from a 'pre-physical and pre-vital' reality, because pre-individual. Moreover, Simondon envisages applying the idea of neoteny to the passage of the non-living towards the living: vital individuation would be the perpetuation of an inchoate phase of physical individuation itself. I will not have the opportunity to return here to this question of the non-living origin of life, and will dedicate myself instead to the question of apoptosis as the second form of 'non-life' rendering life possible. I will analyse the text of Simondon's that expresses an intuition in the direction of this reality that has recently been confirmed and accepted by biology, after a century of dispersed inquiries.

2. The artefacts produced by animals other than humans, such as, for example, the bird's nest or the beehive, do not aim at making possible a *psycho-social* life, but only a *bio-psychic* or *bio-social* life; as Simondon remarks, the 'pure social', that we must understand in opposition to the *psycho-social* and not in opposition to the biological, exists in insects because their social character does not nourish a psyche. Reciprocally, birds and, even more so, mammals develop a psyche without passing by the social. Only the primates and, even more so, humans, are psycho-social: that is, a reality in which the *individual* psyche is paradoxically developed *on the basis of the collective*. This paradox is that of what we call 'interiority' or rather, with Simondon, 'personality', of which Simondon said that it could precisely not be thought on the basis of the opposition exterior / interior (or transcendence / immanence).

3. When I affirm that artefacts make possible a psycho-social life and
   that this is only fully realized with the human, I do not put language
   next to artefacts, nor do I forget the artefacts produced by our
   'psycho-social cousins', the primates. Because, *on the one hand*, language is itself also an artefact, undoubtedly moreover indispensable
   so that other artefacts can become supports for our psycho-social
   personality. Through language, in which thought is elaborated, the
   artefacts produced in the 'external world' nourish in return the
   human mind. This thesis corresponds in fact to Bernard Stiegler's
   extension of works that were already a major source for Simondon;
   I speak of the works of Leroi-Gourhan on the *parallelism* between
   the development of language and that of tools. *On the other hand*,
   the artefacts produced by primates are not preserved by them after
   use, and thus cannot define a historic world coming to nourish
   mind, even if these artefacts are certainly an extension of the living
   body.

THE ARTEFACT, OR THE 'NON-LIFE' THAT MAKES A
PSYCHO-SOCIAL LIFE POSSIBLE

I will pick up the order of the complexification in a reverse direction
and begin with the question of the transindividual regime of individuation in so far as it is a *psycho-social* life conditioned by this ultimate
form of 'non-life' that is the artefact. That it is a matter here of a question, including when one starts with Simondon, sticking with the fact
that psycho-social life and culture seem to have technique as a 'phase',
as Simondon magisterially demonstrated in *Du mode d'existence des
objets techniques*.[7] But the question is knowing if this necessary phase
would not be even more: that is, *a foundation and a frame* for the other
phases of culture. We know that with Simondon technique is only a
phase issuing from the 'phase difference' [*déphasage*] of the 'primitive
magical unity', which for him does not seem to contain the presence of
artefacts but only that of natural 'key points'. This is, moreover, what I
criticized Simondon for at the end of the second volume of my polemical
exegesis.[8] But I want to come back here to the elements of his thought,
and perhaps also to its *tensions*, which may themselves call for a revision
of this thought in the direction of a *foundation* of the transindividual or
of the psycho-social *upon* artefacts.

In the secondary thesis [*Thèse complémentaire*] for his doctorate,
Du mode d'existence des objets techniques, Simondon returned to the
question of the transindividual that he had treated in his main thesis

[*Thèse principale*], *L'Individuation à la lumiere des notions de forme et d'information*. He writes:

> The technical object taken according to its essence, that is, the technical object insofar as it was invented, thought and willed, assumed by a human subject, becomes the support and the symbol of this relation that we would call *transindividual*. [. . .] Through the intermediary of the technical object an interhuman relation that is the model of *transindividuality* is created. We can understand by this a relation that does not put individuals in relation by means of their constituted individuality separating them from each other, nor by means of what is identical in each human subject, for example the *a priori* forms of sensitivity, but by means of this charge of pre-individual reality, of this charge of nature that is preserved with individual being, and that contains potentials and virtuality [*virtualité*]. The object that comes from technical invention bears with it something of the being that produced it, expressing of this being what is the least attached to a *hic et nunc*; one could say that there is human nature in technical being, in the sense that the word nature could be employed to designate what remains original, anterior even to the constituted humanity in the human.[9]

Why is the thought of the transindividual taken up here from the point of a thought of technique *none the less absent* from the main thesis? Before I respond, two preliminary remarks should be made on the very letter of the text. First, what the *end* of this passage says about the meaning of the word 'nature' allows us to understand that, in making the technical object the 'support' of the transindividual relation, the *beginning* of the passage does not envisage detaching the human from 'nature' and contradicts the main thesis. It is even rather *because* the technical object is elevated to the status of support of the transindividual relation that Simondonian thought escapes from what it combats under the name of essentialist 'anthropology'. Indeed, the technical object is for Simondon *nature in the human* – and not human 'nature' or the essence of the human: 'the human invents by putting to work his own natural support, this *apeiron* that remains attached to each individual being.'[10] It is therefore in subverting the opposition *nature / technique* that Simondon understands here to subvert the opposition *nature / humanity*, just as the Introduction to the work announces a subversion of this third opposition that is the opposition *humanism / technicism*.[11]

Second, the passage cited is itself inhabited by a tension, since it makes the technical object *at once* the 'support' and the 'symbol' of transindividuality, which does *not* exactly come back to the same thing. None the less it is the idea of symbol that prevails in the book, the 'interhuman *relationship*' that is made 'through the intermediary of the technical object', being, moreover, 'the model of transindividuality', as Simondon says. The proposal of *Du mode d'existence des objets techniques* more generally consists in making the technical object a paradigm for the comprehension of what Simondon, following Merleau-Ponty rather than Heidegger, names our 'being in the world', a paradigmaticism that considers the technique, however, only as being, in 'human reality', a 'phase' that comes from the 'phase difference' of the 'magic unity' in technique and religion.

But the sensed theoretical tensions here could only be the translation, in the secondary thesis, of tensions present at the heart of the main thesis. Above all, the idea of the technical object as the *support* of the transindividual relationship should *to my mind* be revalorized, because it is this that allows the resolution of the *ultimate difficulty* whose presence it is now a question of revealing at the heart of the main thesis. Undoubtedly, what is at once the most profound and problematic text on the transindividual is in fact that dedicated to the 'problematic of reflexivity in individuation', in which we find the following passage:

> In fact, neither the idea of immanence nor the idea of transcendence can completely account for the features of the transindividual in relation to the psychological individual: transcendence or immanence are indeed defined and fixed before the moment when the individual becomes one of the terms of the relation in which it is integrated, but of which the other term has already been given. But if we accept that the transindividual is auto-constitutive, we will see that the schema of transcendence or the schema of immanence only accounts for this auto-constitution by their simultaneous and reciprocal position; it is indeed at each instant of auto-constitution that the relation between the individual and the transindividual is defined as what *exceeds the individual all the while extending it*: the transindividual is not external to the individual, yet is nevertheless detached to a certain extent from the individual.[12]

In order to problematize this passage, I will first refer to what appeared in the survey of the last chapter of my *Penser l'individuation*: with Simondon, the *psychosomatic* split of the *living* manufactures the *psychic* 'transitory way' that concerns the 'subject', whose 'personality' is, after a 'provisory emotional de-individuation', *transindividual* actualization, the paradoxical place of the greatest individuality *as at once* the most accomplished subversion of the opposition individual / milieu – the social *no longer* even being a milieu. This is why the transindividual or 'real collective' is the actualized type of the psychic itself: 'Psychological individuality appears as being what is elaborated in elaborating transindividuality.'[13] Simondon specifies that this subversion of the opposition between immanence and transcendence by the transindividual draws from the fact that 'there is an anteriority of the transindividual in relation to the individual', this anteriority being indeed what 'hinders defining a relation of transcendence or immanence'.[14] But such an anteriority can not signify that there would be an equivalence between the transindividual and the pre-individual, even if certain passages favour the confusion, as is the case in these lines: 'The psycho-social is of the transindividual: it is this reality that the individuated being transports with it, this charge of being for future individuations.' This possible confusion is only another aspect of a crucial insistence on the fact that transindividual *individuation* – because it is certainly such – constructs radical individuality beyond even the individual, because it is the 'subject' as a pre-individual-individual ensemble that individuates 'itself'. It is this that renders transindividual individuation *thinkable with difficulty*, except by saying with Simondon, in a passage cited above, that 'the transindividual is defined as what *exceeds the individual all the while extending it*: the transindividual is not external to the individual and is nevertheless detached to a certain extent from the individual.'

It remains that the difficulty represented by the idea of the anteriority of the transindividual is not thereby resolved. If the anteriority of the transindividual over the individual does not signify that there would be an equivalence between the transindividual and the pre-individual, *how* then to give it [any] *sense*? It is here that the idea of the technical object as support of the transindividual seems to me able to work. Because this support is first of all the 'symbol' that 'expresses', as Simondon says, the pre-individual part attached to the 'subject'. From there, to pass from the idea of the technical object as 'symbol' to that of the technical object as 'support' is to conceive that the technical object receiving the pre-individual part of the 'subject' is also and reciprocally what makes this 'subject' accede to transindividual individuation in its distinction from the pre-individual. The technical object would thus be this mediation by which the transindividual is constituted in its incomprehensible psycho-social indissociability, *because it would give the place sought by Simondon in his major thesis under the name of what 'interiorises the exterior'*[15] *and 'exteriorises the interior', and which as such is 'anterior'.*

But Simondon thinks the technical *beyond* the simple artefact, under the pretext that the technical is only truly 'concretized' in the modern machine, and will thus never posit the technical object as at the same time an 'expression' of the pre-individual attached to the 'subject' *and as foundation of the transindividual individuation*. He writes, on the contrary, that between the human and nature is created a technogeographic milieu that becomes possible only through the intelligence of the human being: the autoconditioning of a schema through the result of its functioning necessitates the use of an inventive function of *anticipation* that finds itself neither in nature nor in technical objects already constituted.[16]

If it is therefore necessary to recognize here my 'infidelity' to the letter of Simondon's text, the question *at the very least* proposes itself of knowing if the transindividual, such as Simondon *himself* attempts to think it through his main, *then* his secondary thesis – that is, such that he is *embarrassed* by it and finds himself plunged into *theoretical tensions* – is not in fact artefactually founded. In such a perspective, one could say with Stiegler that the *finitude* of the living requires the latter not to be able to be transindividually individuated, therefore in psychosocial 'personality' to speak with Simondon, *except by resting* on those 'crutches of the mind' that are non-living artefacts.

THE TWO MEANINGS OF DEATH AND APOPTOSIS AS 'VITAL DEATH'

I come now to this living [being] itself before its psycho-social individuation, to demonstrate in which way it is also rendered possible by *a type* of 'non-life': the life of the living is only developed by passing by apoptosis or 'cellular suicide'. Simondon himself had, in a passage from *L'Individu et sa genèse physico-biologique*, divided the idea of death in order to think a certain *constitutivity of death* in relation to life:

> Death exists for the living in two senses that do not coincide: it is adverse death . . . But death exists also for the individual in another sense: the individual is not pure interiority: it weighs itself down with the residues of its own operations; it is passive in itself; it is itself its own exteriority . . . In this sense, the fact that the individual is not eternal should not be considered as accidental; life in its ensemble can be considered as a transductive series; death as final event is only the consummation of a process of deadening that is contemporaneous with each vital operation as operation of individuation; every operation of individuation lodges death in the individuated being that is progressively charged with something that it cannot eliminate; this deadening is different from the degradation of the organs; it is essential to the activity of individuation.[17]

Because death, understood in the second sense, is here only a deposit [*dépôt*] for vital individuation, it could seem to be confused with death understood in the first sense. Indeed, the idea of a deposit – even necessary rather than accidental – does not yet allow thinking a constitutivity of death in relation to the living. This is because the deposit, as such, is 'stripped of potentials and can no longer be the basis of new individuations'.[18] But the difference resides in that death in the first sense 'translates the very precariousness of individuation, *its confrontation with the conditions of the world*', while death in the second sense 'does not come from the confrontation with the world, but from the convergence of internal transformations'.[19] Nothing could be further from my mind than the idea that Simondon would have thought apoptosis as condition of life for an epoch in which biology was yet to ask itself as to the nature of apoptosis. Simply, he enters into the logic of a thought of the individuation by wanting, as Simondon had in effect wanted, to subvert all the classical oppositions – and even that between life and death – for the little that we distinguish between *scales* of individuation.

Contemporary biology is in a position to affirm, as does Jean-Claude Ameisen in his work *La Sculpture du vivant*, that death is at the very heart of life. Ameisen's work in fact seems to me to reveal *two* different aspects of this presence. *On the one hand*, the construction of the embryo implies the auto-destruction of a great number of cells. Whence the metaphors of 'sculpture' and of its condition – the cellular 'suicide', applied not only to the formation of the brain and immune system, but also to that of the organism in its entirety:

> From the first days that follow our conception – at the very moment our existence begins – cellular suicide plays an essential role in our body in the course of construction, sculpting successive metamorphoses of our form in becoming. In the dialogues that are established between different families of cells in the course of being born, language determines life or death. In the sketches of our brain and our immune system – the organ that will protect us from microbes – cellular death is the integrative part of a strange process of apprenticeship and auto-organisation whose accomplishment is not the sculpture of a form but that of our memory and our identity . . . It is cellular death that, in successive waves, sculpts our arms and legs on the basis of their sketches, to the extent that they grow, from their base towards their extremities. At the interior of our pre-arms, it creates the space that separates our bones, the radius and the cubitus. Then it sculpts the extremities of our members: our hand is first of all born in the form of a mitten, of a palm, containing five branches of cartilage that project themselves from the wrist and prefigure our fingers. Death thus brutally makes the tissues that join the superior portion of these branches disappear, individualising our fingers and transforming the mitten into a glove.[20]

On the other hand, and this second aspect verifies at the same time that the first aspect is really an *auto*-destruction of cells, every cell is equipped at the same time for auto-destructing and hindering this auto-destruction, in such a way that the life of the organism once formed is only an *inhibited death* [*mort empêchée*], and that it is moreover not long for the cells that should be renewed each day or close to it, like the cells of the skin:

> Whatever their duration of normal life in our bodies, from forty-eight hours to several weeks, from several months to several years, from some decades to perhaps more than a century, each of the cells that constitute us is, permanently, at each instant, capable of auto-destruction. And it will trigger its suicide within hours – at most in several days – if it is deprived of signals that allow it to survive. At the beginning of the 1990s, a new notion of life emerged: living, for each cell that composes our bodies, is, at each moment, to have succeeded in restraining the triggering of suicide. The differenciation that leads, in different cell families, to the locking mechanism of most genes – including, in numerous cell families, for example the neurones, and the locking mechanism of genes that allow the cells to divide themselves – never obliterates, it seems, in any cell, throughout our life, certain genetic information allowing the triggering of the implementation of suicide . . . The daily suicide of hundreds of billions of cells in our bodies only represent the visible manifestation of a permanent potentiality, anchored in each of our cells.[21]

CONCLUSION: LIFE AS DIFFERENCE FROM ITSELF OR 'NON-ESSENCE'

At the end of this rapid examination of types of 'non-life' that condition life as biological evolution, then as psycho-social history, we can make a hypothesis regarding the nature of what we have thus named 'life': this 'nature' of life is perhaps precisely an anti-nature or a 'non-essence', because life will be defined as *difference from itself* if:

1. it is anchored in what is not it (the chemical non-living [being]);
2. it evolves by using death as potentiality inscribed in each cell;
3. it is capable of sublimating itself into a psycho-social life where it fully accomplishes its character of non-essence, since [hu]man, of whom it is said that he is historical and has no 'nature', constructs his mind and personality through a process of 'exteriorization' in artefacts that paradoxically condition the development of his 'interiority'.

NOTES

1. This text is from a paper given in Paris on 16 June 2007 at the colloquium 'Actualité de Simondon', organized by the Centre Georges Canguilhem of the University of Paris 7–Denis Diderot and the Collège International de Philosophie.

2. TN: This utterly untranslatable phrase, which in fact functions as the original title of this article, *'Du mort qui saisit le vif'*, is, as Barthélémy explains in his next paragraph, derived from Karl Marx's *Das Kapital*: to be precise, from the 1867 Preface to the first German edition, where it appears, naturally enough, in the original French. The phrase originally arises in the context of medieval French law, where it denominates the instantaneous transmission of sovereignty to the heir on the death of the previous monarch, or of property to the inheritor – a transmission which is considered to have taken place whether or not anybody marks the death-transfer with a speech-act or, indeed, whether or not anybody is aware of that death at the time. As such, the maxim is at the origins of the notorious utterance *'Le Roi est mort, vive le Roi!'*, which crystallizes one biopolitical way in which the dead affect the living. Not only a fundamental principle of law and sovereign power, however, the specific translation problem here hinges on the currency of the word *'vif'*, which, though retaining etymological links to the sequence that interests Simondon and Barthélémy, including *vivre* (to live), *vivant* (the living [being]), *vie* (life), *vivace* (vivacious), *viable* (viable) and so on, has lost in modern French the meaning of the 'living', meaning something more like 'vivid', 'bright', 'lively'. While it is thus tempting to leave the phrase in French throughout – as I have done sometimes here – this proved unworkable, given its consistent and dedicated repurposing in the article as a whole. I have therefore essayed to keep something of the etymological and the operational in my translating, preferring to render *'vif'* as 'live', in the sense of both what lives and what is 'lively'. Given Barthélémy's retranscription of this phrase into that of evolutionary ontology, it may well be worth noting Marx's own analogies, in the very same Preface, to microscopic anatomy and to physics. The other term here that has proven particularly frustrating to translate is the common *'actualité'*, which refers to 'current events', to what is 'topical' or 'present', and which, in the plural *'actualités'*, is simply 'the news'. Unfortunately, the word also retains links to an entire rat's nest of philosophemes, such as the distinction between the 'actual' and the 'virtual', among others. I have tried to mark this when possible and appropriate; otherwise, I have simply gone for idiomatic English.

3. G. Simondon, *L'Individuation à la lumière des notions de forme et d'information* (Grenoble: Jérôme Millon, 2005).

4. J.-H. Barthélémy, *Penser l'individuation: Simondon et la philosophie de la nature*, preface by J.-C. Beaune (Paris: L'Harmattan, 2005).

5. K. Marx, *Capital*, trans. B. Brewster, intro. E. Mandel (London: New Left Review, 1976), p. 91.

6. Ibid., emphasis in original.

7. G. Simondon, *Du mode d'existence des objets techniques* (Paris: Aubier, 1958). See also my commentary in the second part of *Penser la connaissance et la technique après Simondon* (Paris: L'Harmattan, 2005), as well as the more recent final chapter of my work of synthesis *Simondon ou l'encyclopédisme génétique* (Paris: PUF, 2008).

8. See *Penser la connaissance et la technique après Simondon*, Part 2, Chapter II.4.

9. Simondon, *Du mode d'existence*, pp. 247–8 (emphasis in original).

10. Ibid., p. 248. The non-contradiction between the Simondonian critique of essentialist anthropology and the idea of a technical support of the transindividual has been developed in my *Penser la connaissance et la technique après Simondon*, on the occasion of the polemical exegesis of *Du mode d'existence des objects techniques*.

11. Simondon in fact writes:

> The opposition erected between culture and technique, between [hu]man and machine, is false and without foundation; it only covers over ignorance or resentment. It masks behind a facile humanism a reality that is rich in human efforts and natural forces, and that constitutes the world of technical objects, mediators between nature and the human. (*Du mode d'existence des objets techniques*, p. 9)

It is truly the three oppositions mentioned that are here combated *in a single gesture*. For 'facile humanism', Simondon substitutes, not a technicism – nor at least a 'naturalism' – which would be an anti-humanism, but a *difficult humanism* because it wagers on the subversion of interlaced oppositions between nature, humanity and technique. This is why I cannot agree with Daniel Colson's presentation in *Petit lexique de l'anarchisme, de Proudhon à Deleuze* (Paris: Livre de Poche, 2003). Besides, if Deleuze did the first review – even laudatory – of *L'Individu et sa genèse physico-biologique* and was personally inspired by this work, this is evident on all other points, relative to his thought of 'difference' and of the 'impersonal and pre-individual transcendental field' – even if one could also denounce a recuperation there. As far as anti-humanism and anarchism are concerned, Simondon is less close to it than to the excellent *Pour l'homme* of his friend Mikel Dufrenne, whose subtle critique – addressed to anti-humanism – would be in the service of this 'difficult humanism' that corresponds to the subversion, of utmost importance to a phenomenologist like Dufrenne, of classic alternatives. On this question, see my *Simondon, ou l'Encylopédisme génétique*.

12. On *a certain* anticipation, notably by the Merleau-Ponty of *Signs*, of the Simondonian thought of technology, see Xavier Guchet, 'Theory of the social bond, technology and philosophy: Simondon as reader of Merleau-Ponty', *Les Etudes philosophiques*, 2, 2001.

13. G. Simondon, *L'Individuation psychique et collective* (Paris: Aubier, 1989), p. 156 (emphasis the author's). We recall that this work of Simondon's forms the last third of his main thesis, which appeared in a unified and complete fashion under the title of *L'Individuation à la lumière des notions de forme et d'information*.

14. Ibid., p. 157.

15. Ibid., p. 195.

16. Ibid., p. 157 (emphasis in original).

17. *L'Individu et sa genèse physico-biologique* (Grenoble: Jérôme Millon, 1995), pp. 213–14. We recall that this work of Simondon's is left to the first two-thirds of the main thesis. Regarding the passage cited, it is undoubtedly not by chance if Simondon wrote it when he anticipated a second time – after its first anticipation in the sub-chapter 'The Successive Levels of Individuation' – on the treatment of the 'collective' in its relation to 'the individuation of the living.'

18. Ibid.

19. Ibid., p. 213, my emphasis.

20. Jean-Claude Ameisen, *La Sculpture du vivant. Le Suicide cellulaire ou la mort créatrice* (Paris: Seuil, 2003), pp. 16 and 40.

21. Ibid, p. 138.

Chapter 8

The Aesthetics of Gilbert Simondon: Anticipation of the Contemporary Aesthetic Experience

Yves Michaud, translated by Justin Clemens

Gilbert Simondon is not only the author of an original reflection on technology and technical objects. As the systematic publication of his courses on psychology shows, his project was to constitute a general anthropology, studying perception, imagination, memory, invention, by situating human originality in each case within the set of living beings. He aimed in fact – which is already legible in the third part of the book on the technical object – to elaborate nothing less than a metaphysics that would define the human manner of being-in-the-world in all its manifestations. For those who had the chance to follow his courses, he always had something of the frankness and power of the pre-Socratic philosophers; he spoke Being, the presence of man to it as living being, producer, thinker and artist.

I will proceed in this text in three unequally developed moments. I will first present the general conception of Simondon's aesthetics. I will next examine several more particular points on the arts and on works [of art], and finally I will underline the aspects under which Simondon's thought seems to me to have today a particular import.

I

The conception of aesthetics in Simondon is expressed in the third section of his 1958 thesis, *On the Mode of Existence of Technical Objects*,[1] titled 'Essence of technicity'. This section, highly speculative, undertakes to give the sense of the genesis of technical objects in relation 'to the set of thought, the existence of man, and his manner of being in the world' (MEOT 154). The analysis of technicity makes the mode of technical being appear as fundamental, but other geneses engender other realities. Simondon uses the notion of genesis, not in the standard sense of temporal development or historical evolution, but as a process affecting the relation of human being to the world at the heart of a system. Genesis permits the resolution of tensions and conflicts because it is a succession of phases ending up in metastable states.

Simondon therefore exposes a sort of dialectic in which the potentials of the system, with their incompatibilities, produce successive individuations of this system, but none of these individuations is a stable state 'on the basis of which no transformation is thereafter possible' (MEOT 155). Simondon was a thinker of forms and forces: 'The potentials of a system constitute its power of becoming without deterioration' (ibid.). The potentials are part of reality, and becoming is the sequence of metastable states of the system, including when they overlap or return to each other. I say this because if for Simondon aesthetics comes after technicity, it also returns us to the heart of technicity.

To be simple at the risk of being schematic, we will say that there is first the relation of the living to its milieu, this relation that Simondon studied most particularly in his psychology courses on the human 'faculties' (perception, imagination, invention, memory), a term that he uses while objecting to it because of its rigidity and the blindness to geneses that it induces.

When one next passes to the study of the properly human modes of being-in-the-world, there is first a magical phase – that is, pretechnical and prereligious – a phase in which the organization of the relation to the world comes about in 'a first structuration, the most elementary of all, from which emerges the distinction between figure and ground in the universe' (MEOT 156). It is from this elementary couple of ground and form that the subsequent phases emerge. Forms do not cease forming themselves on grounds through games of forces and potentials. Technics is one of the forces that operates in these processes, but it is not the only one. There is also religion, art and thought.

In the magical phase, the vital liaison between human being and world, their primitive unity, is made without distinction of subject and object; the universe is experienced [*éprouvé*] as a milieu with only the difference between ground and form. The term 'to experience' [*éprouver*] is not anodyne; through it Simondon seeks to express that situation anterior to any separation of object and subject. But the magical universe knows a first structuration. Space and time are neither continuous nor undifferentiated. There appear key-points that regulate the world and provide it with polarities; 'the whole capacity of the world to influence human being is concentrated in these places and in these moments' (MEOT 164).

A reticulation of space in places and moments that concentrate and express the forces contained in the ground of reality is thus produced. The living being is concentrated on these points. Mountains, summits, promontories, gorges, the heart of the forest, have this sort of magical pregnancy through which the exchanges between man and world are effectuated. In the same way, in becoming there are similar salient points: beginnings, inaugurations, strong transitions and passages, all moments that allow human being to inscribe itself in becoming, apprehended as ground.

This unity of ground and form knows a phase difference. The key-points of structure separate and objectivize themselves; technics turns it into figures and technical objects become functional, instrumental, whereas the powers of the ground are subjectivated under the form of the divine and the sacred (gods, heroes, priests). A distance is introduced between human being and world. This distance is mediatized by technics on the one hand, and religion on the other. Where there was only a unity of the living being and its milieu, a difference between man and world appears. Not only does the figure detach itself from the ground, but figure and ground 'detach themselves from their concrete adherence to the universe and follow opposed routes' (MEOT 168); there is an auton-omization of categories of figure and ground. Figures are fragmented and the forces of the ground are universalized.

Technics concentrates itself on the schematism of structures. It divides, separates, detaches objects from the world to render action efficacious. Often it begins by technically occupying salient key-points of the magical space. It takes natural realities for their figural power; it isolates and extracts fragments of the world to act upon it. The techni-cal object is not part of the world but permits relating efficaciously to it. Technical thought is a thought of availability that potentially applies itself to everything everywhere, including by violence: 'There are in fact three types of reality: the world, the subject and the intermediary object between the world and the subject, whose first form is that of the technical object' (MEOT 170).

Religion takes possession of the ground with its qualities, its tensions, its forces: homogeneity, qualitative nature, indistinction of elements at the heart of a system of mutual influences, action with a long bearing in space and time. It thinks in terms of transcendence, englobement, totality. Religion represents the exigency of the totality, technics that of analysis. Religion sees always beyond unity towards absolute unity, absolute norms, a total knowledge [*connaissance*]. The content of tech-nics, on the other hand, is always below unity, in the fragmentary, the partial and plurality. The form of thought of technics is induction that seeks to exceed plurality, whereas religion deduces, or contemplates, absolute unity.

In relation to these two poles of technics and religion, aesthetic thought presents itself as an effort to reconstitute a reticular universe. It is a question, so to speak, of magic after the loss of magic. Simondon's approach is not an approach of the aesthetic object, even if the aesthetic object seems all the more important when art is institutionalized. In fact, it is a theory of the inscription of objects in a register of aesthetic thought. Aesthetic thought is not 'of a limited domain nor a determined species, but only of a tendency' (MEOT 179). It would be better to speak of what is today called 'artialization' or, in a more general fashion more conformable to Simondon's thought of 'aestheticization'. In order for there to be works of art such as those we recognize at the heart of different cultures, it must be that they 'are rendered possible by a fundamental tendency of human being' (MEOT 180). Art and works of art remake a reticular universe, by immersing it not in a disappeared primitive magical unity but in the real universe that issued from the phase difference of the magical world, in the technical world and in the religious world:

> The aesthetic impression implies the feeling of the complete perfection of an act, a perfection that objectively gives it a radiance and an authority by which it becomes a noteworthy point of lived reality, a knot of experienced [*éprouvée*] reality. This act becomes a noteworthy point of the network of human life inserted into the world; from this noteworthy point to others a superior kinship is created that reconstitutes an analogue of the magical network of the universe. (MEOT 180)

In this sense, every act, every thing, every moment can become a noteworthy point of this sort, all can therefore be 'aestheticized'. Cultures select these points, but less positively than negatively – through what they exclude from aesthetics: 'culture intervenes as a limit more than as creator' (MEOT 181).

Aesthetic thought thus aims at restoring continuities, but it does not do so by restoring magic; it operates in a world divided between objects and spirits, between figures and ground. It produces a world at once technical and religious: technical, because it is not natural and uses technics; religious, because it incorporates the 'forces, qualities, ground characters' of religion. 'Aesthetic thought, remaining in the interval between religious subjectivation and technical objectivation, is limited to concretising ground qualities by means of technical structures' (MEOT 182). Differently from that produced by religion, the work [of art], however, remains artificial and localized; it is not transcendent to the world but in the world. 'The maturity of technics and religions tends towards the reincorporation of the geographic world for technics, the human world for religions' (MEOT 182).

What defines the aesthetic object is therefore its insertion, and not the fact that it is an imitation of whatever there is. What characterizes art is its pregnancy and its salience, its manner of generating places, points, moments and exceptional instants. Simondon thereby defends an aesthetics of the local and the *in situ*, an aesthetics of sensitivity to places and moments, an aesthetics of structures grafted on to reality to give it form and signification; the aesthetic object depends on the gesture of placing, inscribing, inserting a mark in the natural or technical or religious world. To organize a natural reality as a park, to modulate the voice, to give a particular turn to language, to clothe oneself in a certain manner, are all cases of the production of aesthetic objects: 'there are in the world a certain number of notable places, exceptional points that attract and stimulate aesthetic creation, as there is in human life a certain number of particular moments, radiant, distinguished from others, that are called the work' (MEOT 184). The aesthetic work prolongs the saliences of world and life: it creates a new network of key points.

Simondon shows on this basis that technics, which begins by detaching from the world a set of objects, can aesthetically reinscribe them in nature: 'There appears the aesthetic impression, in this accord and this overcoming of technics which once again becomes concrete, inserted, reattached to the world by the most notable key points' (MEOT 181). The beauty of technical objects is not a beauty superadded through design – when this is produced, it has to do with two superadded objects ('every distortion [*travestissement*] of technical objects in aesthetic objects produces the embarrassing impression of a fake, and appears a materialised falsehood' [MEOT 185]).

On the other hand, the technical object takes on its own beauty when it is reinscribed in nature, in the geographic or human world. Aesthetics is always the business of insertion and inscription. Thus the technical object takes its aesthetic sense in making a singular point of the world stand out. Simondon thus praises – surprising in these times of Green militancy – high-tension lines crossing valleys and mountains, of dams in gorges, of lighthouses on rocks: 'the technical object is not beautiful in just any circumstances; it is beautiful when it encounters a singular and notable place of the world . . . The technical object is beautiful when it encounters a ground that agrees with it, of which it can be the proper figure, that is, when it completes and expresses the world' (MEOT 185).

The aesthetic object is therefore a prolongation of the natural world or the enclosed human world – it is a noteworthy point of a universe. The religious act can itself make the object of this aestheticization when it is inserted into reality in place of being a pure ritual: 'there are places of the natural world that call for a sanctuary, as there are moments of human life that ask for a sacramental celebration' (MEOT 189). Aesthetic reality therefore superadds itself to given reality, but according to lines that already exist in reality.

In these conditions, the beautiful is a process, not a quality of things: 'it is never, properly speaking, the object that is beautiful: it is the encounter operating a propos of the object between a real aspect of the world and a human gesture' (MEOT 191). One can therefore have an aesthetic impression without an aesthetic object: such would finally be the key phrase of Simondon's thought. In fact, the aesthetic object 'is not properly speaking an object; it is also partially the depository of a certain number of signal characteristics [*caractères d'appel*] that are of subject-reality, gesture, awaiting the objective reality in which this gesture can exercise and accomplish itself' (MEOT 191–2). The aesthetic object therefore emerges from a genesis; it calls on our tendencies, 'on our primitive existence in the world before perception' (MEOT 192). Simondon is less interested in the aesthetic object than in the aesthetic impression of which the object is only the support, the pretext or the accompaniment: 'the real aesthetic impression cannot be subjugated to an object; the construction of an aesthetic object is only a necessarily vain effort for refinding a magic that has been forgotten' (ibid.). Or again, 'the aesthetic object is what prepares, develops, entertains the natural aesthetic impression' (MEOT 194).

II

Once the general orientation of this theory is understood, Simondon's dispersed reflections in this current of his work on certain forms of art, on the arts in general or on aesthetic objects can be better understood. For convenience, I will regroup them under three headings: the dispersed remarks on aesthetic properties, those on the arts and those on aesthetic objects.

Simondon's texts abound in remarks on aesthetic properties, notably concerning technical objects, design and architecture. He underlines, regarding architecture, the way in which certain architects, Le Corbusier or Eiffel in particular, arrive at grafting nature and art in perfect accord with his conception of salience and reticulated space. This goes together for him with a critique of decorative or architectural camouflage; there must on the contrary be a 'phanerotechnics' that shows the logics of the material and the inscription *in situ*. Simondon extends his consideration right up to tools, cars and everyday technical objects (radar, keys, bolts).

In the same way he underlines that certain works consist in the dynamic superposition of structures. Thus he treats opticalization by the adding on of microstructures to the object in the baroque, in Op Art, including its sartorial variants.[2] In other cases, there are two 'images' that superpose themselves to produce a dynamism. Such is the sense of the analysis that Simondon gives to the famous Mona Lisa. This painting is, says Simondon, a superimpression in relation to itself:

> there is certainly the same and unique canvas, a beginning of the smile and an end of the smile, but not the full smile, the entelechy of the smile. There are only the two extreme terms of the smile that are painted and revealed. But the complete chain of the smile is the contemplation that brings it and constitutes it in its own proper interiority whether individual or personal . . . The smile deploys itself and nonetheless also the smile is already disappearing.[3]

As ever with this dynamic and genetic approach, one must note the reflections on the conditioning of commodities and objects: what to do for products to be presented in such a way as to provoke the sensation of the basis under the perceptive conditions of a culture? Simondon suggests even extending these reflections beyond 'products' properly called to 'non-object' phenomena like electricity, waves and sounds.

As far as the arts are concerned, Simondon sees there the technical forms of the production of objects and aesthetic impressions. Inventions are the amplification of learning [*apprentissages*] and they then give rise to formalizations and normalizations through the constitution of symbols. There are formalizations for operatory finality, for communicating, to give orders and obtain coordinated actions. There are others for what is of an affectivo-emotive order (II 157). It is thus a question of favouring participation and action by the communication of a feeling, an emotion. The arts and religious life correspond to this 'formalisation of a subjective type' (II 157).

Simondon maintains that 'the successive inventions of symbolic forms recruit by means of the enlargement of effects and modes of appearing of reality that have no primitive acceptance in the artistic domain' (II 159). The arts, in their development, invent compatibilities between heterogeneous givens. Simondon leads this analysis towards cinema and television, and he intuits the integration of the digital. (He only speaks of recordings on magnetic strips.) There is, in each epoch, an art that conducts the procession of arts and integrates them: architecture in the seventeenth century when buildings united gardens, paintings, cabinet work, fountains, sculptures; literature at the beginning of the nineteenth century when the book sought to forge means for the compatibility of the arts (engraved reproductions, lithography). Today it would be cinema, television and, of course, the computer, 'symbolic systems of compatibility resting on a technical invention in the course of its development, as previously printing joined lithography and engravings for mass circulation' (II 160). This implies that, for Simondon, there is a historical relativity of the arts and their classifications. It is also clear that these are the aptitudes of the arts to freight contents that count. There is no place for formalism with Simondon, except if we understand by this, in a barely theoretical manner, the abstract and avant-gardiste characteristics of certain 'modern' works applying to the incorporation of new materials and media, and to inscription in new saliences.

In so far as aesthetic objects are concerned, Simondon shows that they are made from several layers. The superficial layer is that of 'predetermined and predetermining finality' (II 180): picturesque or decorative or sentimental finality, whether it is in a painting of a landscape, a typical decorative object or a fashionable song. The middle layer is that of a ritualized elaboration, picking up the accepted rules of the genre and putting them to work in a manner authorized by the group of experts [*connaisseurs*]. There is finally the 'futurist' layer, which can also appear archaic in other regards, notably for the conventional cultivated amateur, which consists in recruiting for the work unforeseen, local, surprising and heterogeneous effects:

> every inventor in the matter of art is futurist to a certain extent, which means that he exceeds the *hic et nunc* of needs and ends by enlisting in the created object sources of effects that live and multiply themselves in the work; the creator is sensitive to the virtual, to what demands, from the ground of time and in the tightly situated humbleness of a place, the progress of the future and amplitude of the world as a place of manifestation. (II 182)

III

What now is the import of this theory and about what can it today say something to us?

I will not discuss the metaphysics of this hylomorphic conception, renovated by the physics of phases and transitions. It has its beauty, but also very certainly its limits – to the extent to which it imposes a very systematic and even mechanical frame on thought, even if in a pre-Socratic manner. I will concentrate on aesthetics and art.

What is most important in Simondon's thought is that it is precisely an approach to aesthetics rather than to art; there is a register of 'aesthetic' thought, as there is a register of technical, religious, metaphysical thought, and, even if art is one of its manifestations, it is not the only one. Aesthetic impressions pass before and largely overflow the domain of aesthetic objects which are inscribed in culture and history, which are therefore held in the relativity of cultures and the manner in which they institutionalize aesthetic production and intention.

At base, what Simondon tells us, rediscovering simple poetic intuitions, is that anything can be the object of an aesthetic experience, provided that the gaze dwells on its formal characteristics and its salience on a ground, whether this is in space or time (the value of instants and key moments). Other thinkers, in analytic philosophy, as in so-called continental philosophy, have discussed the aesthetic attitude that suspends technical interests and beliefs, which detaches us from the real and suddenly gives way to aesthetic feeling – it is precisely of this that Simondon speaks. This experience is open to all; it belongs to humanity, whether it is an elevated and refined experience, or a banal one. Simondon, however, does something other than propose another variant of the aesthetic attitude: he adds to it his own consideration on the saliences of experience. If there is aesthetic experience, this is because something suddenly detaches itself in space or time, surges from the ground and imposes itself. Then a human being (or a group of human beings) could either let the aesthetic moment be lost in the fugitive impression or elaborate it, rendering it durable, communicable, thus giving it a consistency in objects or symbolic marks by inscribing it in a larger construction. Someone hears a nightingale late at night, or sees a rock with strange forms, and all that remains is the happiness of this experience. A musician captures this song or those sounds to inscribe them in a work of '*musique concréte*', a sculptor makes a statue *in situ*, a religious group builds a chapel in a place.

Simondon thus makes room for an aesthetics of the banal, the slim, the light, the fugitive, as for an aesthetics of elaboration and enrichment. He also makes a place for recuperation by the arts of the weak, banal, natural, of all that comes 'in passing'. Aesthetic experience is not reserved for those who can have the experience of art. It is not only an affair of sophisticated elaboration. It can even be present in a non-worked manner in sophisticated art. The neo-dadaist practice of the

1950s make considerable use of this recuperation of the simple, banal, light, what Duchamp even called 'the infra-slim' at the heart of the most sophisticated art, whether in music, in the visual arts, in dance. In the same way the Dadaists used voice, cries, onomatopoeia in their recitals of phonetic poetry and their performances. A significant part of the most contemporary visual art plays with these banal aesthetic impressions, in the range of everyone, in performances (Francis Alÿs), photography (Sophie Calle), installations (Ann Veronica Janssens, Tracey Emin). Arthur Danto has spoken of the transfiguration of the commonplace; this transfiguration has operated in art since the 1970s, and since the 1950s for music (electro-acoustic music).

Simondon's thought has yet another interest, that of underlining the importance of practices *in situ*, in the environment and in nature, in public space. The major part of art since the 1970s is *in situ*: whether in nature (*land art*, *earth art*), in urban space or simply in the space of the museum or gallery, marking salient geographical points or creating them from nothing in space (*land art*), in time (holidays, festivals, commemorations, inaugurations, grand opening ceremonies for the Olympic Games, celebrations) or again in the social space of art ('installations').

Simondon has obviously the merit of proposing a theory that enables us to comprehend at which point technical objects and complexes of technical objects make art today. There has been an incredible proliferation of the world of technics, to the point that this second world has, in many regions of the world, obliterated the greater part of the natural world, not only with urban proliferation, the sprawl of housing, the crossing of landscapes by communication routes and energy transports of all kinds. In a first moment, decorative art was a way of 'rendering beautiful' technical objects, whether in prettifying them with tacked-on elements, or with putting on a sort of bodywork that dissimulated their machinery. Simondon has some very harsh judgments about this decoration before modern design. His analysis of progressive integration of the technical object comes at the right time to explain the beauty of 'lean' [*pauvre*] design when form follows function and follows the integration of function. Today, on the other hand, it would be in default, now that functions and forms are again separated, not by the default of form (as in the past for decoration), but by the technological hermeticism of functioning and the liberation of capacities of formal invention (see new design freed or almost so from material constraints); the design of an iPod, an iPhone, a computer or even of a train is no longer in relation with technical functions but only with the ergonomics of usage or energy constraints.

On the other hand, the Simondonian theory of reinvestment of key points of space and time by technical objects and equipment is more pertinent than ever. Conforming to what Simondon said, technique does not stop reinscribing itself in nature and time as art; there is an artialization of technique. One could even go much further than he did. Not only do technical objects inscribe themselves in space and becoming as saliences in often grafting themselves on to natural saliences (dams, motorways, high-tension lines, aerials, illumination of monuments), but very often they produce these saliences through their existence alone: a nuclear station, a field of windmills, an international airport in themselves constitute saliences in an otherwise indefinite space.

A final point, of extreme importance: this theory of aesthetic saliences is in perfect sync with the hitherto indissoluble bond between aesthetics and tourism. Tourists travel the world in quest of geographical, memorial, sentimental saliences that render the world worthy of being visited and travelled. Tourists are always in this sense in a state of aesthetic quest, even when their aesthetic impressions are limited to a speedy trip to saturated monuments and to eating standardized typical meals that never existed in the form that they take for the tourist. This is because the low quality of an aesthetic experience does not kill its nature as aesthetic experience. Tourists are therefore in a quest for attractors that structure space to give a direction [*sens*] to their travels. One goes to see the Taj Mahal, the Eiffel Tower, the Ryoanji Garden, the *Mona Lisa*, the *Demoiselles d'Avignon* or the site of the destroyed Twin Towers. Simondon's aesthetic theory gives a perfect account of the solidarity between the touristification of the world and aesthetics, between real attractors – and even more so the symbolic ones (one does not go to see the *Mona Lisa*, one goes to see the city for which one of the symbolic markers is the *Mona Lisa*) – and tourist movements.

The import of Simondon's theory of aesthetics could be summarized in three keywords: aesthetic impression (rather than the aesthetic object), techno-aesthetics (rather than natural aesthetics) and aesthetic attractors (rather than masterpieces). Through these words and what they implicitly object to, we measure the eminently current character of a thought that wanted to be pre-Socratic – and the importance of the displacements that it operates.

NOTES

1. Gilbert Simondon, *Du mode d'existence des objets techniques* (Paris: Aubier, 1958), hereafter designated MEOT.

2. Gilbert Simondon, *Imagination et invention (1965–1966)* (Paris: Les Editions de la transparence, 2008), pp. 90, 91; henceforth designated II.
3. Gilbert Simondon, *Sur la techno-esthétique* and *Réflexions préalables à une refonte de l'enseignement* [unpublished text on techno-aesthetics, 3 July 1969].

Resonances

Gilles Deleuze, a Reader of Gilbert Simondon

Sean Bowden

Several years ago, at a conference on the work of Gilbert Simondon,[1] Bernard Stiegler announced that an English translation of Gilbert Simondon's *L'Individuation psychique et collective* (*Psychic and Collective Individuation*) was being undertaken and would be published with the University of Minnesota Press.[2] According to Stiegler, the publishers were convinced of the viability of the project thanks to the following argument: 'if we love Deleuze, then we *need* Simondon'.[3] Indeed, not only does Gilles Deleuze's 1966 review of Simondon's work already mention several concepts which Deleuze would later develop in his own particular way – the concepts of 'singularity' and 'intensive magnitude', for example – we also find Simondon cited in support of key arguments in works such as *Difference and Repetition*, *The Logic of Sense* and *A Thousand Plateaus*.[4] These citations, however, contain very little explication of the precise way in which Deleuze understands and appropriates Simondon's work. It is thus clear that, in line with Stiegler's argument, a full appreciation of these Deleuzian texts will require some knowledge of Simondon, a knowledge which has so far been denied Deleuze's English-language readers.[5]

It is nevertheless the case that Stiegler's argument would be better applied to the publication of a translation of Simondon's *L'Individu et sa genèse physico-biologique* (*The Individual and its Physico-Biological Genesis*), since this is the only Simondon text to which Deleuze explicitly refers.[6] In the – let us hope, temporary – absence of such a translation, what we would like to do here, whilst avoiding the highly technical analyses that Simondon undertakes in relation to developments in twentieth-century physics and biology, is to outline for the English-language reader the main concepts and arguments of *L'Individu et sa genèse physico-biologique* and to indicate how Deleuze takes up certain aspects of this work in his 1968 *Difference and Repetition*. In doing so, we shall also refer to some of the French secondary literature surrounding Simondon's work, in order to give the reader an appreciation of the attention currently being paid to Simondon in France.

GILBERT SIMONDON AND THE THEORY OF PHYSICO-BIOLOGICAL INDIVIDUATION

Simondon's *L'Individu et sa genèse* is an attempt to think the individual as the result of ontologically prior 'processes of individuation', as opposed to thinking individuation with reference to already constituted individuals. According to Simondon, such a project runs counter to the Western philosophical tradition which has generally always taken one of two paths: the substantialist path or the hylomorphic path (see INFI 23–5 on this). On the one hand, metaphysicians of substance tend to begin with the already constituted individual and subsequently ask about its coming to be, thereby thinking the nature of individuation uniquely in terms of the characteristics of this already given individual. But as Simondon asks, what if processes of individuation 'overflow' what we ordinarily think of as individuals? What if processes of individuation are not exhausted in the production of individuals and simultaneously produce something more than the individual? If this were the case, then by beginning their investigation on the basis of the already constituted individual, the metaphysician of substance risks masking a more fundamental reality.

On the other hand, taking their inspiration from Aristotle, some philosophers have tended to begin with a 'principle of individuation' whose function is to explain that the individual is an individual because, for example, it is a particular combination of matter and form (or sensation and *a priori* spatio-temporal and conceptual form, and so on). In this case, whilst it is a principle of individuation and not the individual itself which is presupposed, the principle is nevertheless a 'first term': that is to say, an individual which the philosopher gives him or herself, in thought, in order to explain individuation. Once again, therefore, philosophy fails to think individuals in general as the result of prior processes of individuation.

In order to avoid presupposing anything already individuated, either in reality or in thought, Simondon proposes to think individuation through a simultaneous and corresponding individuation of the thought of individuation. As he puts it, this task 'consists in *following being in its genesis*, in accomplishing the genesis of thought at the same time that the genesis of the object is carried out' (INFI 34). So how is this 'immanent double genesis' of being and thought to be achieved?[7]

First of all, in order to account for individuation without recourse to an already constituted individual, Simondon hypothesizes the existence of what he calls the 'pre-individual' and a corresponding operation of individuation which will be carried out in relation to it (INFI 149). As will be examined more fully below, the pre-individual internalizes a difference or potential which the individual will be said to have structured or resolved, although not without remainder, through a process of individuation (INFI 25). Now, at first glance, it appears that Simondon has once again postulated an individual 'thing' with certain determinate characteristics – a type of dynamized 'primordial soup' – in order to think individuation, thereby failing once more to think the ontological priority of individuation with respect to individuals in general. More precisely, however, Simondon bases his hypothesis of the pre-individual and its corresponding operation of individuation on an 'encyclopedic', but in principle open, series of investigations into the processes of individuation of entities in different domains: physical entities, but also biological, psycho-social and technological.[8] As will be seen below, he will then argue that his concept of 'transduction', which picks out the characteristic general features of processes of individuation in these diverse domains, also characterizes the individuation of the very thought of individuation in these domains (INFI 36). In other words, individuation will be 'known' through transduction understood as a process which generates both individuals and the thought of their individuation, rather than by means of a fixed concept of transduction.[9]

In the second place, Simondon affirms what he calls a 'realism of relations', whereby a relation is not an accident with respect to a substance but rather a prior and constitutive condition of substance (INFI 82–3).[10] As he puts it, the 'individual is the reality of a constitutive relation', a constitutive relation which does not depend for its existence upon already given terms, but rather refers only to other relations (INFI 62).[11] Granting primacy to relations over individuals 'all the way down' is a consequence of Simondon's commitment to an anti-substantialist approach to individuation. Indeed, it is for this reason that, for Simondon, being is not a unified 'one', identical to itself. As he writes,

[a] relation must be grasped as a relation in being, a relation of being, a manner of being and not a simple relationship between two terms that could be adequately known by means of concepts because they would have effectively separate existences ... If substance is no longer the model of

being, it is possible to think of relations as the non-identity of being with respect to itself, the inclusion in being of a reality which is not identical with it, with the result that being as being, before individuation, can be grasped as more than a unity and more than an identity. (INFI 32)

So what is the link between pre-individual processes of individuation and this realism of relations? Simondon argues that the first characteristic of the pre-individual is that it is distributed according to different 'orders of magnitude' (INFI 31–2). These orders of magnitude take a variety of different forms depending on the domain under consideration: for example, the different inter-elemental forces in the clay and in the mould in the operation of casting a brick (INFI 43–4); the different potential energies corresponding to two different structures such as a supersaturated solution and a seed crystal (INFI 76–7); the difference between, on the one hand, different species of chemicals in the earth and atmosphere and, on the other hand, solar energy, in the case of the individuation of a plant (INFI 34, n. 12); the difference between an organism's internal organization and its external environment in the case of the individuation of an animal (INFI 28, 225–6), and so on. Following Simondon, what we are dealing with in each of these cases is a pre-individual which is comprised only of disparate orders of magnitude that may be, primitively, without communication (INFI 34). What is crucial, then, is that relations are established between these orders by processes of individuation (INFI 26). In other words, following Simondon, the pre-individual will form a system of relations governing the genesis of the individual, but only in so far as the individual, in its coming to be, actualizes or structures these relations.[12] Indeed, this manner of conceiving the pre-individual both allows us to think the individual in terms of relations, and prevents us from postulating Simondon's 'orders of magnitude' as themselves the types of already individuated things between which there could be relations.[13]

Now, Simondon talks about pre-individual relations between different orders of magnitude in a variety of ways. In thermodynamic terms, Simondon speaks of a 'metastable system' wherein there is a 'potential energy' between different orders of magnitude and where the process of individuation corresponds to the progressive degradation of this potential energy through a series of transformations (a potential energy is said to be actualized by these transformations) (INFI 26). In terms of the theory of vision, Simondon speaks of a 'disparation' between two orders of magnitude, whereby two twin sets which are not totally superimposable, such as left and right retinal images, are seized together in a system and allow the formation of a single set of a higher degree which integrates all their elements (INFI 205–6, n. 15). Indeed, it is in light of these various characterizations that Deleuze says that we may, in speaking of individuation, speak as much of the establishment of interactive communication between different orders of magnitude or disparate realities, as the actualization of a potential energy or the integration of singularities, as the resolution of the problem posed by disparate realities by the organization of a new dimension of a higher degree.[14] In any case, what is important is that a pre-individual relation between different orders of magnitude both is established by and governs a process of individuation which actualizes or structures these relations.

But now, what brings these orders of magnitude into communication if it cannot, strictly speaking, be the individual? To be sure, since the individual does not exist prior to the relation that it will have been said to actualize, it cannot be what initially establishes the relation. For Simondon, then, it is a 'singularity' which begins individuation (INFI 62, 97). As he writes, concretely, a singularity may be 'the stone that begins the dune, the gravel which is the seed for an island in a river carrying sediment' (INFI 44, n. 5); or again, it may be the 'information' contained in a seed crystal such that it induces further crystallization when added to a supersaturated solution (INFI 78).[15] In other words, the individual which is coming about is said to 'prolong' a singularity. But interestingly, it also appears that an already constituted individual may play the role of a singularity when it enters into another system in a state of metastable equilibrium and brings about a transformation (INFI 82, n. 9). As Deleuze notes in this regard, however, it is important to distinguish carefully between singularity and individual, for singularities are by definition pre-individual.[16] Indeed, it appears that the capacity of an individual to function as a singularity for a pre-individual metastable system ultimately depends on the nature of the metastable system in question. In other words, a singularity is simply whatever is capable of bringing about a 'break' in a metastable system and of causing its heterogeneous orders to communicate in a process of individuation which actualizes the system's potentials and transforms it in the production of new individuals (INFI 78). A singularity is thus 'pre-individual' in the sense that it has a local and functional definition which is strictly relative to the different orders between which it brings about communication.[17]

It is in this manner that, for Simondon, a singularity is also 'information' (INFI 48, n. 8; 97), in a sense that can be generalized from cybernetics and information theory. In the theory of information, information is what 'passes' between an emitter and a receptor (or a cascade of such emitters and receptors) when the receptor can be said to make a 'deci-sion' with respect to the state of the emitter (whether this decision be a reaction, an adaptation, a decoding or some other transformation, depending on whether one is dealing with systems that are physical, biological, technological and so on). However, it is essential to note that information must not here be equated with a 'message'. Information rather depends upon relations between the natures of the emitter and the receptor: that is, upon relations between the 'possible states' or 'events' which define each of them, and factors such as the background interference or 'noise' due to the nature of the information channel. In this sense, then, information is essentially, in the words of one early cybernetician, a 'set of possibilities', and the problem which cybernet-ics and information theory were originally designed to deal with is that of formalizing the probabilistic conditions under which the correct or intended message can be reliably selected from a set of possible mes-sages.[18] Technical details aside, what is important for Simondon's philosophical concept of information or singularities is that it must obey certain purely relational (or again, 'purely operational' – INFI 220) con-ditions with respect to the different orders between which it functions. On the one hand, information must be in some sense 'unforeseeable' for the receptor if it is not to be received as the simple external repetition of an already existing internal state or simply confused with background 'noise'. (In information theory, the total probability for the receptor of a particular state of the emitter, as much as the non-distinction of the information signal due to noise, means no information: that is, no 'deci-sion' or transformation on the part of the receptor with respect to the emitter.) On the other hand, information must be in some sense 'fore-seeable' if it is to be meaningful for and capable of being integrated by the receptor, since the receptor already has its own possible states and mode of functioning with which to make a 'decision' with respect to the state of the emitter (or again, more technically, if all states of the emitter are equiprobable for the receptor, then there is no information) (INFI 221–3). It is thus clear that there is information only when what emits the signal and what receives it can form a differential system in relation to something 'non-immanent' to, but 'almost entirely' coinciding with, that particular system (INFI 79, 223). As Simondon writes, 'information is *between* the two halves of a system in a relation of disparation' (INFI 223, n. 30), meaning thereby that, if there is information, a system is formed which integrates the elements of the two disparate realities in a common process. In other words, 'information is *that through which the incompatibility of the non-resolved system becomes the organizing dimension in its resolution*' (INFI 31, emphasis in the original). And indeed, extrapolating from this, in so far as it refers to the system's 'constitutive difference', information is something like the sense or meaning (Simondon typically writes, '*signification*') of this system, provided that one also adds that this 'sense' only emerges in the concrete transformations that actually take place in the system.[19] Sense, for Simondon, is relational (INFI 223).

But precisely how, for Simondon, does the individual emerge from such communication between heterogeneous orders? The concept that Simondon introduces in order to account for the emergence of the individual is that of 'transduction'.[20] As he writes,

> We understand by transduction an operation, physical, biological, mental, social, through which an activity spreads step by step within a domain, this propagation being founded on a structuring of the domain which is carried out from place to place: each region of the constituted structure serves as the principle for the constitution of the following region, in such a way that a modification is thus progressively extended at the same time as this structuring operation . . . A crystal which, from a tiny germ, grows and spreads in all direction in its solution furnishes the simplest image of the operation of transduction: each constituted molecular layer serves as the structuring basis for the layer which is currently being formed. (INFI 32–3)

In effect, transduction is the name given to the ongoing actualization or structuring of the potentials of a metastable system whose constitutive, heterogeneous orders have been brought into communication by a singularity functioning as a 'structural germ'. It is in this way that, as mentioned above, the structured individual which emerges from this process is said to 'prolong' this singularity (INFI 78, 82, 532). For Simondon, a 'complete' individuation would correspond to the total use of potential energy contained in the metastable system before structuring. 'Incomplete' individuation, on the other hand, corresponds to a structuring which has not absorbed all of its potential energy (INFI 79–80). But in fact, incomplete individuation is the general case, since the individual always tends to emerge at the same time as a characteristic 'milieu' or environment (such as a crystal and its solution) (INFI 24–5). This milieu emerges precisely because the individual is not capable of exhausting all of the potentials of the pre-individual reality from which it emerges. And indeed, this is why Simondon says that the milieu is itself a system, synthetically grouping together two or more levels of reality (INFI 30, n. 6). It can thus be considered the individual's 'reserve' of pre-individual charge (INFI 62–3). In any case, the picture that emerges here is of a world composed of heterogeneous orders between which there exists a 'potential energy' which may be actualized in various ways by appropriately structured singularities. The individuals which are produced by these transductive operations may in turn serve as singularities for other systems or even as relatively amorphous structures (in themselves, or in relation to their milieus) which may be restructured in encounters with other singularities. As Simondon writes, a being

> is genetically constituted by a relation between an energetic condition and a structural condition which prolong their existence in the individual, an individual which can at any moment behave like a structural germ or like an energetic continuum; its relation differs depending on whether it enters into a relation with a milieu which is equivalent to a continuum or with a milieu which has already been structured. (INFI 110–11)

Of course, these processes of individuation may be more or less complex, depending on the number of systems and subsystems involved. For example, transduction is direct and at a single level in physical systems, and indirect and hierarchized in the living being (INFI 160).[21] And things are even more complex when we consider the relation between the physical and the biological, or again, the biological and the psychic. At the limit, such a conception of transduction would 'consider the energetic regimes and the structural states as convertible into each other through the becoming of the whole' of Nature (INFI 148–9). It should be noted, however, that this 'whole' does not dissolve the difference between, and the specificity of, the different domains of individuation. The individual does not have a direct relationship with the whole of Nature (INFI 65). On the contrary, each regime, as we have seen, is characterized by the type and number of relations and processes it implicates or in which it is implicated. This is precisely what allows Simondon to specify the difference between, for example, the biological and the physical in terms of information and transduction:

> [T]here is *physical* information when the system is capable of receiving information just once, then develops and amplifies this initial singularity. If the system is capable of successively receiving several contributions of information, of compatibilizing several singularities instead of repeating the initial singularity, the individuation is vital. (INFI 152)

So we have our characterization of processes of individuation via the concept of transduction. However, Simondon also gives us another and at first sight unrelated definition of transduction:

> Transduction is a mental process [*procédé*] and, even more than a process, a movement [*démarche*] of the mind which discovers. This movement consists in *following being in its genesis*, in accomplishing the genesis of thought at the same time that the genesis of the object is carried out . . . Transduction is thus not only movement of the mind; it is also intuition, since it is through transduction that, within a problematic domain, a structure appears as bringing about the resolution of the problems posed. (INFI 34)

So how is this second definition of transduction to be reconciled with the first? We have already examined two aspects of Simondon's thought which allow us to see how these two aspects of transduction are to be thought together. The first is Simondon's anti-substantialist assertion that being is through and through relational. In other words, if relations virtually precede their terms in all domains, then not only will we have to characterize concrete processes of individuation in systems that are physical, biological and so on in a relational way, but also the very thought of these processes, and thus the determination of the terms in which these processes are characterized, must emerge in a relational way. It can thus be said that Simondon's dual definition of transduction as both objective and mental is in line with this requirement for a relational description of processes of all kinds. Indeed, even the relation between the objective and the mental – the relation typically called knowledge – must be described in relational terms. What this means is that, as Simondon writes, 'knowledge is not a relation between a substance object and a substance subject, but the *relation between two relations*, one of which is in the domain of the object and the other in the domain of the subject' (INFI 82–3).[22]

The second and related aspect of Simondon's thought which shows us precisely what Simondon means by 'transduction' is his method: that is, as has been seen, his encyclopedic, if in principle open, investigation of processes of individuation in diverse domains. This method incorporates both the objective and the mental aspects of transduction in a single, speculative philosophy. Indeed, as a number of commentators have noted, Simondon's initial analysis of the formation of crystals through transduction functions as the 'elementary paradigm' for the individuation of the thought of individuation. In other words, the use of this paradigm in different and increasingly complex, 'problematic' domains of knowledge acts as a 'structural germ' for the gradual transformation of our understanding of transductive processes of individuation in these other domains, and in turn leads to an ongoing individuation of our knowledge of individuation (INFI 33, 83–4).[23] As Simondon describes his method:

> Having thus attempted to seize, on the one hand, the epistemological role of the notion of the individual in this domain, and on the other hand the phenomenological contents to which this notion refers, we will try to transfer the results of this first test to domains which are logically and ontologically subsequent . . . [This method] is founded . . . on the search for a structure and an operation which is characteristic of the reality that one may name the individual; if this reality exists, it can be applicable to different forms and levels, but must authorize the intellectual transfer from one domain to another, by means of necessary conversions; the notions that it will be necessary to add in order to pass from one domain to the next will thus be characteristic of the order of reality which makes up the content of these domains. (INFI 555)[24]

Or more simply, as Jean-Hugues Barthélémy has put it, if we are dealing with relations 'all the way down', as it were, then 'to pass from the polarization of the *crystal* to that of the living being, is *to pass from one degree of individuality to an other by a multiplication of the relation*.'[25] In short, transduction thus describes, at once, 'real processes of individuation in their analogically connected diversity *and* the kind of thought which allows them to be understood'.[26]

But what now of Deleuze's relation to the philosophy of individuation which Simondon establishes in *L'Individu et sa genèse physico-biologique?*

SIMONDON IN DELEUZE'S *DIFFERENCE AND REPETITION*

Although it will be necessary to remain schematic in our comments, we can indicate several points at which Simondon's influence on Deleuze's *Difference and Repetition* can clearly be felt. First of all, in terms of general aims, Deleuze, like Simondon, wants to think of 'identities' as ontologically derived entities. What Deleuze calls 'identities', here, have traditionally been understood to be ontologically primary, self-identical individuals, differing from all others, and whose differential 'criteria of identity' can be conceptually specified using an appropriate means (Platonic division and dialectic, Aristotelian generic and specific difference, Leibnizian compossibility, Hegelian contradiction and so on). Deleuze, however, wants to think identity in terms of difference rather than difference in terms of identity. In other words, as opposed to thinking difference as a relation between two, already given, self-identical individuals, Deleuze want to think a differential difference from which all apparently self-identical individuals would ultimately be derived. As he writes, '[d]ifference is the state in which one can speak of determination *as such*.[27] The task is thus to show how this differential determination or individuating difference ontologically precedes constituted individuals 'all the way down' (DR 38).

In relation to this aim, as is well known, Deleuze posits two intimately related 'halves of difference': a purely differential, problematic or virtual 'Idea' made up only of differential relations and singularities, which is actualized or differenciated by 'spatio-temporal dynamisms' or 'intensive processes of individuation' (DR 279–80). This parallels, quite precisely, the way in which Simondon posits transductive processes of individuation as actualizing a purely relational pre-individual, made up only of different orders of magnitude and singularities. Indeed, Deleuze himself makes this parallel explicit when he writes that:

> Gilbert Simondon has shown recently that individuation presupposes a prior metastable state – in other words, the existence of a 'disparateness' such as at least two orders of magnitude or two scales of heterogeneous reality between which potentials are distributed. Such a pre-individual field nevertheless does not lack singularities: the distinctive or singular points are defined by the existence and distribution of potentials. An 'objective' problematic field thus appears, determined by the distance between two heterogeneous orders. Individuation emerges like the act of solving a problem, or – what amounts to the same thing – like the actualization of a potential and the establishing of communication between disparates. The act of individuation consists ... in integrating the elements of the disparateness into a state of coupling which ensures its internal resonance. The individual thus finds itself attached to a pre-individual half which is not the impersonal within it so much as the reservoir of its singularities. In all these respects, we believe that individuation is essentially intensive, and that the pre-individual field is a virtual-ideal field, made up of differential relations ... Individuation is the act by which intensity determines differential relations to become actualized, along the lines of differenciation and within the qualities and extensities it creates. (DR 246)

This, then, is Simondon's second influence on Deleuze. In short, Simondon provides Deleuze with a means of speaking about the concrete actualization of those purely problematic Ideas through which every difference can be determined as a difference of difference. Indeed, it would appear that Simondon's work directly inspired two of Deleuze's philosophical concepts bound up with his conception of the actualization of virtual Ideas: 'intensity' or 'intensive magnitude', and 'singularities'. To speak, first of all, about the concept of intensity, we do not think it is a coincidence that both Simondon and, subsequently, Deleuze make use of a thermodynamic vocabulary in order to speak about the way in which relations or differences are primary in relation to 'things'. As was seen above, Simondon speaks of 'orders of magnitude', 'metastable systems' and 'potential energy' in order to characterize the pre-individual and defend his commitment to an anti-substantialist 'realism of relations'. Similarly, Deleuze employs the concept of 'intensive quantity' precisely in order to talk about the purely differential basis of 'what happens' and 'what appears'. As he writes:

> Everything which happens and everything which appears is correlated with orders of differences: differences of level, temperature, pressure, tension, potential, *difference of intensity* . . . Every intensity is $E - E'$, where E itself refers to an $e - e'$, and e to $\varepsilon - \varepsilon'$, etc.: each intensity is already a coupling (in which each element of the couple refers in turn to other elements of another order). (DR 222)[28]

In terms of the concept of 'singularity', it is again clear that Deleuze's concept resembles Simondon's in many respects. We know that while Simondon privileges an 'informational' model for his concept, Deleuze refers primarily to Weierstrassian analysis (at least implicitly) and Albert Lautman's analysis of Henri Poincaré's 'qualitative theory' of differential equations (DR 175–7; 324, n. 9).[29] However, what both of these models have in common is that they define the concept of singularity entirely in relational terms: that is, as that which allows for the communication and actualization of a purely differential or problematic relation within a new form or individual. More precisely, for both thinkers, a singularity refers to the differential conditions of a purely problematic instance; for Simondon, as has been seen, a singularity is defined by the way in which it 'almost coincides' with the different orders between which it establishes communication, just as, for Deleuze, singularities correspond to the 'values' of the relations between the purely differential elements of the virtual Idea (DR 175, 278).[30] Furthermore, this same singularity is immanent in the real solutions which 'resolve' this problematic or differential instance; for Simondon, the individual resolving or structuring the relation between different orders of magnitude is said to 'prolong' the singularity which brought them into communication and initiated a transformation, while, for Deleuze, singularities are said to be 'enveloped' by the intensive series of individuating factors which determine the differential relations of the Idea to be 'actualized' in new forms (DR 246, 279).[31] In other words, for both philosophers, the singularity refers to both pre-individual relations and to the real forms and individuals which specify the 'actual' nature of these pre-individual relations.

A third point of convergence between Simondon's and Deleuze's respective projects is the claim that intensive processes of individuation concern all of the domains of being: physical, biological, social, psychological, perceptual, linguistic and so on.[32] In Chapter 5 of *Difference and Repetition*, Deleuze discusses a number of 'intensive systems' belonging to diverse domains, and the various ways in which they have been and ought to be thought. He discusses, for example, classical thermodynamics (DR 222–4, 228–9, 240–1), Curie's work on symmetry (DR 222–3, 234),[33] the visual perception of space (DR 229–31), number theory and order theory (DR 232–3, 237–8), embryogenesis (DR 249–52), biological evolution (DR 255–6), and the relation between self and other in psycho-social systems (DR 256–61). In Chapter 2, Deleuze also analyses language in intensive terms, in particular in relation to literary systems (DR 121–4) and psychic systems (DR 122–6).[34] In fact, Chapter 2's discussion of the passive synthesis of habit in terms of the contemplations and contractions of elementary 'repetitions' is a discussion of the way in which individuals are constituted by syntheses of series of intensive differences, wherein each element of a contracted couple refers to (or 'repeats') coupled elements from other orders:

> What we call wheat is a contraction of the earth and humidity . . . What organism is not made of elements and cases of repetition, of contemplated and contracted water, nitrogen, carbon, chlorides and sulphates, thereby intertwining all the habits of which it is composed? . . . [E]verything is contemplation, even rocks and words, animals and men . . . even our actions and our needs. (DR 75)

Now, Deleuze further argues (as does Simondon, it can be recalled, when he argues that the individual does not have a direct relationship with the whole of Nature) that, even though all the systems and domains of being he discusses have a common 'intensive character', this 'should not prejudice them being characterized as mechanical, physical, biological, psychic, social, aesthetic or philosophical and so on. Each type of system undoubtedly has its own particular conditions' (DR 117–18). It is nevertheless clear that, for Deleuze as much as for Simondon, a number of systems from different domains can be conjoined in the production of certain individuals. For example, biological, social, psychic and linguistic intensive processes combine to produce modern human beings. What is more, it is evident that if, as Deleuze claims, difference must account for 'determination as such', the relation between these different systems must also be thought 'differentially': that is to say, in relation to purely differential or problematic Ideas (the Simondonian pre-individual).[35]

Of particular relevance with respect to this question of the relation between different intensive systems is the question of the relation between those systems implicated in the production of the individual human being and those systems producing the individuals making up this being's 'world'. Indeed, it is clear that the determination of this relation will have some bearing on how we are to think about knowledge. The question is, in other words: how are we to determine the relation between the development of 'knowledge' embodied in concepts, the intensive constitution of the individuals which are 'known' in various domains, and the intensively constituted 'knowing' subject? We saw that, for Simondon, knowledge is the structuring of a relation between two relations in pre-individual tension, one of which is in the object and the other in the subject. Similarly, Deleuze speaks of a complex differential relation between knowledge, the known and the knowing subject.[36] He argues that intensive processes of individuation progressively determine the actualization of virtual Ideas within concepts corresponding to the resulting individuals, through the intermediary of a 'divided subject' who, while thoroughly dissolved in intensive processes, thinks itself, its world and the relations between them in purely differential terms. With respect to the actualization of Ideas by processes of intensive individuation, Deleuze writes that 'the role of dramas [i.e., intensive processes of individuation] is to specify concepts by incarnating the differential relations and singularities of an Idea' (DR 218). Or again:

> It is because of the action of the field of individuation that such and such differential relations and such and such distinctive points (pre-individual fields) are actualized – in other words, organized within intuition along lines differenciated in relation to other lines. As a result, they then form the quality, number, species and parts of an individual, in short, its generality. (DR 247)[37]

As for the 'divided subject', on the one hand, it is a 'dissolved self', which is to say 'an event which takes place in pre-existing fields of [intensive] individuation: it contemplates and contracts the individuating factors of such fields, and constitutes itself at the points of resonance of their series' (DR 276). On the other hand, it is a 'fractured I' who does not so much actively and spontaneously think (since psychic systems are, properly speaking, systems of intensive individuation), as stand in a relation to those pre-individual and impersonal problematic Ideas wherein the psychological self, its intensive world and the relations between them can progressively be thought: that is to say, differentially determined 'all the way down' (DR 86).[38] As Deleuze writes,

> the individual in intensity finds its psychic image . . . in the correlation of
> the fractured I with the dissolved self . . . [W]hat swarms around the edges
> of the fracture are Ideas in the form of problems – in other words, in the
> form of multiplicities made up of differential relations and variations of
> relations, distinctive points and transformations of points. These ideas,
> however, are expressed in individuating factors, in the implicated world of
> intensive quantities which constitute the universal concrete individuality of
> the thinker or the system of the dissolved Self. (DR 259)

As with Simondon, then, Deleuze understands 'knowing' to be the actualization of a relation, in pre-individual or differential 'tension', between two systems of differential relations, one constitutive of the known individual and the other of the knowing subject. More precisely, knowing is an ongoing, open-ended and differential process involving the simultaneous actualization of ideal, pre-individual relations in persons, individual things, and the concepts corresponding to these persons and individuals.

These striking parallels between Simondon's and Deleuze's philosophical projects, some of them explicitly recognized by Deleuze, can leave us in no doubt as to the immense influence which Simondon had on this latter. Indeed, several recent commentaries on Deleuze have pointed out this philosophical debt. Alberto Gualandi, for example, signals very clearly Simondon's importance for Deleuze, and in particular for his *Difference and Repetition*.[39] Anne Sauvagnargues analyses in detail Simondon's 'decisive contribution' to Deleuze's philosophy more generally.[40] Finally, even though he cautions against taking any of Deleuze's privileged references as the 'key' to his thought, Alberto Toscano has usefully mapped a number of ways in which a philosophical relation between these two thinkers can productively be thought.[41] It is hoped that our above analyses have been able to contribute in some small way to this growing literature on Simondon and on Simondon's influence on Deleuze. In particular, it is hoped that we have been able to supply English-speaking readers of Deleuze with a solid overview of a number of the themes to be found in Simondon's yet-to-be-translated *L'Individu et sa genèse physico-biologique*, and how these themes have been taken up by Deleuze in his *Difference and Repetition*.

NOTES

1. 'L'Individuation de Simondon', Ecole Normale Supérieure, rue d'Ulm, Paris, France, 15 December 2007.
2. This text, consisting of the second part of Simondon's 1958 *doctorat d'état*, was published for the first time in French in 1989 with Aubier. A more recent edition

can now be found in the collection *L'Individuation à la lumière des notions de forme et d'information* (Grenoble: Jérôme Millon, 2005).

3. Stiegler was, however, also at pains to insist that we need to begin reading Simondon *without* reference to Deleuze, no doubt taking him in those directions indicated in Stiegler's own work.

4. See Gilles Deleuze, 'On Gilbert Simondon', in *Desert Islands and Other Texts 1953–1974*, trans. Michael Taormina, ed. David Lapoujade (New York: Semiotexte, 2004), pp. 86–9; 'Asymmetrical Synthesis of the Sensible', in *Difference and Repetition*, trans. Paul Patton (London: Athlone, 1994), esp. p. 246; and 'Fifteenth Series of Singularities', in *The Logic of Sense*, trans. Mark Lester and Charles Stivale, ed. Constantin V. Boundas (New York: Colombia University Press, 1990), pp. 100–8 and in particular p. 344, n. 3. Simondon is also cited in 'The Geology of Morals' and 'Treatise on Nomadology – the War Machine', in Gilles Deleuze and Félix Guattari, *A Thousand Plateaus*, trans. Brian Massumi (London: Athlone, 1988), pp. 39–110 and pp. 351–423.

5. The only published English translation of Simondon's work is of the introduction to *L'Individu et sa genèse physico-biologique*, which has been published in Jonathan Crary and Sanford Kwinter (eds), *Incorporations* (New York: Zone, 1992), pp. 297–319, and more recently under the title 'The Position of the Problem of Ontogenesis', in *Parrhesia*, 7 (2009), pp. 4–16.

6. Originally published at Presses Universitaires de France in 1964, *L'Individu et sa genèse physico-biologique*, the first part of Simondon's *doctorat d'état*, was reprinted in 1989 with Aubier and in 1995 with Krisis, and can now be found, reunited with *L'Individuation psychique et collective*, in *L'Individuation à la lumière des notions de forme et d'information*. Citations of this text will hereafter be referred to in the body of the essay as INFI, followed by the page number. All translations of this and other French language texts are my own.

7. On the 'immanent double genesis of being and thought', see Jacques Gareli, 'Transduction et information', in Gilles Châtelet (ed.), *Gilbert Simondon – Une Pensée de l'individuation et de la technique* (Paris: Albin Michel, 1994), pp. 55–6; Muriel Combes, *Simondon: Individu et collectivité* (Paris: PUF, 1999), pp. 18–20; Bernard Aspe and Muriel Combes, 'L'acte fou', *Multitudes*, 18 (2004); Jean-Hugues Barthélémy, *Penser L'Individuation – Simondon et la philosophie de la nature* (Paris: L'Harmattan, 2005), pp. 37–8.

8. On Simondon's 'encyclopedism', see Pascal Chabot, 'L'encyclopédie idéale de Simondon', in Jacques Roux (ed.), *Gilbert Simondon: une pensée opérative* (Saint-Etienne: Publications de l'Université de Saint-Etienne, 2002), pp. 149–61.

9. It is in this sense, as Barthélémy notes, that Simondon's 'genetic ontology' is neither a science nor a philosophical Knowledge of the kind claimed by German idealism. In other words, it is not *objectivizing*. It represents a 'knowledge' of individuation, but this knowledge is inseparable from a process of the individuation of knowledge. See Jean-Hugues Barthélémy, *Simondon ou l'encyclopédisme génétique* (Paris: PUF, 2008), p. 37.

10. See also Didier Debaise, 'Les Conditions d'une pensée de la relation selon Simondon', in Pascal Chabot (ed.), *Simondon* (Paris: Vrin, 2002), pp. 53–68; Didier Debaise, 'Qu'est-ce qu'une pensée relationnelle?', *Multitudes*, 18 (2004); Barthélémy, *Penser l'individuation*, p. 100.

11. Indeed, for Simondon, a particular relation is only ever an aspect of the '*internal resonance*' of the system (INFI 28–9): which is to say, of the entire set of relations constituting the system.

12. In this sense, the pre-individual does not, strictly speaking, come 'before' the operation of individuation. Barthélémy discusses this question of temporality in

Simondon ou l'encyclopédisme génétique, pp. 45–9. See also on this, Combes, *Simondon: Individu et collectivité*, p. 37.
13. On this, see Barthélémy, *Penser l'individuation*, p. 103.
14. Deleuze, 'On Gilbert Simondon', p. 87.
15. As Muriel Combes writes,

> 'a physical system is said to be in metastable equilibrium (or false equilibrium) when the slightest modification of the system's parameters (pressure, temperature, etc.) is sufficient to break this equilibrium. It is in this way that, in supercooled water . . . the slightest impurity having a structure which is isomorphic to the structure of ice plays the role of a seed crystal and is capable of causing the water to turn to ice.

See her *Simondon: Individu et collectivité*, p. 11.
16. Deleuze, 'On Gilbert Simondon', p. 87.
17. On singularities, see also Didier Debaise, 'Le Langage de l'individuation', *Multitudes*, 18 (2004).
18. For useful introductions to cybernetics and information theory, see W. Ross Ashby, *An Introduction to Cybernetics* (London: Chapman & Hall, 1957); Francis Heylighen and Cliff Joslyn, 'Cybernetics and second-order cybernetics', in R. A. Meyers (ed.), *Encyclopedia of Physical Science and Technology*, 3rd edn (New York: Academic, 2001); John R. Pierce, *An Introduction to Information Theory – Symbols, Signals and Noise*, 2nd edn (New York: Dover, 1980); and Kenneth M. Sayre, *Cybernetics and the Philosophy of Mind* (London: Routledge, 1976).
19. As Simondon writes,

> 'an information is never relative to a unique and homogeneous reality, but to two orders in a state of *disparation* . . . [I]t is *the sense* [signification] *which will emerge when an operation of individuation discovers the dimension according to which two disparate realities can become a system* . . . [I]nformation is *this through which the incompatibility of the non-resolved system becomes the organizing dimension in its resolution*; information presupposes a system's change of phase, for it presupposes a primary preindividual state which is individuated according to the organization which has been discovered. (INFI 31, emphasis in the original)

20. Gilbert Hottois suggests that Simondon derives the notion of 'transduction' from that of the 'transducer', which is any apparatus which is capable of transforming energy (for example, a microphone). See his *Simondon et la philosophie de la 'culture technique'* (Brussels: De Boeck, 1993), p. 45. See also Barthélémy, *Penser L'Individuation*, pp. 131–2. However, it should be noted that the notion of 'transduction' is also used in genetics and physiology in a sense which is analogical to its technological one.

21. > [T]he structure of a complex organism is not only integration and differentiation; it is also this institution of a transductive mediation of interiorities and exteriorities, going from an absolute interiority to an absolute exteriority through different mediating levels of relative interiority and exteriority. (INFI 226)

22. It is in this way that relational being is said to have unity: not the unity of identity, but rather 'a *transductive unity*' (INFI 31).
23. This point is attested to in Combes, *Simondon: Individu et collectivité*, pp. 24–8 and Hottois, *Simondon et la philosophie de la 'culture technique'*, p. 39. This is also, though with some reservations, the thesis of Isabelle Stengers in her 'Pour

une mise à l'aventure de la transduction', in Pascal Chabot (ed.), *Simondon* (Paris: Vrin, 2002), pp. 137–59. With regard to the 'problematic' nature of the domains of knowledge where the paradigm of crystallization will play the role of a structural germ, Barthélémy has pointed out certain 'relational' tensions that Simondon effectively exploits: the coexistence and reciprocal limitation of the individuality and interaction of particles in the physical world (following De Broglie's concerns over the definition of 'potential energy'); the opposition between mechanism and vitalism in biology; the problem of the relation between perception and action in the living creature; the opposition of 'psychologism' and 'sociologism' in thinking the 'becoming-transindividual' of the living creature; and the opposition of subject and object in epistemology. See, respectively, his *Penser L'Individuation*, pp. 110–11, 151–2, 174, 187, 224, 235 and 239–40. We could also add to this list: the problematic relation between the physical and the living in biochemistry, the problematic postulation of a neoteny between different species, and the problem of the different levels of individuality applicable to the study of collectivities in biology (INFI 152, 171, 157–8). It can also be noted that this understanding of Simondon's method also explains his use of scientific notions outside of their usual contexts, for names such as metastability, order of magnitude, potential energy, singularity, information and so on stand for concepts which must now be understood, not in relation to the scientific domains from which they have been extracted, but from the point of view of an anti-substantialist, relational and *transductive* conception of being.

24. As Combes explains, 'logical subsequence' here refers to the process of going from the simple to the complex, while 'ontological subsequence' refers to the different levels of being which emerge as ongoing and related resolutions of the pre-individual: from the physical to the biological to psychic and social individuals and finally to the technological (even if higher levels are irreducible to lower ones, since each domain has its own particular characteristics). See her *Simondon: Individu et collectivité*, p. 27. It should also be said that, at each 'ontological' stage, the earlier paradigm does not determine a later process as such. Rather, in accordance with our relational definition of information and singularity, the transposition of the paradigm-germ from level to level is simultaneously a 'construction' of this germ.

25. *Penser L'Individuation*, pp. 176–7.

26. Hottois, *Simondon*, p. 44.

27. Deleuze, *Difference and Repetition*, p. 28. Citations of this text will hereafter be referred to in the body of the essay as DR, followed by the page number.

28. In his review of Simondon's *L'Individu et sa genèse physico-biologique*, published two years before *Difference and Repetition*, Deleuze explicitly notes that Simondon's concept of 'orders of magnitude' is very close to that of 'intensive quantity'. See Deleuze, 'On Gilbert Simondon', p. 87.

29. An in-depth study of these mathematical resources in Deleuze's *Difference and Repetition* can be found in Simon Duffy, *The Logic of Expression: Quality, Quantity and Intensity in Spinoza, Hegel and Deleuze* (Aldershot: Ashgate, 2006).

30. On this particular point, see also Deleuze, *The Logic of Sense*, p. 50.

31. As Alberto Gualandi puts it,

> [the] process of individuation actualizes the elements, relations and singular points which constitute the Idea . . . It is intensity which determines the Idea to be actualized, for the distinctive feature of intensity is to resolve its differences in a process of individuation which creates new individuals.

See his *Deleuze* (Paris: PUF, 2003), pp. 67–8.

32. Gualandi also makes this point in his *Deleuze*, p. 66.
33. In Curie's work on symmetry, it is understood that a certain minimal *dissymmetry* is a necessary condition for physical phenomena in general. Simondon also discusses Curie's principle of symmetry (see INFI 88–90).
34. See also DR 118: 'words are genuine intensities within certain aesthetic systems'.
35. In fact, Deleuze argues that all intensities are differentially 'implicated' in one another, to one degree or another depending on the domain in question, and thereby express 'the changing totality of Ideas' (DR 252, 280–1).
36. Strictly speaking, Deleuze uses the terms 'learning' and 'apprenticeship' rather than 'knowing', in order to emphasize that 'coming to know something' should not be thought, as it traditionally has been, as the grasping of some pre-existing identity (by correctly specifying the criteria of its identity or essence). Rather, it should be thought of as a contingent and provisional 'effect' of a differential and open-ended process in which the student or apprentice is implicated (see DR 164–7, 192).
37. It should be noted that difference is here not so much represented in the concept in accordance with the requirements of establishing the criteria for recognizing pre-given identities. Rather, in its two 'halves' (indi-different/ciation – DR 246, 279), difference is what drives the progressive development of differentiated systems of concepts corresponding to individuals constituted by intensive processes. As Deleuze writes,

> [q]ualities, extensities, forms and matters, species and parts are not primary; they are imprisoned in individuals as though in a crystal. Moreover, the entire world may be read, as though in a crystal ball, in the moving depth of individuating differences or differences in intensity. (DR 247)

The allusion to Simondon's paradigm of both individuation and the thought of individuation – crystallization – should not go unnoticed here.
38. Gualandi puts this same point in more ontological terms when he writes that '[i]f the Idea is the capacity [*puissance*] that Being has to give itself to thought, intensity is the capacity that Being has to exist and affect us.' See his *Deleuze*, p. 70.
39. See Gualandi, *Deleuze*, pp. 62–7.
40. See Anne Sauvagnargues, *Deleuze: l'empirisme transcendental* (Paris: PUF, 2009), p. 240.
41. See Alberto Toscano, 'Gilbert Simondon', in Graham Jones and Jon Roffe (eds), *Deleuze's Philosophical Lineage* (Edinburgh: Edinburgh University Press, 2009), pp. 380–98. See also his *The Theatre of Production – Philosophy and Individuation between Kant and Deleuze* (Basingstoke: Palgrave MacMillan, 2006), pp. 136–98.

Science and Ontology: From Merleau-Ponty's 'Reduction' to Simondon's 'Transduction'

Miguel de Beistegui

If philosophy today must, as I believe it does, posit itself as ontology *again*, it cannot do so without engaging in a close confrontation with the natural sciences. Why? First of all, because many of the questions and issues that traditionally fell under the authority of philosophy, and which helped clarify the fundamental meaning of that which is, now fall under that of science. More importantly, though, and as a result of the evolution of science itself, because such questions and issues have been radically transformed in the hands of science, especially in the last hundred years. Does this mean that, henceforth, philosophy must become philosophy of science, and let its own problems and methods be determined by those of science? Not at all. In the light of the event of science, philosophy must avoid a twofold trap: that of philosophizing without taking into account the challenge of science for thought; and that of subordinating philosophical thought to scientific procedures and 'facts'. In other words, it can be a question of neither blissfully ignoring such a challenge, nor turning it into the sole measure of thought and an unquestionable paradigm. The task, rather, consists in setting a new ambition for philosophical thought against the background of the event of contemporary science. It is a question, in short, of allowing thought to advance in and through a genuine *dialogue* with science.

This ambition was already formulated by worthy predecessors, especially in France. This is perhaps no coincidence, as many French philosophers of the last century inherited a double tradition, which they treated with equal respect: the history of metaphysics and of metaphysical problems, on the one hand; and the scientific rationalism and the philosophy of science of the last two centuries on the other. In what follows, I would like to isolate just two such philosophers, in order to show how they have helped forge the terms of an encounter with science against the backdrop of a philosophical commitment to ontology. They are Merleau-Ponty and Simondon. Simondon was Merleau-Ponty's doctoral student. Simondon's monumental doctoral thesis, however, does not reveal any traces of influence on the part of Merleau-Ponty. And Merleau-Ponty's comments on Simondon amount to virtually nothing. Does this mean that the two approaches are incompatible? Such would seem to be the case: where Merleau-Ponty insists that philosophical questioning be rooted in perception, and finds his impetus as well as his method in Husserlian phenomenology, Simondon simply ignores phenomenology. Yet, a closer look at Merleau-Ponty's later thought, which aims to overcome the Cartesian dualism still present in Husserl, reveals a certain proximity to Simondon's problematic of pre-individual being. It is mostly in the context of his long confrontation with the natural sciences, and their *propaedeutic* role for philosophy, that Merleau-Ponty sets the stage for an encounter with the thought of Simondon. It is indeed in the context of these lecture courses that a subtle yet decisive shift takes place, one that takes Merleau-Ponty's thought away from the 'reduction', which designates the very possibility of thought for phenomenology, and into the Simondonian 'transduction'.

The influence of Husserl's phenomenology on Merleau-Ponty's thought could never be sufficiently stressed; decisive from the start, it remained crucial until the very end. The thematic of perception, which unifies that thought, and which is meant to signal the origin of subjectivity as well as that of the world, remains incomprehensible without referring to the manner in which Husserl himself privileged it. By way of caution, let me emphasize from the start that Husserl never equated perception with sensation alone.[1] Perception is an intuitive act: that is, according to Husserl's own definition, a sense-fulfilling act. This, in fact, is what distinguishes it from the merely sense-bestowing – or signifying – act, which refers to an object without presenting it in person or in the flesh (*leibhaftig*). Intuition, on the other hand, does not merely represent the object, but allows it to be there, bodily present, as it were. With the notion of fulfilment, Husserl is able to extend our conception of perception beyond the merely sensible object. As a result, a given category is thought to be actually present in categorial intuition. Similarly, an essence is present 'in its corporeal identity' in eidetic intuition.[2] Perception is an act that is broader than sensation. Merleau-Ponty takes up and explores further this fundamental feature of Husserlian phenomenology. Only on the basis of such a feature can we understand the 'perceptual faith' that is spoken of in *The Visible and the Invisible*.[3] It is synonymous with actual, bodily givenness, and encompasses virtually every experience or act.

This being said, there is no doubt that, within this originary givenness, sense perception – that is, perception of the *sensible* world – is
granted a certain privilege. On this point, too, Merleau-Ponty follows
Husserl very closely. It is indeed Husserl who first granted sense perception a prominent role; in sensation alone is the intention actually,
completely fulfilled, and the object *bodily* given. This, however, and by
virtue of the determination of perception as actual, bodily givenness, of
which sensation is only an exemplary case, does not mean that categories or essences, which in themselves are not sensible, and therefore real,
cannot be said to be perceived in a broader sense; whilst not objects of
sense perception, they are indeed given *in* and *as* themselves. Let me
summarize this point: only in sense perception can something be truly
and completely given; yet there is an intuition of the non-sensible also.
Merleau-Ponty draws the conclusion of this idea by claiming that perception extends and exceeds itself in something other than itself; it is the
'archetype of the originary encounter' that is 'imitated and renewed in
the encounter with the past, the imaginary, the idea'.[4] In what amounts
to a genuine reversal of Platonism, the idea, the imaginary – in short, all
that is not immediately sensible and that, within Platonism, used to fall
within the domain and under the authority of the intelligible – is now
envisaged as essentially derived from a single origin: namely, the sensible. Merleau-Ponty's phenomenology of the sensible world puts him at
odds with the intellectualist or Platonist school, for which the sensible
world is only the perversion and degradation of an intelligible reality
that is in principle accessible to a purely intellectual intuition. Rather
than reiterate the opposition of the sensible and the intelligible, of sense
perception and intellectual intuition, Merleau-Ponty chooses to speak
of the visible and the invisible. Between the two, there is no longer an
opposition or a hierarchy, but a movement of deepening and extension
of a single structure; the invisible is the invisible *of* the visible itself, and
accessible only in and through the visible. In so far as all experiences
are rooted in the sensible, it remains, however, that sense perception
constitutes the exemplary or *archetypal* sense of what is bodily given,
and not one of its modalities only. Perception is essentially sense perception. At the same time, it is irreducible to – and potentially always
more than – sense perception. It is this chiasmic structure, indicative of
a new sense of being beyond the disputes of idealism and empiricism,
which Merleau-Ponty precisely calls the flesh. Hopefully, it has become
clear why the concept of the 'sensible', which we find throughout *The
Visible and the Invisible*, designates at once a dimension of the world
and the world itself. Similarly, it is now clear why Merleau-Ponty

equates the flesh, the perceived (*le perçu*) and the sensible, even though he now prefers to speak of a 'brute' or 'wild' being, rather than of the perceived.[5] This is because 'to see is always to see more than one sees.'[6] It is the sensible itself that transcends itself in its own sense and not, as Husserl believed, the transcendence of sense that is realized in bodily givenness. The transcendence in question is no longer vertical and super-sensible, but horizontal; the sensible overcomes itself in a movement of self-deepening, and its 'sense' is precisely this depth. Sense is the hidden side, the lining of the sensible.

Where Merleau-Ponty departs from Husserl, and progressively intro-duces a new sense of being, is in his conception of bodily givenness (*Leib*), which he understands in terms not of a full and total presence of the object, not, therefore, of a fulfilment of an intention that, up until then, had remained empty or only partially fulfilled, but of an awaken-ing and an initiation to a world, an experience of a 'there is' which, because it is no longer equated with the full presence of the object, does not exclude a dimension of withdrawal and absence. It is the very meaning and function of bodily givenness that has undergone a certain transformation; where the flesh used to provide an access to the satu-rated presence of the phenomenon – envisaged as an object of knowl-edge and the horizon of all acts – it now awakens the sensible body to a world and a sense of being as 'there is'. The move, then, is one that takes us away from the 'ontology of the object', which characterizes modern metaphysics, including aspects of Husserlian phenomenology, and clas-sical physics (in the broad sense of the science of nature of Descartes, Galileo and Newton), and into an ontology of the flesh as the proper and originary mode of givenness of the world, the outline of a 'there is' from within which the very being of the human emerges. Bodily given-ness is no longer a function of an intentional, intuitive act, albeit that of an *incarnate* consciousness. If anything, it is rather the 'subject' who is now intended and constituted within the world, in what amounts to a reciprocal and co-originary opening up. To the reversal of Platonism previously mentioned, and which did not result in a mere empiricism, we must now add the suspension of all idealist theses, including that of Husserl himself (for, whilst not a matter of representation, the transcen-dental consciousness remains *constitutive*). More fundamentally still, we must note the advance that consists in overcoming the dualist ontology of the sensible and the intelligible, as well as that of the subject and the object, through an ontological monism that is rooted in the notion of perception and unveils the world as carnal reality, a reality to which I myself belong, a fabric woven with the same threads as those of my body. Idealism and realism both find their point of departure in a world that is divided from the start, and are left to wonder how to reduce the gap. To overcome this separation, however, all they would need to do would be to see how the flesh, as the originary presence on the basis of which all givenness can be thought, constitutes their common origin. The flesh *exists* only as this self-transgression and self-differentiation. It is entirely contained within this doubling of itself (the visible and the invisible, body and mind, the life-world and that of science), which gives the illusion of two separate worlds, or of a rigid division of the world. When thought according to its essence, however, the world always appears in its originary doubling or difference.

Merleau-Ponty never called this primacy of perception into question. It continues to guide his lecture courses on the concept of nature from the late 1950s.[7] The questioning that unfolds in those courses is itself motivated by the desire to elaborate a philosophy of nature on the basis of the theory of perception. It is now a question of showing that the perceived object that was described in *Phenomenology of Perception* has an ontological meaning, that it corresponds to the fundamental meaning of being and that, to use Barbaras's own formulation, it 'defines the conditions to which everything that has a claim to reality is subjected'.[8] Let me emphasize this point: that which 'is' or is 'real' is everything that can be *perceived*. Perception, which defines the fundamental structure of reality, is the key to the understanding of the sense of the being of beings as a whole. Despite Merleau-Ponty's claim, however, and his ambition to think outside the opposition of empiricism and idealism, I would like to ask to what extent the sense of being I have just identified does not reintroduce a kind of transcendental subjectivism – no longer that of the sense-bestowing consciousness, which constitutes a world of objects in principle reducible to their essence, but of the sense perception and the corporeality through which the world occurs as sensible. Despite the methodological reversal to which Merleau-Ponty subjects his own project, and which consists in taking his point of departure in nature itself, in order to reveal the identity of being and of perceived beings, rather than envisage nature as the completion or the correlate of the acts of an incarnate consciousness, I want to question the value and the chances of success of an ontology that, from the start, will have subjected the sense of being to that of a subjectivity, albeit reformulated in that way. The question of science, and of ontology's relation to the sense of nature it discloses, will turn out to be crucial.

It is in the context of this 'passage' from transcendental phenomenology to ontology, or from the sense of the being of consciousness as the 'origin' of the world to the sense of the being of the world as 'flesh' that Merleau-Ponty engages in a close dialogue with the natural sciences. The word 'dialogue' is, I believe, appropriate, inasmuch as Merleau-Ponty does not seek to ascribe to science a particular place in relation to philosophy, and one that, naturally, philosophy alone would be in a position to determine, but to ask whether certain developments in the natural sciences, far from obscuring the task of ontology, can confirm the hypothesis developed in his later thought. Unlike the Husserl of the *Crisis*, Merleau-Ponty sees in the recent developments of the natural sciences (from relativity to quantum theory and biology) a profound attempt to call into question the very ontology of the object that he himself is trying to overcome. The question, in other words, is one of knowing whether the world of twentieth-century science is still a world of mere *things*, of inert objects, or whether it is in the process of becoming a world of living *phenomena*. Such an evolution on the part of Merleau-Ponty's phenomenology with respect to science is decisive, and deserves close attention. It is an evolution that consists in a quasi-reversal of the initial phenomenological presupposition: far from constituting an obstacle to the formulation of the new ontology – one that is no longer of the object, but of the flesh, no longer a dualism, but a monism – contemporary science and its general 'attitude' would seem to set us underway to the sense of being as sensible being. The phenomenological 'reduction' of the world that is required would thus no longer take us from the natural world to its transcendental origin, but from the transcendental philosophy itself to the very being of nature, which today's science would help to clarify. More than an evolution, this transformation amounts to a revolution, in the double sense of a reversal and an upheaval. Indeed, once science is no longer viewed as merely naive – that is, as presupposing its own object, and the world itself *as* object, without calling into question the manner in which that object is constituted and its relation to the object in question; once it begins to revise and redefine its own fundamental concepts in the light of a different and emerging sense of nature, we can only wonder about the necessity to uphold the phenomenological reduction and the fundamental distinction between the 'life-world' and the 'scientific worldview'.

A number of Merleau-Ponty's claims from the lecture courses on nature and *The Visible and the Invisible* seem to confirm the hypothesis I have just formulated. 'Modern science', he writes, 'often criticises itself and its own ontology.'[9] The opposition between a rational subject and nature as an object spread out before it, which for so long characterized it, 'is valid only in the case of Cartesian science' and 'not in the case of modern science'.[10] Quantum mechanics, for example, 'deprived the old mechanics of its own dogmatism'[11] by signalling the 'emergence of a new scientific ontology' that will make us 'forever unable to re-establish Laplacean ontology, at least not with the same dogmatism'.[12] Does this mean that we should rely on science completely in order to isolate the concept of being of life and of nature in general? Is ontology itself destined to be nothing but the metaphysics of physics, as was the case for Descartes and, possibly, although in a different sense, for Kant? Is Merleau-Ponty slowly converting to something resembling the neo-Kantian position or, more radically still, the very scientific positivism that phenomenology, himself included, began by opposing so strongly? This is the point at which Merleau-Ponty's subtle, if not ambiguous position with respect to science becomes manifest. Whist remaining faithful to phenomenology's thesis, according to which philosophy is the science of pre-science, he claims that the pre-science in question is itself accessible through science alone, and this means through a detailed and demanding confrontation with it. It can no longer be a question of suspending or neutralizing the scientific attitude altogether, and of accessing the life-world that underpins it directly. Rather, it must now be a question of immersing oneself in the natural attitude, and of extracting its hidden truth, which philosophy alone can reveal. The scientist is himself too busy looking for 'ways to grasp and get a grip on the phenomenon' ('*des "prises" par où saisir le phénomène*') to be able really to 'understand' it.[13] Yet it is the phenomenon itself that the scientist has in mind, not its mere image or representation. The thought of the scientist is not motivated by the concern to see – and *a fortiori* to see, as Merleau-Ponty claims, that one always sees more than one sees – but to 'intervene' and to 'find a foothold' ('*trouver des prises*'). In this effort to get a firm grip on things, however, 'the scientist discloses more than he sees in fact.'[14] It is this excess that becomes the object of philosophy. In a way, the philosopher is an opportunist guided by the question regarding the sense of that which is. He sees 'behind the back of the scientist what the scientist himself does not see'.[15] Scientific thought is essentially interventionist and efficacious; it is a thought that measures and predicts. But science does *think*, and its thought is one that increasingly maps on to the phenomenality of phenomena – that is, to the reality of the world as we perceive it: it is a world of flux and becoming, and one that is often opaque. It would seem, therefore, that the distinction between the world of phenomena and the world of scientific objects no longer holds, at least no longer in the same rigid and absolute way. In the context of philosophy as ontology, and of the need to extract the meaning of nature as *sensible* nature, science is a *propaedeutics* for philosophy. What does this mean? That in order to extract the sense of being in question, philosophy cannot proceed directly.[16] Phenomenology called for a 'return to the things themselves' beyond naturalism and the scientific worldview. This is a call to which Merleau-Ponty still wishes to respond. His response, however, brings science back into the task itself. Science has become uncircumventable for philosophy itself: '*One cannot construct a direct ontology.* My "indirect" method (being in the beings) alone corresponds to being – "negative philosophy" like "negative theology".'[17]

Only as the way that takes us through the scientific attitude, and not simply as the suspension of that attitude, can the phenomenological reduction still designate the mode of access or the method that corresponds to the phenomenon in question (the being of beings). The method is now a *via negativa*. At the end of this indirect voyage alone will the matter at hand become positively manifest. All of this is summarized in a working note of *The Visible and the Invisible*:

> The search for the 'wild' view of the world nowise limits itself to a return to precomprehension or to prescience. 'Primitivism' is only the counterpart of scientism, and is still scientism. The phenomenologists (Scheler, Heidegger) are right in pointing out this precomprehension which precedes inductivity, for it is this that calls in question the ontological value of the *Gegenstand*. But a return to pre-science is not the goal. The reconquest of the *Lebenswelt* is the reconquest of a *dimension*, in which the objectifications of science themselves retain a meaning and are to be understood as *true* . . . the pre-scientific is only an invitation to comprehend the meta-scientific and this last is not non-scientific. It is even disclosed *through* the constitutive movements of science, on condition that we reactivate them, that we see what left to themselves they *verdecken*.[18]

What Merleau-Ponty is indicating here is a circular structure between the pre-scientific and the scientific levels, between the *Lebenswelt*, to which phenomenology wants to turn, in so far as it constitutes the originary phenomenon in which all acts, practices, values and institutions are rooted, and science, as one such discourse and practice – indeed, a dominant one. It is precisely in so far as science has become the dominant discourse regarding the sense of nature that phenomenology must itself go through the movements of science, and extract the pre-scientific in it. Science, and the attitude that characterizes it, cannot be set aside or suspended in the task that consists in returning to the things themselves. Those things, and the unifying, fundamental meaning that underlies them, must be wrested from science itself, in which they are implicated – enveloped, as it were. Philosophy does not merely repeat or even clarify the movements and concepts of science. It is not metascientific in that sense. Rather, it seeks to extract from science what science itself does not think: namely, its implicit ontology, itself indicative of the meaning and the place of the human *being*. There is always something that science covers over (*verdeckt*) in disclosing its object. This, Merleau-Ponty insists in the same working note, has nothing to do with the lived experience, and philosophy itself with the desire to reduce scientific facts and data to a phenomenology of the *Erlebnisse*. Philosophy must not believe in consciousness as in a criterion and measure of truth; it too deceives us about ourselves, the world, and the nature of language. The phenomenology of lived experience is itself naive, and not radical enough. The turn to science can itself enable phenomenology to radicalize itself. Science itself can point us in the right direction and indicate the sense from which it emerges – on the condition, of course, that we manage to disclose the soil it covers over and know where and how to *look*. It is this origin and its discovery (*Entdeckung*) that is the object of philosophical questioning. The task of philosophical thought, then, is to *see* where scientific thought measures and predicts, to find again the meaning of the phenomena through the objectifications of science itself.[19] It is now possible to find the being of *phusis* through physics, the being of life through biology and so on, in such a way that 'all the particular analyses concerning Nature, life, the human body, language will make us progressively enter into the *Lebenswelt* and the "wild" being.'[20] Merleau-Ponty seems to be going even further, when he warns philosophy itself against its own impatience to see and understand, and even against the ease with which it can generate concepts and become complacent with the language it forges to interpret scientific data. Philosophy must become aware of the traps of its own, natural language (what Merleau-Ponty calls 'gnosis', especially in relation to Heidegger), and not only of the objectivistic tendencies of science. If Nature is an all-encompassing something (*un Englobant*), he writes, it cannot be thought on the basis of philosophical concepts alone, and least of all 'by way of deductions'.[21] This reservation, formulated with respect to a certain philosophical danger, this re-evaluation of scientific experience in the context of a philosophical problematic, are, to say the least, surprising, and take us further away from Husserl's attitude to science.[22]

Let me now turn, albeit briefly, to the specific way in which key developments in contemporary science can be seen to open the way to an ontology of the sensible, and reveal the sense of being of nature as perception. To a large extent, contemporary science can be seen to have presided over a radical revision of its subjectivistic and objectivistic presuppositions, thus facilitating the task of a philosophical questioning directed towards the being of natural phenomena. It can be argued that the scientific object is precisely no longer an object in the sense that Husserl, and Merleau-Ponty after him, initially criticized as an abstraction. In addition, it can be argued that the scientist himself is no longer this Laplacean demon: that is, this omniscient being who describes the world from the viewpoint that would be that of God Himself. If the scientist is no longer a 'subject' in the classical sense, and nature an 'object' in the sense of what stands there before us, *partes extra partes*, how can we begin to describe the nature of the relation between the scientist and his object? How can we conceptualize our relation to nature as it emerges from the new scientific data?

Let me begin by analysing the manner in which twentieth-century science called into question its own objectivistic presupposition. In the first sketch of the last lecture course devoted to the concept of nature, Merleau-Ponty mentions three ways in which contemporary science overcame the modern, classical conception of nature. Each is to serve as an indirect access to philosophy's own goal: that is, to the possibility of extracting a new ontology from the scientific discourse itself. We should mention, to begin with, the overcoming of the Euclidean (metric) thought of space in Riemannian geometry, and its application in the theory of relativity; Euclidean space is only a particular instance of a larger space, to which we ourselves belong. In fact, Euclidean space, which, as we know, underpins the Cartesian conception of space, and of physics up until Einstein, is only one aspect which non-Euclidean space takes on over relatively short distances. We can even envisage it as *emerging* from a continuity that is itself non-metric. Thus, Riemannian space contains and envelops Euclidean space, which seemed to exclude it at first. By disclosing gravity as the force that gives space its metric properties, the theory of general relativity provided this geometry with a concrete, physical reality. The emergence of gravity as one of the four forces of the universe suggests that at a certain temperature – the temperature approximating that of the universe at the time of its creation – the forces in question lose their individuality and merge into one another, in what amounts to a unique and highly symmetrical force, the geometry of which has led to intense mathematical and physical speculations in the last three decades.

Next, we should mention the overcoming of the classical conception of the atom as an indivisible substance and an irreducible kernel of matter in the purely statistical being of the quantum object. This new kind of object has no status outside this statistical measure. Whilst real, it is not actual in the classical sense. Unlike the classical physical object, it does not occupy a precise position at a precise moment, predictable in advance, but a number of positions, which can be predicted only statistically. Quantum mechanics claims that the universe evolves according to a precise and rigorous mathematical formalism. At the same time, however, it claims that this framework determines only a probable future. It cannot predict whether or when this future will actually take place. By appealing to this intrinsically statistical dimension of the quantum object, Merleau-Ponty is right in emphasizing the fact that it challenges the classical conception of natural beings as substances: that is, as self-present and self-identical things to which corresponds a specific position and speed. The quantum object is indeed ontologically distinct from the pure Cartesian thing. But does it confirm Merleau-Ponty's hypothesis regarding the being of natural beings as *perceived*?

Finally, the most decisive transgression, at least that to which Merleau-Ponty devotes the largest amount of pages, is that of biology, and of ontogenesis and phylogenesis in particular. According to Merleau-Ponty, the impossibility of identifying life with its organized state alone, and the necessity to define a sense of being that no longer coincides with actuality alone, is really what is at stake in the question of ontogenesis. In embryogenesis, the emphasis is indeed on the progressive emergence of structures and functions through a cascade of bifurcations and differentiations. Against the advocates of preformation, for whom the tissues and organs of the fertilized egg are supposed to be present from the start in the egg itself, at an embryonic level, precisely, Merleau-Ponty agrees with the idea, popular amongst most biologists, that the differentiated structures of the complete organism emerge progressively as the embryo develops.[23] If such an idea has become acceptable, it is because it no longer presupposes what for a while seemed to be the only alternative to preformism: namely, epigenesis, or the idea of an amorphous and completely undifferentiated embryo, which was somehow thought to possess the spontaneous ability to generate its own final, fully organized state. We know today that the egg possesses a structure defined by zones of biochemical concentration and by polarities established through the asymmetrical position of the kernel. The embryo goes through various phase transitions that correspond to as many breaks of symmetry. This is the structure that clarifies and resolves itself as it unfolds. We are now confronted with a situation where the egg does indeed possess the biochemical elements and the genetic information it needs to develop into a fully formed organism, without, for that matter, possessing a clear and distinct picture of that organism. Merleau-Ponty is echoing those debates when writing of 'the progressive determination' of life that is 'production starting from a predominant equipotentiality'.[24] He also speaks of 'the profound equivocity of place in the living substance'.[25] This is because the organism, as an individuated being, comes from this space 'where there is not yet "visible" differentiation (anatomy) nor "functioning" for that matter'.[26] If life is indeed to be characterized in terms of its potentiality or capacity, it cannot be a question of understanding the possible as 'simple preformed reservoir' to which a principle of choice would be added. In addition, the potentiality or the possible that characterizes life, and which needs to be asserted in its precedence and difference from the complete, actual organism, 'eliminates actualism'.[27] In other words, 'it is simply not the case that all is actual'; we must indeed recognize a genuine reality to the power of becoming and transformation that constitutes the organism, yet this reality is distinct from mere actuality. The fully differentiated structure, or the complete genesis alone is actual. This is the fundamental meaning of Driesch's following claim, which Merleau-Ponty cites: 'There are more morphogenetic possibilities in each part of the embryo than is actually realised in a morphogenetic case.'[28] This, still according to Driesch, explains how the eyes of crustaceans can be regenerated identical to themselves when the optical ganglion has been left untouched. On the contrary, if the ganglion is taken out, an antenna develops.[29] What does this mean with respect to the category of possibility, which the organism is supposed to illustrate? That it can no longer be taken in its classical sense: that is, as the prefiguration or preformation of actuality. Similarly, actuality can no longer be seen as the realization and the perfection (the *entelecheia*) of the possible. In the move from the possible to the actual, a change occurs. The actual constitutes only one possible realization of this potential. There is, therefore, an excess of the potential over the actual, and a dimension of being of the organism that remains latent in the complete organism. It is no longer possible to consider life, and nature in general, as a mere 'bag of possibilities'. It is not as if the crustacean had a reservoir of eyes. Rather, it is itself a 'virtual' field that can evolve and resolve itself in various ways.[30]

What conclusions can be drawn from this brief survey of twentieth-century physics and biology? One decisive conclusion concerns the change of emphasis from a nature that was essentially fixed and immutable, made of beings grasped in what we could call their final, already made or fully individuated phase, to a nature that is essentially evolving, in the making, and thus irreducible to its actual realization in a fixed time-space. What emerges from Merleau-Ponty's analyses is the impossibility of grasping the essence of the organism on the basis of its organized state alone, the essence of metric or Euclidean space on the basis of its sole extension, the essence of the atom on the basis of a concept of indivisible substance. We could summarize this new problematic with the concept of emergence, or that of genesis. Whether in the case of Euclidean space with respect to Riemannian space, of gravity with respect to the other forces, of the particle with respect to its field or, most of all, of the formed organism with respect to the embryo, the emphasis is now on the operation through which the fully individuated being, which ordinarily we tend to take as our point of departure for the investigation of the sense of being, emerges progressively from a pre-individual, pre-phenomenal horizon. Merleau-Ponty's critique of actualism, inspired by scientific developments, leads to a kind of geneticism, or a philosophical ontogenesis. At the same time, and more discreetly still, this geneticism is coupled with a structuralism. One does not need to choose between genesis and structure. Why? Because the structures in question do not govern processes of identity but of differentiations, do not produce substances but events. If we consider the biological example of ontogenesis, we realize that beneath 'life' as an enveloping phenomenon (*phénomène-enveloppe*) lies a 'cumulative structure'.[31] In addition, Merleau-Ponty claims, 'the being of science and the being-perceived of the embryo amount to less than its Being, which is structure.'[32] Implicitly, and besides the problematic of perception, with which he began, Merleau-Ponty recognized a sense of being as genesis *and* structure, which, it seems, he did not have time to develop. Were we to extend and clarify Merleau-Ponty's own analyses, often only partially developed, especially in the last lecture course, and draw the necessary conclusions, we would need to wonder about the compatibility of the ontology of perception and of the flesh with that of genesis and structure. We need to ask whether, in order to be realized as ontology, philosophy must not go beyond the phenomenological standpoint. This is the point at which Simondon's thought, to which we shall turn very shortly, turns out to be decisive.

As for the subjective pole of contemporary science, we see the extent to which it is modified with the transformation of the objective pole. For this new gaze turned towards the world is a gaze that comes from the world, and a gaze that affects the world; this living being that I am describing is also this being that I am, and it is the gaze of a living being that interrogates it, and interrogates itself in interrogating it. The destabilization of the scientific object as a pure, external thing goes hand in hand with our ability to call ourselves into question as existing outside it, or as linked to it by a difference in kind. The worldview according to which man and nature face one another is no longer tenable. As a living being, the human partakes in what it describes; as a sensible being, its approach to nature is always an intervention carried out from within it, and one that modifies nature, as quantum theory testifies. His curiosity, rationality and scientificity he holds from nature itself. By illuminating it, he illuminates himself; by analysing himself, he discloses it. His power of thought and analysis is that of nature itself, and his reflection on nature is always the self-reflection of nature itself, or what Merleau-Ponty calls the 'hyper-reflection' of nature. It is perhaps this notion of reflection – and not that of reduction – that now delineates most precisely the philosophical attitude according to Merleau-Ponty; it no longer consists of a gaze directed towards the lived experience, of a phenomenology of *Erlebnisse*, but of nature's self-reflection, through which its brute being surfaces.[33] Between the human and nature, there is a common destiny and a mutual encroaching. It is this reciprocity and this co-belonging, this common origin which philosophy needs to clarify. And that, Merleau-Ponty believes, it can do only by revealing the sense of being as *sensible*. Everything, including the world of spirit and of science, of history and of language, follows from the sensible, brute being.

Let me finish by indicating, albeit briefly, how Simondon's ontology enables us to extend this genetic and structural dimension of being, but at the cost of a challenge to the phenomenology of perception.

Simondon's conception of being is contained entirely in his notion of individuation. The thematic of individuation is very old. The classical, mostly Aristotelian concepts, however, which hitherto oriented the question of individuation, turn out to be of very little use when it becomes a question of thinking the process of individuation itself as the defining feature of being. With Simondon, the ontological problematic undergoes a remarkable shift; whilst the tradition began with already individuated beings, and raised the question of their individuation in terms of principles, Simondon emphasizes the *process* of individuation through which they become individuated, and identifies this process with their very being. Instead of taking the individual as his point of departure, and asking how it became what it is, Simondon chooses to interrogate the reality that *results* in the individual as we know it. Where the word 'being' used to stand for a thing or a principle, it now stands for an operation. The shift, then, is from beings as things to being as event. If there is indeed a phenomenon in the narrow sense of the term – that is, in the sense of what is perceived in an immediate intuition, there is also, and more significantly, a broader phenomenon, which contains the pre-phenomenal or pre-individual horizon of every individuated being. This is the phenomenon that philosophy needs to think. Every being contains and expresses a horizon of being that it can call its own and that is not immediately apparent. In order to define this horizon, Simondon discards the classical concepts inherited from the tradition – those concepts that presuppose the ontology of the object Merleau-Ponty wishes to overcome: substance (which indicates the self-identity and self-presence of being, and a non-generated reality that is closed to everything that is not itself), form and matter, as well as the principles normally associated with such concepts (of identity, the excluded middle and sufficient reason):

> Unity, characteristic of the individuated being, and identity, authorising the use of the principle of the excluded middle, do not apply to the pre-individual being. This explains why it is impossible to reconstitute the world, retrospectively as it were, with monads, even by adding new principles, such as that of sufficient reason, so as to organise them in a universe.[34]

Only when considering the *individual* as the ultimate reality does it become necessary to posit and call upon principles, and to think the coherence of the world as an aggregate of units. Both the monism of substance and the dualism of form and matter (which Simondon calls 'hylomorphism') presuppose the existence of a *principle* of individuation that is prior to the individuation itself; the individual, as the reality to be explained, is the point of departure, and the question regarding its coming into being is raised only subsequently. It is the very notion of principle that is problematic, in so far as it locates the conditions of existence of the individual outside the individual itself, thus denying itself a genuine access to the *genesis* of the individual.

The question of individuation will no longer be raised in terms of principle, then, but in terms of genesis. Principles are instruments of logic. Genesis, on the other hand, is an ontological category. It aims to grasp the individual as it emerges, and to follow it in its own becoming. It refuses to posit or postulate a power of being that is independent of the individual itself, and of which the latter would be the emanation. On the contrary, it will allow the individual to emerge from out of the pre-individual horizon of being that characterizes it. In place of the old concepts inherited from the tradition, Simondon creates a new conceptuality aimed at bringing to life the reality that unfolds 'before' that described in those concepts. The individual is now envisaged on the basis of its own operation of individuation, and the reality that is now to be thought, the 'ultimate' phenomenon, is the assemblage individuation-individual. The individual – the phenomenon in the narrow sense of the term – is not the whole of being, but only one of its phases, and actually the final one only. Far from constituting the origin and the completion of philosophical thought, then, the perception of the phenomenon, as the fully individuated thing we are for the most part familiar with, only provides a point of entry into the process that unfolds prior to it, and of which it is itself the completion. It is the operation of individuation that is now primordial. The individuated entity is only secondary and derivative with respect to it. Simondon's approach is somewhat reminiscent of that of Merleau-Ponty. We saw how Merleau-Ponty wanted to wrest ontology from the metaphysics of substance, actuality and identity. He too emphasized the genetic dimension of natural beings. Yet, unlike Simondon, he could not conceive of an ontology that would not, somehow, remain attached to a pole of subjectivity, albeit redefined in terms of perception.[35] As a result, the question of genesis, as indicative of the horizon of being of *all* natural beings, remained in an awkward position with respect to the dualism that Merleau-Ponty set out to overcome. Everything happened as if, as a result of his confrontation with the new science, in the margins of the thematic of perception as it were, and almost despite himself, Merleau-Ponty had discovered another ontology, one that would no longer unfold *between* a subject and an object (this is the in-between of the Flesh), but *within* every individual (including within ourselves), between the individuated and the pre-individual being. It is this other sense of being that Simondon extends and interrogates further.

Upon leaving the familiar shores of individuality, and of identity, for those – as yet uncertain but more promising – of the pre-individual and the differences that constitute it, a new conceptuality becomes necessary. Like the Merleau-Ponty of the lecture courses on nature, Simondon finds the necessary resources to overcome the classical ontology of the object in a number of scientific developments. His concepts are often derived from those of science. Thus, he prefers to speak of 'systems' rather than 'substances'. This allows him to privilege the *relationality* of being, as opposed to its identity, and its *potentiality*, as opposed to its actuality. In doing so, he too criticizes 'actualism' in philosophy. He envisages the individual on the basis of a horizon of problematicity, and as a solution to a pre-individual problem: it is a 'mode of resolving an initial incompatibility that is rich in potentials [*riche en potentiels*]' and the last phase of a 'tense, oversaturated phenomenon, above the level of unity'.[36] The pre-individual horizon or stratum is thus defined in terms of an incompatibility, an imbalance between potentials of energy, from which the constitution of an individual emerges progressively. The individuated individual emerges as the solution to a problem that is itself of a different nature. Let me emphasize that the individual always retains its pre-individual reality, even when fully individuated, and that its individuation does not exhaust all of its potentials at once. It is, to use Merleau-Ponty's own conceptuality, a *phénomène-enveloppe*. An organism, for example, and as Merleau-Ponty himself made abundantly clear, is always 'more' than its organized and fully differentiated reality. This excess signals a *virtual* reality that can be observed at the embryonic stage.

At the most basic level, however, the system that best illustrates the process of individuation – and which Simondon eventually shows to be operative in the psychic and collective individuation of the human – is the crystal.[37] Starting with a unique and very small germ immersed in water, a crystal grows and extends progressively; once constituted, every molecular layer becomes a *structuring* base for the constitution of the following layer. The result, Simondon claims, is an 'amplifying reticular structure'.[38] A paradigmatic value can be derived from the study of the genesis of crystals, inasmuch as it allows one to grasp at a macroscopic (or molar) scale a phenomenon that relies on system states that belong to the microphysical (or molecular) domain. Such a study makes it possible to grasp the activity that takes place *at the limit* of the self-forming crystal. It becomes possible, then, to witness the emergence of a solution within a system that is neither actually stable, nor simply unstable, but, to use Simondon's vocabulary, 'metastable'. By that, we need to understand a system that is rife in potentials. The individual – the crystal – emerges as the solution to a pre-individual problem constituted by internal tensions, and which it continues to express once individuated. It is not enough, therefore, to claim that Simondon replaces the notion of substance with that of system. The system in question remains to be thought as *metastable*. This metastability alone accounts for the individuation of the phenomenon. The stable state designates the level at which transformations of the system are no longer possible. This happens when the potential of the system has been exhausted, when all its potentialities have been actualized. It is the state that corresponds to the lowest possible level of potential energy, beyond which the system can no longer transform itself. Remarkably, the Ancients recognized it as Being itself. They could not conceive of a sense of being other than individuated beingness. Outside it, they could conceive only of its negation – namely, becoming – which they associated with instability and chaos. But the metastable system is neither order nor chaos, neither rest nor motion, neither pure being nor random becoming. A metastable system is a system that, whilst not contradicting the second law of thermodynamics, which stipulates that, in the long term, all differences of energy will be cancelled, harbours within itself a sufficient amount of energy – of differences of potential, in other words – to create order. Most of the existing systems are of that kind. Even though the 'law' is that dictated by thermodynamics, and even though, in the long term, entropy can only increase, the 'rule' is that of negentropy, and of information. There is no form that presides over the organization of matter; there is simply a series of processes of in-formation through which matter organizes itself. Against the background of inert and self-identical being, a flourishing of differences and a remarkable power of becoming unfold. A general ontology can emerge from this scientific context. Like Merleau-Ponty, Simondon sees the study of natural phenomena as a stage towards ontology. To be more precise, I would say that it is a stage of ontology itself, inasmuch as the physical and biological individuation eventually leads to *l'individuation psychique et collective*, each level revealing the same type of operation, the same meaning of being.

Yet, let me repeat, this ontology is not one of *perception*. The sense of being that is disclosed is not that of the *perçu*. This is because the being that I myself am does not escape this process of individuation. As a result, it is only on the basis of the pre-individual horizon that is my own that my own being can be grasped. Now this horizon presupposes the physical and biological individuation from which the psychic and collective individuation emerges, as a new domain of reality, and a solution to a problem that is in itself not human. It cannot be a question, therefore, of referring the being of the natural world to its perception, since perception itself follows from it, and constitutes one of its phases. This, however, does not mean that we need to fall back into the old dualism; to define the world as sensible world, made of the same fabric as myself, is not the only way to overcome the abyss that separated me from the natural world. For as soon as being is envisaged in its pre-individual and constitutive (or genetic) dimension, a unique process unravels, from which all individuals follow, including this individual that I am; if I am, to use Merleau-Ponty's own terminology, *of* the world and *of* being, it is not, first and foremost, because I perceive, but because of the pre-individual and impersonal singularities that I share with the natural world as a whole. In a way, the thematic of perception is already too advanced in the operation of individuation. It grasps subjectivity at a stage that presupposes too much already, and which the thematic of individuation is precisely there to make explicit.

A method follows from the task that Simondon sets for thought. This method differs from the phenomenological reduction, and even from the 'reflection' Merleau-Ponty develops in his later thought. The reason why the reduction is no longer required as a method is because, in a sense, it has already taken place at the level of the phenomenon itself. What phenomenology calls a phenomenon – that is, the reality that manifests itself to a consciousness or a lived body in an immediate intuition – is actually the completion of an internal process of formation, the progressive emergence of an actual being from within a field of problematicity. The phenomenon in the phenomenological sense is only an *epiphenomenon*, the ontological reduction of a pre-individual and pre-phenomenal field of differences and potentials. The problem with phenomenology is that it has too much faith in appearances, and subordinates the task of thinking to clarifying the meaning of our primitive, perceptual faith in the validity of such appearances. It rejects traditional scepticism, which is obsessed with the question regarding the existence of the world, in order to raise the question of the meaning of that existence. Unlike Husserl, who located such a meaning in the essence of the phenomenon, accessible only to the transcendental consciousness, Merleau-Ponty locates it in the sensible itself, accessible to the lived body. His 'faith' in intuition and perception as the origin of our being in the world forbids it to call into question the phenomenality of the world as a principle of knowledge. Now if the truly modern dimension of scepticism – which leads to the certainty of the world as a world reduced to its extension and its mathematical reality, and to that of the I as a thinking thing – is one that Simondon rejects with phenomenology, he is, in turn, quite sceptical of phenomenology's commitment to the world as a world of appearances, and its belief in the *perceived* world as the only valid world. Simondon's own scepticism, in turn, aims to guide us further into the being of the phenomenon, and further away from any essentialism. The being of the phenomenon that is here in question does not refer back to a horizon of transcendence, but of immanence, in so far as it designates the internal genetic dimension of the phenomenon itself.

The unity of being, Simondon tells us, is 'transductive'. By that, he means that a being is essentially characterized by its ability to dislocate or 'dephase' itself (*se déphaser*) with respect to itself and from either side of its centre. Transduction designates the structure of dislocation and '*déphasage*' of being with respect to itself, through which a being is individualized. If every process of individuation amounts to an operation of transduction, it is because it consists of a series of *déphasages*, each triggering a new phase of being, or a new state of the system. Thought is itself an operation of this kind; it is the self-reflection of transduction, the doubling of transduction back on itself – much in the way that Merleau-Ponty's thought of the flesh signalled the hyper-reflection of nature itself. Transduction is not only an ontological category, then. It also designates the method of thought itself. As a method, the transduction does not remain outside thought. It is not a preliminary stage that would set thought under way. Rather, it is philosophy itself, and itself an enactment of being. It is at once an instance of being and its reflection, a material process and a spiritual event. This identity of subject and object, of thought and being will come as a surprise only to those who, too used to linking thought to already individuated entities – the thinking thing and the extended thing, the mind-thing and the body-thing – and abstract principles, such as form and matter, fail to dive into the depths of the pre-individual, for which such a dualism no longer makes any sense.

Philosophy need not shy away from the challenge of science. Yet the challenge in question is a challenge *for* philosophy. It is a challenge that, if taken up, makes philosophy richer. If philosophy becomes richer in the process, it is by remaining philosophy. It remains philosophy to the extent that it develops an eye for what science itself cannot see, and yet discloses. It is concerned to disclose the being of the phenomena science analyses. The question regarding the being of phenomena is the question of philosophy. It cannot be developed, however, independently of science. Philosophy is neither within nor outside science. It traverses it. The questions it puts to science are not the questions of science. Yet the answers to such questions can be found only in and through a certain mode of engagement with science. With Merleau-Ponty and Simondon we witnessed two fine examples of the spirit and the manner in which such a philosophically productive encounter can take place. It is an encounter that needs to be taken up again, and further. The task of thinking demands a dialogue with science.

NOTES

This chapter was originally published in *Angelaki*, 10.2 (2005), and is republished by kind permission.

1. See R. Barbaras, 'Le Dédoublement de l'originaire', in *Le Tournant de l'expérience* (Paris: Vrin, 1998), pp. 81–94.
2. E. Husserl, *Gesammelte Werke (Husserliana)* (The Hague: Martinus Nijhoff,

1984), vol. XIX/2, *Logische Untersuchungen*, VI, §45, A 614/B142; *Gesammelte Werke (Husserliana)* (The Hague: Martinus Nijhoff, 1976), vol. III/1, *Ideen zu einer reinen Phänomenologie und Phänomenologischen Philosophie, I, Allgemeine Einführung in die reine Phänomenologie*, §24, 43–4.

3. *Le Visible et l'invisible* (Paris: Gallimard, 1964), p. 209; trans. Alphonso Lingis, *The Visible and the Invisible* (Evanston: Northwestern University Press, 1968), p. 158. Henceforth VI, followed by French and English pagination.

4. VI 210/158.

5. VI 300/247.

6. VI 300/247.

7. M. Merleau-Ponty, *La Nature. Notes. Cours du Collège de France* (Paris: Seuil, 1995); trans. Robert Vallier, *Nature. Course Notes from the Collège de France* (Evanston: Northwestern University Press, 2003). Henceforth *Nature*, followed by French and English pagination.

8. R. Barbaras, 'Merleau-Ponty et la nature', *Chiasmi International*, 2 (2000), p. 59.

9. *Nature*, 120/85.

10. *Nature*, 120/85.

11. *Nature*, 125/89.

12. *Nature*, 125/90.

13. *Nature*, 120/86. Quite obviously, Merleau-Ponty is making a crucial distinction here between the 'concepts' of science, which make sense of phenomena by taking hold of them, by finding a foothold in them, grasping them in the sense of a *Begriff*, and the concepts of philosophy, which do not seek to intervene amongst phenomena, but 'understand' them in a way that remains to be clarified.

14. *Nature*, 121/87.

15. *Nature*, 121/87.

16. Let me nuance this statement: through a close dialogue with the natural sciences, philosophy can access the sense of being as flesh indirectly. That being said, a more direct experience of the world as flesh is given in the relation to the work of art. This distinction, I believe, allows one to understand the nature of Merleau-Ponty's critique of science in the opening pages of *Eye and Mind* – a critique that may otherwise be seen as contradicting his appreciation of science in the lecture courses, delivered at about the same time at which *Eye and Mind* was written.

17. VI 233/179. Translation modified.

18. VI 235–6/182. Translation modified.

19. See VI 220–1/166–7.

20. VI 221/167.

21. *Nature*, 122/87.

22. And further away still from 'the false etymologies of Heidegger, his gnosis'. We must resist 'the illusion of an unconditional treasure of absolute wisdom contained in language' (*Nature*, 122/87).

23. *Nature*, 305–7/240–2.

24. *Nature*, 305/241.

25. *Nature*, 306/241.

26. *Nature*, 306/241. Translation modified.

27. Quantum mechanics too eliminates actualism by granting the subatomic particle a statistical reality outside actuality.

28. *Nature*, 295/232. The French translation of the citation in question can be found in Hans A. Driesch, *Philosophie de l'organisme*, trans. M. Kollmann (Paris: Rivière, 1921), p. 65.

29. *Nature*, 297/233.
30. *Nature*, 307/242.
31. *Nature*, 304/239.
32. *Nature*, 304/239.
33. See VI, note from February 1959, 235/181–2.
34. G. Simondon, *L'Individu et sa genèse physico-biologique* (Grenoble: Jérôme Millon, 1995), p. 23.
35. In two short unpublished notes (317 and 319), Merleau-Ponty comments on the marginalization of the thematic of perception in Simondon's work. As expected, his appreciation of it is ambiguous. On the one hand, he goes as far to recognize that it cannot be a question of formulating 'all problems in terms of perception' and that such a tendency characterizes 'the phenomenological attitude as Fink criticises it'. Life, he goes on to say, exceeds the framework of perception, and 'we don't perceive all the time.' At the same time, he insists on the fact that it cannot either be a question of simply discarding perception as the origin of philosophical questioning: 'we no longer know what we are talking about if we *take root* in the metaperceptive [*si l'on* s'installe *dans le métaperceptif*].'
36. G. Simondon, *L'Individu*, p. 23.
37. See G. Simondon, *L'Individuation psychique et collective : à la lumière des notions de forme, information, potentiel et métastabilité* (Paris: Aubier, 1989).
38. Simondon, *L'Individu*, p. 31.

Chapter 11

The Question of the Individual in Georges Canguilhem and Gilbert Simondon

Dominique Lecourt, translated by Arne De Boever

Is the individual a reality? An illusion? An ideal? There is no *single* science, not even biology, that can answer this question. And if *all* sciences can and must contribute to the answer, it is doubtful that the problem is properly scientific, in the sense in which this word is commonly used.[1]

These are the questions and considerations that Georges Canguilhem associates in 1945 with the problem of biological individuality – posed, according to him, by the concept of the cell. From his medical thesis on *Quelques problèmes concernant le normal et le pathologique* (1943) [Some Problems Concerning the Normal and the Pathological] until his last lectures at the Collège Philosophique in 1947, one can see an ambitious philosophical programme establish itself whose spirit can be summed up in a striking formula: 'The problem of individuality is itself indivisible.'

The essential part of Canguilhem's *œuvre* is not so much the successful execution of this initial programme. It is, rather, this programme's dismantling, and then, as if by surprise, its reconstitution through the transfer of concepts. It is from this singular trajectory that it drew – and still maintains – its exceptional force of intellectual solicitation. This essay will discuss Canguilhem's work, focusing on its relation to the work of one of Canguilhem's students, Gilbert Simondon.

In the life sciences where he chose to establish himself, Canguilhem was in the same situation as Gaston Bachelard in physics in the 1920s: because of an unexpected leap of scientific progress, he was forced to 'reeducate himself several times'. As is well known, the biological sciences went through their major revolution at the moment when he published his first texts. In 1944, O. T. Avery and his collaborators showed that the transforming substance of the pneumococcus is constituted of

DNA. It was around this time that molecular biology took off. This development put in perspective the entire history of the biology that preceded it; it redrew the past. This immediately forced Canguilhem to suspend the philosophical elaboration of the notion of the individual that he had undertaken. Under the influence of this shock, he set out on a terrain of new research on the individuality of the human being. That his thought is thus carried quite far from his initial 'biologism' cannot leave one indifferent, especially in a time when a certain militant materialism dominates the intellectual scene, and medical ideology finds itself called on – at the expense of the doctors, who feel very conflicted about this – to furnish the certain (biologistic) bases of an 'ethics' whose traditional, philosophical ties to law and juridical ideology are clearly in the process of becoming undone.

But let us return for a moment to 1945 and to the programmatic formula that Canguilhem announced at that time. It consists of two aspects. One should recall, on this occasion, that the notion of the 'individual' refers to an 'indivisible', but that, when one is talking about a living individual, it is not a negative notion, contrary to what the etymology and the historical use of this notion suggest. (Cicero introduces the word '*individuum*' in Latin to refer to Democritus's atom.) Far from referring to a minimal, evanescent being, a minimum of being, the notion is entirely positive here. This positivity carries the entire charge of Canguilhem's 'vitalism'. With reference to Auguste Prenant, he writes that 'life is not possible without the individuation of that which lives'. To this he adds that the living, at whatever level it is conceived, can be considered as a 'centre' (CV 96) that structures the milieu with which it enters into a debate. Life manifests itself in the activity of this centre as the 'dynamic principle of surpassing oneself'.

In his extension of these theses, all of which receive lengthy argumentations, Canguilhem inscribes the idea of a general theory of 'degrees of individuality' that would lead from the cell to the person, and from the person to society. He evokes the work of Espinas on animal societies, and of Maeterlinck, Wheeler and Bergson. But his primary source of inspiration, which is cited and praised multiple times, is Kurt Goldstein. *La Structure de l'organisme*[2] – a work that was published in Amsterdam in 1934, at the beginning of the exile of this famous neuropsychiatrist from Frankfurt – is considered to be the first and exemplary sample of what a global philosophy of a biologically founded individuality could look like. The profound influence of this work on postwar French philosophy would merit a separate study in itself. In 1945, three years after his book *The Structure of Behavior*,[3] Maurice Merleau-Ponty publishes

The Phenomenology of Perception.[4] Both are books that interpret and popularize Goldstein's thought.

What interests us here is that Canguilhem takes from his reading of Goldstein the idea that only the totality of the organism, as an integrating and individuating form, gives meaning to the elements that compose it. Canguilhem brings this thesis to bear on the ensemble of the living. Thinking with but also after Goldstein, he is moving towards 'Gestalt-theory' (CV 143). And it is in this way that he can give the first formula of the particular version of 'vitalism' that he believes he must defend:

> Biology must first take the living to be a meaningful being; it shouldn't take individuality to be an object, but a character in a meaningful context. To live means to radiate out from a centre of reference that cannot itself be referred without losing its original meaning. (CV 143)

This vitalism encompasses a theory of knowledge, which generalizes Goldstein's thesis that 'biological knowledge is a creative activity, an intervention that is essentially similar to the way in which the organism enters into a composition with the ambient world so as to be able to realize itself.' Against Bergson, Canguilhem holds that science only has meaning when it is an 'adventurous enterprise of life'. To attain its proper aims of conservation and expansion, it creates its own meaningful 'forms' – which is to say, concepts. A theory of technics as the extension of the organism complements this position; backed up by Leroi-Gourhan's research, such a theory includes the discipline of medicine, which is presented by Canguilhem as life's attempt to establish its normal appearance by means of instruments.

But the notion of the individual that is thus constructed includes a second aspect that has a very marked, tense relation with the first. It is worth noting that this aspect was borrowed from Goldstein as well. The individuality of the living, Canguilhem writes, 'does not stop at the ectodermic borders, no more than it begins with the cell' (CV 144). It is not the ultimate (indivisible) term that would make any analysis impossible; it is not a 'being' or a 'thing' in the way in which things were conceived in the eighteenth century. It always appears as a simple 'term in a relation', with the other term being constituted by the 'milieu'. At each level of the living, one would discover such a relation that is constitutive of its proper terms. This is why the 'internal milieu of the organism' cannot be identified to the 'exterior' physical milieu, as Claude Bernard first proposed. This also clarifies why the human being, which is situated the highest, does 'not [know], as individual, a pure physical milieu', or even a milieu that is biologically pure. As a historical, geographically situated being, its milieu appears to be a milieu that is first and foremost cultural. Canguilhem relies on the work of Vidal de la Blache and the French school of human geography to give some features of this particular milieu.

In a way, these two types of analysis could appear to be entirely in line with each other. Canguilhem formulated the wish that what he called a 'general theory of the milieu from an authentically biological point of view', encompassing 'the technician and the man of knowledge, in the way that von Uexkull had tried to do for the animal and Goldstein for the sick person', would come to correspond to the generalized philosophical notion of individuality.

But how to reconcile the primacy of the relation between these terms with the idea that one of these two terms – namely, the living individual – constitutes, in each order of magnitude, a centre of absolute reference? It seems that, in reality, the good 'form' of the living being governs only too much over the ensemble of 'the living' in order to be able to give it order and meaning. And thus Canguilhem's text is saturated with anthropomorphism and anthropocentrism:

> If the originality of the biological must be claimed, it should be claimed as the originality of a governance over the entirety of experience and not over isolated parts of experience. In the end, and paradoxically, classical vitalism would commit a sin only if it were too modest, through its reluctance to universalize its conception of experience.

How can one speak of the 'experience' of a cell? Would the 'polarization' of vital activity be its 'elementary form'? This is what Canguilhem insistently suggests. It happens, for example, that he writes that, rising up from an undifferentiated milieu, life 'makes the difference'. Could this originary polarizing difference be held for the prefiguration of the 'analysis' of which, according to the same text, knowledge consists? ('To know is to analyse': that is the aphorism with which *La Connaissance de la vie* begins.)

To understand what is at stake in the project of making the two theses that are defended here cooperate, one must observe their 'play'. Canguilhem is clearly attached to this 'play' because it appears to him naturally to overcome the gap that still exists between the two great theories that had dominated the sciences of the living for almost a century: cellular theory and the theory of natural selection, both formulated independently from each other in 1859. What does Canguilhem retain of Darwinian theory? The reversal of the traditional relation of the individual to the type, the recentring of the problematic of evolution on the notion of the individual. This explains why he blames Claude Bernard's disinterest in Darwinian theory on his incapacity to 'conceive the relation of the individual to the type in any other way than as that of an alteration starting from ideal perfection that is thought of as completed'. Whatever the value of this judgment may be, Canguilhem celebrates Darwin over and against Bernard for having conceived of individuality as a try-out, an attempt in relation to which the – biotic – milieu plays the role of the judge. 'Living forms', he explains in his typical style, appear as 'individual organizations whose validity is referred to their possible success of life.' The generality of the thesis is emphasized in the following passage:

> All successes are threatened because individuals die, and even species do. All successes are thus belated failures, and failures are aborted successes. It's the future of forms that will determine their value.

Resisting the vulgar 'evolutionism' of Spencerian or Lamarckian descent, one can ask whether Canguilhem does not place too much emphasis on the interest of Darwinian theory for the debate of the individual and the milieu, at the cost of its interest in the creation of forms. This would also explain his slightly distorted and biased take on embryology: morphogenesis must materialize the junction that he establishes philosophically, and it is teratology that will interest him first and foremost. Teratology's way of providing counter-evidence allows him to understand 'monsters' as the failures of a vital dynamic that is regulated by a process of progressive individuations.

The second aim of the speculative 'game' in relation to the notion of the individual is to root the essential theses on medicine that are defended in *On the Normal and the Pathological*[5] in a general conception of biology. These theses are the following: normality is always second to the divergent; any objectivist conception of the norm as an objectively held fact that is statistically identified with an average should be challenged; therapy could not have been conceived as the simple application of a previously given physiological knowledge; medicine cannot present itself as a science but merely as 'an art at the crossroads of several sciences'. This art always presupposes as its principle the claim of the individual who declares her- or himself ill through a comparative 'judgment' that bears on her or his proper history. But, thus rooted in biology, these theses are weighed down by Goldsteinian ontology.

The best example of this is without a doubt the definition of health at which Canguilhem arrives. If illness is 'a negative behaviour for a concrete living individual in a relation of polarized activity with her or his milieu' (NP 156), health is indicated by a 'margin of tolerance in relation to the unreliabilities of the milieu' (NP 130), of which 'the individual is the sole judge.' By the 'living milieu', Canguilhem refers to the work of the living itself which, as he writes, 'withholds itself selectively from or offers itself selectively to certain influences' – in other words, the concrete human individual as a totality defines by her- or himself the always singular meaning that one must give to the word 'health'. This is why, he concludes, there is no 'objective pathology'; the scientific discourse of the pathologist merely translates in abstract terms what was in the consciousness of the individual who feels her- or himself to be 'ill' through the shrinking of the 'margins' of her or his relation to the milieu. Put differently, health is indicated by the maintenance or the establishment of a 'form' that is the single title-holder of an authentically vital 'meaning'. And the existence of medicine merely translates the presence in the 'human individual, as in any other instance of the living [*vivant*], of a polarized reactivity to the variations of the milieu' (NP 80). A medical ethics of the humanist type thus appears at the horizon of Canguilhem's thought; it is the patient who judges according to her or his feeling, and not the doctor on the basis of her or his science. One understands why this thesis resonated with the doctors, at a time when 'scientific medicine' subordinated to the laboratory began to put in place a system that carried the very real threat of an insidious iatrocracy. Indeed, one wishes that this thesis would continue to resonate with the most advanced doctors today.

But it is at this point that the arrival and development of molecular biology in the 1950s appears to have shaken this impressive construction. The 'lottery of heredity' brought in the triumph of the discrete over the continuous, of the uncertain multiple over the substantial unity of meaning. Every biochemist knew from then on that the problem of individuality could very well be divided. As a result, the notion of the individual would no longer play the central and totalizing role in Canguilhem's texts that it had in the early works.

The last published text (*Idéologie et rationalité dans les sciences de la vie*, [Ideology and rationality in the life sciences], 1977) ends by taking stock of this situation, with this simple claim of coexistence: 'There is room, next to the biochemists, for a Buytendijk and a Goldstein.' More importantly for our purposes, in the second edition of *La Connaissance de la vie* (1965) – which is the text that I cited at the beginning – Canguilhem adds a note in which he tips his hat to the 'insights' that Gilbert Simondon's thesis on 'the individual and its psycho-biological genesis' had brought the year before. Simondon's argument consists in emptying the individual of its Aristotelian, ontological force [*charge*]. The individual, for Simondon, is never more than the result of a process of individuation whose principle cannot be found in the form that it takes. This process is continuously shaped by the 'pre-individual', from which the individual detaches itself only partially and intermittently, and the transindividual, in which the individual needs to insert its being.

It is worth noting that in Canguilhem's own texts, the notion of the individual is from now on reserved for the human being as such; and it is in medical philosophy that it continues to play a major part – but a part that has been rewritten, in a new tone that is openly Nietzschean. The human individual is desubstantialized; its normativity affirms itself as a capacity, without common measure, to create new forms that institute themselves in a relation of forces that traverse the individual. Along the same lines, health is redefined in the most daring sense of the 'great health': no longer as a simple 'margin', but as a risk that the individual affirms and assumes in order to break its limits and open up new horizons. The specifically human 'milieu' is thus rethought, and the specter of Vidal de la Blache vanishes.

What appears instead is the face of Michel Foucault, who, from *Birth of the Clinic* (1963)[6] until his last works, will place himself on the path thus opened up by Canguilhem, in order to think the intricate history of knowledge and power. In stark opposition to all morality of equilibrium and conservation, an ethics of risk begins to outline itself.

Goldstein wrote in 1934: 'The meaning of an organism is its being.' Ten years later, Canguilhem extends the formula and turns it around: 'The being of the living is its meaning.' The project to inscribe meaning into the intimacy of the living as its being and as the measure of its unity – even if this project can no longer, at the time of molecular biology, be taken up by the notion of individuality – therefore remains at the heart of Canguilhem's philosophy. One can see it re-emerge in a new form, in the texts that were written and published between 1963 and 1966 under the title *Nouvelles réflexions concernant le normal et le pathologique* [New Reflections on the Normal and the Pathological]. It is brilliantly reaffirmed in the study entitled 'La Nouvelle Connaissance de la vie' [The New Knowledge of Life] in 1966 and published in 1968 in the *Etudes d'histoire et de philosophie des sciences* [Studies of the History and Philosophy of the Sciences].

There can be no doubt that we are dealing with the same project. Canguilhem writes: 'But we must not forget that the theory of information does not operate through division!' (NP 209). In his own way, through a simple transfer of concepts, Canguilhem welcomes the recent developments of genetic code theory; to him, they seem to realize, through ways that had appeared impossible to him, his own programme from 1943! This explains his strange tone of broken triumph when he is showing the 'concept' inscribed in 'life' in the form of the code. With its discrete structure, information substitutes for the signifying totality of the form, but the signifying aim can once again be mirrored into the origin as signification!

Canguilhem thus ends up celebrating the triumph of Aristotle. Exactly where 'vitalism' should have forced him to ring the alarm bell, the ontology with which he had charged it carried him into the jubilatory forgetfulness of the critique of Aristotelianism in biology that he himself began. There is no doubt that he gave too much credit to a certain formalism of the code; molecular biology, on the other hand, did not get stuck in the milieu of the 1960s. François Gros has convincingly shown how even the most illustrious biologists had to detach themselves from these pseudo-linguistic abstractions to 'rise' towards superior organisms and find a track of research that would be suited to the 'organic' realities of the living.

As a result of this renewal, developmental neurobiology has shown that the human individual cannot be taken as an 'individual' in the same way that a bee or even a primate can. Alain Prochiantz has emphasized this: epigenesis weighs in so heavily here on the realization of the genetic programme that – we should not hesitate to say – even the theory of information itself appears to be divisible! In reality, and in the most general way, one can only speak of a 'language of cells' metaphorically; we are dealing here with a 'language' neither in the sense of that which allows us to speak, nor in the sense of 'information', nor in the physico-mathematical sense in which 'language' is turned into 'theory'.

The affirmation of, and the defiant insistence on, 'vitalism' as an intellectual demand to recognize the originality of the living continues to resonate today, when the conjunction of a certain biochemical materialism and a certain mathematical formalism aims to negate it, so as to be able to neuronalize thought better. But the misadventures of Canguilhem's vitalism need to be taken seriously; the specificity of vitalism is lost as soon as it is subordinated to a philosophy of Being, even if Being were reduced to the weak pulse of an originary difference. Perhaps it would be better to abandon the very word 'vitalism', which contains too many ambiguities?

Saved in this way from all substantialist ontology, vitalism could give itself the task of contributing to the elaboration of a new – non-Aristotelian – notion of form that would be appropriate to the living. It could spur the effective collaboration within this perspective of mathematicians and biologists.

A final lesson from Canguilhem: philosophers will not be able to keep themselves separate from this work. Whatever one might like to think, there is always philosophy at the heart of inventive scientific thought. It is up to philosophers to recognize this in order to try, at their own risk, to respond to the solicitations from the researchers that discover it. Thus, philosophy would no doubt win back a part of the credit it has lost because of its current literary turn. And, to conclude with a beautiful expression from Canguilhem, science could gain, for its part, something like an 'attitude of freedom'.

NOTES

This essay first appeared under the title 'La Question de l'individu d'après Georges Canguilhem', in *Georges Canguilhem: Philosophe, historien des sciences* (Paris: Albin Michel, 1992), pp. 262–70.

1. Georges Canguilhem, *La Connaissance de la vie* (Paris: Vrin, 1969), p. 78. TN: All translations of quotations from this work have been translated directly from Lecourt's original French text, and are referred to hereafter as CV followed by the relevant page number. The recent English translation is *Knowledge of Life*, ed. Paola Marrati and Todd Meyers, trans. Stefanos Geroulanos and Daniela Ginsburg (New York: Fordham University Press, 2008).
2. TN: *The Organism: A Holistic Approach Derived from Pathological Data in Man*, trans. Heinz Ansbacher, Molly Harrower and Eugene Barrera (Boston: Beacon, 1963).
3. TN: *The Structure of Behavior*, trans. Alden L. Fisher (Boston: Beacon, 1963).
4. TN: *Phenomenology of Perception*, trans. Colin Smith (New York: Routledge, 2002).
5. TN: G. Canguilhem, *Le Normal et le pathologique* (Paris: PUF, 1966), p. 156. All quotations from this work have been translated directly from Lecourt's original French text. The English translation of this work is *On the Normal and the Pathological*, trans. Carolyn R. Fawcett and Robert S. Cohen (New York: Zone, 1989). This work will hereafter be referred to as NP, followed by the relevant page number.
6. TN: *Birth of the Clinic: An Archeology of Medical Perception*, trans. A. M. Sheridan (New York: Routledge, 2003).

Chapter 12

The Theatre of Individuation: Phase-Shift and Resolution in Simondon and Heidegger

Bernard Stiegler, translated by Kristina Lebedeva

We know very well that where Heidegger says that time is the veritable principle of individuation, Simondon responds that there is no principle of individuation, but the process of individuation. Since the reading that I proposed of *Being and Time*, I have maintained that one of the major concepts that has allowed for the philosophical advances of the twentieth century – as much neglected and misunderstood as it has remained, also in Heidegger – is the concept of primary retention discovered by Husserl in 1905. I will not explain again here the reasons that led me to claim that, even if I share with Husserl the point of view that absolutely distinguishes primary retention, which is the 'big now' of perception, to speak like Gérard Granel,[1] from secondary retention, which is, like the second synthesis of the *Critique of Pure Reason*, the result of reproduction and imagination in memory and thus as past,[2] I no longer agree at all with Husserl when he claims that primary retention owes *nothing at all* to secondary retention. I have tried to show that primary retention is always a primary *selection* and that this selection is always brought out in the function of secondary retentions that anticipate the primary retention in the form of *secondary protentions* (with the primary protentions being carried by the temporal object that supports the phenomenon) and that as such filter it. Furthermore and above all, I have attempted to show that the conditions under which secondary retentions perforate primary retentions, which are thus primary selections, are overdetermined by the factical and prosthetic conditions under which the now can have access to its already-there that is past and secondary, through the artifacts in which what I call *tertiary* retentions consist – which is to say, the supports of what we are about to examine as a process of individuation.

My thesis about the primary philosophical sense of *Being and Time* is that Heidegger attempts to free himself there from the Husserlian thought of time by introducing the already-there of historiality – which is very close to Simondonian pre-individuality. However, he does not truly succeed in breaking with Husserl precisely because, like Husserl, he still wants to exclude tertiary retentions – which constitute for him the realm of *Weltgeschichtlichkeit* – from the *originary* realm of *Eigentlichkeit*. Finally, Simondon's relation to the question of time is too inhabited by its intimate penetration of Bergsonian thought in order for it to be able to escape both the metaphysics of vitalism that denounces the geometrization of time – which is to say, its spatialization, precisely in what every tertiary retention consists, and the Bergsonian ignorance of the crucial difference brought about by Husserl between primary and secondary retention. That is why psycho-social individuation is essentially – although perhaps unwittingly – thought with the cone of *Matter and Memory*.

After these elaborations, let me introduce my subject by telling you that, on the one hand, I have always been struck by the *resonance* of Simondon with Heidegger or of Heidegger in Simondon, and that, on the other hand, I have just as much been struck by the immense distance separating the two. And it is in this proximity of distance that joins them that I am going to see today a kind of *transductive relation*, a transduction as Simondon defines it – namely, as that which opens up possibilities of internal resonances in a process of psychic and collective individuation, and thus (re)constitutes its terms.[3] We who still attempt to do philosophy belong to this process that would open us to the possibility of effecting a *leap* in individuation and thus to realize a transindividuation by one of these leaps of which Heidegger also often speaks.

But as for the *manner* of leaping and what *to leap* means, that would perhaps be a question precisely of *leaping beyond the Heideggerian sense of leap*. It would be a question of transindividuating the potential of philosophical individuation in which the pre-individual reserve [*fonds*] of the Heideggerian text consists, in so far as it expands and supersaturates the question of leap by pushing the 'question of being' or the 'question of history' to the extreme. And for this Simondon would be, if I dare say this so, at the same time a catalyst and a springboard in some way, in that he is the thinker of the quantum leap as the full [*plénière*] modality of individuation. It is, of course, necessary to underscore here that Heidegger will have shared with Simondon the philosophical attention to the quantum question. Recall here, also, the reference to Heisenberg in *Being and Time*.

Finally, the leap to be effected in this transduction is that which proceeds, for me, from a *reading* in which the *terms of the reading* – which is to say, the texts of Heidegger and Simondon, *Being and Time* and *Psychic and Collective Individuation* in particular – constitute themselves and each other in the proximity of their distance in such a way that, individuated on the basis of the pre-individuality that they constitute for us, the texts lead to a reading of the ensemble that joins the terms of the relation *by default*: as a relation that is thus dynamic because it is a *phase-shift* [*déphasage*] and that calls forth a *resolution*. This resolution is not a *solution*, but a *decision*. For my part, this decision – which is to say, this reading, in so far as it joins the two texts in their immense distance, but at the same time asks them a common question starting from their very resources – this decision of reading consisted in positing the necessity of situating, as a *transductive* and thus also individuating *element*, what I have called *tertiary retention*. That is to say, just as well, *facticity*, but conceived here as prostheticity and as that which then constitutes the *Wirklichkeit* of the mark of origin's originary default, the accidentality from which proceeds time and where it is a matter – as in the case of *Entschlossenheit* and thus in a *quantum* leap – of *differentiating becoming as future* [*avenir*]: which is also to say, this time in a more Simondonian language, of *negentropizing the entropic becoming* that is constituted by accidental chance.

Such questions do not only have a political interest, or an interest beyond the political, in an *apoliticity* on the basis of which I sometimes attempt to think the future and the beyond of *polis*, in the sense that Bataille spoke of an atheological thought, engendered from the theological itself, from its individuation, or as I myself have said sometimes, even in this very place, a little more than fifteen years ago, at the invitation of Gérard Granel in the name of a thought that I qualify as *atranscendental*, but coming from the transcendental, from its individuation. I explain all of this in the last volume of *Technics and Time*. By political *or* apolitical, I mean: in *or* from the process of psychic and collective individuation that has opened up history as individuation of the West, in the possible *after* of such a Western process if it is true that it is rather a question of thinking how that which – having begun and thus necessarily also having an end – we would essentially be in charge of individuating today, in and as the end of the individuation of the West, the nascent figure of another time, the accidental and yet necessary conditions of a renewed individuation – stating precisely the necessity of such an accident, as 'resolution', but a resolution in so far as it has the capacity for affirming a reinvented phase-shift in the face of an entropic and increasingly hegemonic tendency.

In any case, it is within such a perspective that I situate my intervention. Just as Foucault and Deleuze speak of the end of a Greco-Judeo-Christian apparatus [*dispositif*] (we who are no longer Greeks, not even Christians, as they say),[4] I put forth my capacity for individuation – psychic in the sense of Simondon, existential ipseity in the sense of Heidegger – in so far as it is inscribed at the heart of a *process* that invents itself and in which I attempt to *participate* as an inventor. Whether this process is a 'history of being' or an *ontogenesis* in the sense of Simondon is a big part of the question, but it is not the only one; the *real* question is situated in a *beyond* of this alternative – which is to say, precisely in its surpassing [*dépassement*] as a leap into a new process of individuation. It is thus that I think of philosophy today: as the experience of this *kata-strophe* (that is also a cata-lysis) of what will have been the process of psychic and collective individuation that began from two sources. Of these two, today, the Greek source is, if not accomplished, then at the very least exhausted: that it has *exhausted the resources of its initial conditions* and today it is a question of reinitializing this source (in a hypomnesiac and technical sense, the way one 'initializes' a system) and reinitiating it (in a logical, which is to say, anamnesiac sense, the way a master initiates) or rather reindividuating it from a reinitialization that escapes all decision and all 'resolution', and, *a fortiori*, all solution and all mastery.

The question is then to agree on this point: what are these *resources*? Or rather, what will these resources have been and to what type of new initial resources, constituted quantically [*quantiquement*] by a leap, can they give rise? Such a reinitialization can only yield an individuation as a quantum leap and it is in the worry [*inquiétude*] attentive to the necessity of *this* leap that I attempt the transductive relation of the Simondonian phase-shift and the Heideggerian resolution, with a view to constructing, in one way or another, the new theatre of individuation – understanding that here *constructing* means *individuating* what is already there as pre-individual potential.

The *relation* is established first of all through the striking fact of the proximity of the *already-there* of the historial past of *Dasein*, a past 'which is not something that follows along after [*Dasein*], but something which already goes ahead of it'[5] and the *pre-individuality* from which proceeds the individuation of the Simondonian psychic and collective individual. There are indeed other considerations that are common to the two thinkers. Most notably, there is the consideration – one that perhaps was not reflected upon enough – of the system of objects that, as that which constitutes what I myself called the *whats*, opens up the horizon of a world within which leaps must occur and that is also what

Simondon thinks as *milieu*. The Heideggerian thought of being-in-the-world resonates with the Simondonian *individual-milieu dyad*.

Certainly, the conditions of leaps in which individuation from a world or from a milieu consists, as *Entschlossenheit* or as quantum leap, and as the result of the already immense difference between world and milieu, are very distant from one another. But I think that the conditions are very distant from one another *first of all* because that which is posed in one as an evident *bipolarity that is constitutive of individuation* is in the other the *originary and tragic question of a fall [déchéance] of the individual in the course of individuation*. I mean that the first difference between Simondon and Heidegger, which in truth is constituted as an immense distance, which all of a sudden puts them into the transductive relation of a *very distant mutuality*, if not of a veritable separation, of a disjunction that could never again return to the conjugation of a conjunction, is that one speaks of the *we* and the other of the *they*, the *we* of one lacking the *they* of the other and vice versa. Furthermore, in this regard, Marc Crépon shows in his recent book *Terreur et Poésie* how Hölderlin is in Heidegger the support of a discourse not on the *we*, but on the *people*,[6] and, in this case, not on the proletariat, the Third State, or the *demos*, but indeed on the *German* people – which constitutes, I believe, the price to pay for the nonthought of the *we* in its originary relation to the *I*, the unthought that masks the question of the fall which claims, however justly, in *Being and Time*, to be its thought.

In Heidegger, there is neither difference nor the tension *in Dasein* between the *I* and the *we*; *Dasein* is not an *I*. It is neither, properly speaking, a *we*; it is prior to this kind of distinction, but it does not contain this distinction either. And this is a problem, I think, for it does not allow us to interrogate fully the tension and the dynamic phase-shift that is, by contrast, constitutive in Simondon and allows us to think individuation as process, a process that does not denigrate the collective and that also avoids thinking *Entschlossenheit* as a decision limited by being-towards-death; the stakes – but I will not have time to develop it here – are *overmortality [surmortalité]*: which is to say, that which, when it is thought starting from being-towards-death, nevertheless allows one to account for the fact that psychic individuation always carries itself forward, as originarily collective in this sense, going beyond itself, into a future that exceeds *its own disappearance* and to which it delivers its inadequation because that is the question in the preindividual which it is, from that moment, called upon to constitute in its turn, and in relation to which it is entirely traversed. It is thus that the constitution of a transindividual is possible. But this overmortality is that which presupposes what I call tertiary retentions in so far as they support this transindividual.

Certainly, I use here personal pronouns that are in principle proscribed by precisely everything that *Being and Time* puts in place; it is certainly not a question of making *Dasein* collapse into an *I*. Nor is it a question of reducing it to a *we* that quickly becomes unthinkable, at least by itself – if not precisely as people. Yet it seems to me that *Dasein* oscillates in a permanent denial between the *I* (this is what authorizes a certain interpretation of *Dasein* as ego, in the work of Jean-Luc Marion, for example; the voice of conscience of being-at-fault, of *Schuldichkeit* [sic], is indeed that of an *I*, as Heidegger says explicitly – and the whole question is then to translate *Schuld* not so much as *guilt* or even *debt* but as *default*[7] and to translate-by-default is what every translation is); thus, in a permanent denial between the *I* and the *historial people* (as heir of the 'Greek *Dasein*', the people of the Hymns).

It is here that a transduction between Heidegger's existential analytic and Simondon's processuality of individuation must be carried out. Rethinking existentiality in the way *Being and Time* attempts to designate it analytically as dimension of a *Da-sein* and as being-towards . . . is properly – joining if not an *I* to a *we*, then at least a 'psychic' individuation to a 'collective' one – that which all of a sudden gives *Being and Time* a renewed individuating efficacy, as both reinitialized and reinitiated. But this is only the case in so far as this transindividuating transduction happens, such is my own contribution, through the affirmation of a dimension of individuation that is found *neither* in Heidegger *nor* in Simondon and which is that of what I called the *retentional apparatuses* and that are constituted by tertiary retentions.

I owe much, if not everything, to the pre-individual potential that *Being and Time* will have been for me. But this will only have been truly the case, this will only be individuated, as that which characterizes what I believe I think today, when I am able to mobilize the Simondonian question of the process of psychic and collective individuation in my reception of *Being and Time*.[8] Many years after these connections, after *Le Temps du cinéma*,[9] I ended up telling myself that, contrary to the absence of the difference of the psychic and collective poles in Heidegger – that which inevitably leads the latter to confuse the question of the *we* with that of the *they*, which is to say, of the fall – there is no question of the *they* in Simondon. The possible annulment of the *we* in the *they*, the possibility of the annihilation of the difference between the psychic and the collective, of the *I* and of the *we*, in their confusion does not seem to enter Simondon's thought.

What Heidegger posits as a point of departure, namely *facticity* – such that it always results in the ultimately *inevitable* character of the *temptation to determine the undetermined*, which is to say, to flee the necessity of the resolution contained in the solitude that the *singularity* of *Dasein* necessarily is, that individuates itself only at this price, this *solitude in facticity* – is not really a *question* in Simondon. However, this does not mean that it is not addressed [*abordée*] at all; on the contrary, this question of the tension between psychic and collective, of the necessary opposition of the individual to the group, this question that is the dynamic constraint of transindividuation, of internal resonance as effictivity of the theatre of individuation permanently addresses [*borde*] us. But it is not treated *as such*, and consequently and above all, it does not allow us to pose the question of the *flight* before the necessity of the quantum leap in which effective individuation necessarily consists. That which, in a language too Aristotelian for Simondon, I call its passage into act.

However, I maintain this question as that of a passage into act not only because this expression intimately concerns me and initially allowed me to think philosophy, but because I think that Aristotle in this regard raised a specific question that concerns precisely the conditions of psycho-collective transindividuation in so far as it is not the gregariousness of collective psychology of that which Freud thought he could call the horde, which he hastily assimilated to the crowd.

Sensibility, which was thought as such for the first time by Aristotle, characterizes two different types of 'souls': the sensitive, supposedly animal soul and the noetic, supposedly human soul. The sensibility that is supposedly human is also and in some of its parts noetic: which is to say, inscribed into *logic*. It is in this that the noetic sensible opens up to sense. 'Logic' does not mean here to conform to the rules of rationality, but to be inscribed in a *becoming-symbolic*. For a noetic soul, everything sensible that is in act becomes the support of an *expression*. This expression (which is also, Aristotle says, a discernment, a *krinein*, a judging, a *making-a-difference*)[10] is a *logos* – as speech [*parole*], as gesture: narration, poem, music, engraving, *mimesis* in all of its forms . . . I call it an *exclamation*; the noetic experience of the sensible is *exclamatory*. It exclaims before the sensible in so far as it is *sensational*: that is to say, the experience of an *incommensurable* singularity. The sensitive soul neither exclaims nor expresses itself in this sense, it does not experiment with the sensational singularity of its world, it does not *make* world (*kosmos*), which is to say that it does not expand its sense in exclaiming it symbolically. This noetic expansion of sense is what Simondon calls psychic and collective individuation. It is this process.

The sensational is the intellective sensible. But the passage from the regime of the sensible into the regime of the sensational needs support because, as Aristotle writes in his *Peri psukhes*, the noetic (sensationally intellective) soul is only *sometimes* noetic – namely in those moments when it experiences the extraordinary: that which comes from another plane. Ordinarily, it is sensitive, which is to say that it lives not in the mode of its animality but of what is to be called its *stupidity* [*bêtise*] – its regression to the sensitive stage.[11] Ordinarily, I plunge into the ordinary because I submit myself to the *stupid* [*bête*] *tendency* which makes it possible that *I can participate in the divine only discontinuously*, as Aristotle says. It is this tendency, of which, in any case, I would not know how to free myself (this dream of purity is what best accomplishes the tendency that it believes to fight; it is the stupidest [*bête*] and laziest expression of stupidity), which makes that, in general: which is to say, ordinarily, in this generality of the genre where I am in the perception without exception, in the non-sensational sensibility, I am in the realm of regression.

Heidegger, in referring at the same time to Book A of *Metaphysics* and to *The Nicomachean Ethics*, formulates it as follows: 'The human cannot constantly dwell among the *timiotatâ*; for the human, this autonomous mode of being, forever attending to the *timiotatâ*, is unthinkable.'[12] And Aristotle cites Simonides in this sense: 'God alone can have this privilege.'[13] The stupid tendency that is thought already in Aristotle as the regression of the intellective-sensational soul to the sensitive stage is what contemporary industrial entropy exploits as it exploits the projective and fascinatory capacity of the cinema of consciousness (something Adorno did not understand).[14] It exploits it through the exploitation of the pulsational depth [*fond*] of the body: which is to say, of the unconscious. It is necessary to critique not only reason, but indeed also stupidity [*bêtise*], which is not simply a critique of unreason but, above all and primarily, a critique of laziness. This critique of stupidity [*bêtise*] can be constituted only by rules, ethical maxims and a praxis that are essentially an ethics and a praxis against laziness, an ethics and a praxis of courage.

Such courage is a sensible way to behave, an affirmation of the sensible as sensational and against the becoming-pigsty of the sensational through what I analysed some time ago as a sensationalist press [*une presse à sensations*], a sense-printing machine that has become aesthetic, and that is pursuing the mnemotechniques that forge collective retentions which the second essay in *On the Genealogy of Morals* contemplates, precisely at the moment when these mnemotechniques, having become mnemotechnologies, are functionally integrated in the system of global production and with them *all aesthetic* and *symbolic* life in general. Such is the society of control that Deleuze speaks of as what succeeds the disciplinary societies of Foucault and Marx.

These mnemotechniques and their efficiency are what neither Heidegger nor Simondon allows us to think, even though both call for this thought; and in any case, for me, the transductive relation that is established between them and that establishes them as the pre-individual reserve of the philosophy most necessary and capable of a quantum leap is what leads to the thought of this very mnemotechnicity as what I call tertiary retention. But in order to explicate this point by way of conclusion, let us first return to Simondon and Heidegger.

What Simondon privileges is *transindividuation* as the reality of individuation in general: that is to say, as what accomplishes transindividuation while inscribing it in the essential incompletion of an eternal return. I am currently attempting to show elsewhere (in *De la misère symbolique*) that it is a matter here of the circuit of desire as such. This transindividuation as circuit is not truly thinkable on the basis of and with *Being and Time* – unless as what will later become a 'history of being' ... *Later*, which is to say, *after* that which constitutes the *evidence of a failure of the existential analytic.*

Yet it is a matter of *reciprocally critiquing the two gestures* at the same time: the one that proceeds from the *fact of fall* without positing by way of an equally initial point the *primordial conjunction* of the psychic and the collective, and here I am speaking of Heidegger; and the one that, if not denies, at least occludes or underestimates the *necessity* of *Verfallen*, which is to say, the *essential fragility* of individuation – the gesture of Simondon. But it is only at the price of this possibility of fall inscribed in facticity that the *primordial conjunction is equally a primordial disjunction.* In neglecting it, Simondon does not see that it is a question of struggling, *between* these two tendencies, *for* their articulation and *against* their decomposition, which is the fact of deindividuation. In other words, individuation is essentially the com-position of forces that bind it and that make it a process: which is to say, a dynamic. There is no dynamic without the duality of forces that attempt to annul each other. But it is what Heidegger, just as well as Simondon, ignores – the one by denigrating the psychic-collective duality by collapsing into the fall; the other by ignoring the fall as the tendency to confuse the two poles in the *they.*

That is what remains of the *metaphysics of mastery* in Simondon (and in his mechanological project as foundation of the control of the technical cybernetic ensemble for mechanological power), which has as its political price its inattention to the question of the confusion of the *I* and the *we* and to the *becoming-they* of individuation: which is to say, *deindividuation* in its own right. The latter constitutes a tendency to a *regression toward the sensitive soul: which is to say, the generalization of the gregarious mode* – which is the psycho-social form of entropy. It is what I would like to introduce here first of all by way of a digression on the question of technics in Simondon. There one sees that, even if he does not allow one to think directly what I just called deindividuation, he, none the less, thinks the machine precisely as a loss of individuation. But he does not see coming the question of deindividuation proper to the hyperindustrial cybernetic machine, that which indifferentiates logic and technics, producing a logistics where calculation is put in service of deindividuation as desingularization, with singularity being that which must be reduced to particularity in order that the circulation of merchandises be able to impose itself without frontiers or limits, at the price of destroying the circulation of desire: which is to say, *libidinal energy.*

Simondon thinks the nineteenth century as a loss of individuation where the worker cedes to the machine the status of technical individual. This analysis is obviously very close to that of Marx. However, it is also quite different precisely in that it rests on the concept of individuation that escaped Marx (even though the latter justly underscored against Hegel, in his *Critique of Hegel's Philosophy of Right*, the irreducibility of singularity to particularity as the incommensurability of the *living* in the process of production): an automatic system of machinery – moved by an automaton, the moving force that moves itself – consisting in a large number of mechanical and intellectual organs such that the workers themselves are nothing but conscious articulations of it. The machine that possesses the ability and the force in place of the worker is itself a virtuoso endowed with a soul represented by the mechanical laws which are acting in it and that, in order to maintain its constant auto-movement, consumes coal, oil and so on, just as the worker consumes nourishment (instrumental materials).

Here it is Marx who is speaking. But in Simondon, form does not precede matter, and neither is it the other way around; he is not a 'materialist'. The process of individuation in which technical evolution as differentiation consists must be inscribed into a different categorization; the technical *industrial* object concretizes this dynamic *in itself*, without the intervention of that by which, for instance, Leroi-Gourhan, in his analysis of the realization of technical tendencies, calls the interior social milieu. In Simondon, technical evolution as the dynamic of evolutive tendencies tends towards techno-logical perfection through the integration and overdetermination of functions that is in itself a process of individuation – *but very paradoxically, Simondon does not assign any role to it in psychic and collective individuation.* As for the articulation between this becoming-machinic and the becoming-social, which is, by the way, also a becoming-symbolic, as the support of the transindividu-ation, even though it is not thought, it is historicized as follows. I reca-pitulate here the summary that I have proposed of its position in *The Fault of Epimetheus*:

> Industrial technics is characterized by a transformation of technical indi-viduals, which allows for the comprehension of the genesis and breaking down of the present-day relation of the human to the machine. The drama-turgy of modern technics begins in the eighteenth century with a phase of optimism. A crisis ensues with the advent of industrial technics exploit-ing the resources of the thermodynamic machine. The machine does not replace the human: the latter supplements, up to the Industrial Revolution, the absence of machines. The appearance of the tool-equipped machine, *qua* a new technical individual, however, strips the human of its role as technical individual as well as of its employment. The machine takes the place of the human because the human fulfilled the function of machine – carrying tools. However, a new optimism is ushered in during the twentieth century with the cybernetic machine capable of producing negentropy. More profoundly than the relinquishment of the human's place as techni-cal individual beside the machine, the threat of entropy makes possible the anguish in which the human experiences technical evolution. Against this, optimism is justified through reference to a thought of life, because tech-nical evolution appears as a process of differentiation, creation of order, struggle against death.[15]

However, I attempt to show in *De la misère symbolique 1. L'époque hyperindustrielle* that, for the time being – which is to say, in the hyper-industrial *hegemony*, the cybernetic machine, far from being negentro-pic, is archi-entropic; as the hyper-reactive system that tends to real time, it also tends to a synchronization that constitutes a new stage in the history of the loss of individuation and a fusion in what eventually leads to the hegemony of the *they*.

Dasein always lives in a difference in relation to others – in order to even it out or to accentuate it: this is the 'distantiality'. But this means that *Dasein* stands from the start in subjection to others and that it is not itself. This *who* that *is*, is the *they*, 'the *who* is the neuter.' This *who* entails an *essential tendency* (essential to *Dasein*) to the mediocre level-ling down of all possibilities of being (differences); it is the publicness (or the 'public opinion') that controls *prima facie* 'every way in which world and *Dasein* get interpreted', disburdening '*Dasein* of its everydayness'.

> In one's concern [*Besorgen*] with what one has taken hold of, whether with, for or against the others, there is constant care as to the way one differs from them, whether that difference is merely one that is to be evened out, whether one's own *Dasein* has lagged behind the others and wants to catch up in relationship to them, or whether one's *Dasein* already has some priority over them and sets out to keep them suppressed. The care about this distance between them is disturbing to being-with-one-another, though this disturbance is one that is hidden from it. If we may express this existentially, such being-with-one-another has the character of distantiality. The more inconspicuous this kind of being is to everyday *Dasein* itself, all the more stubbornly and primordially does it work itself out.

> But this distantiality which belongs to being-with, implies that *Dasein*, as everyday being-with-one-another, stands in subjection to others. It itself is not; its being has been taken away by the others. *Dasein*'s everyday possibilities of being are for the others to dispose of as they please.

> 'The 'who' is not this one, not that one, not oneself, not some people, and not the sum of them all. The *who* is the neuter, the *they*.

> In this averageness with which it prescribes what can and may be ventured, it keeps watch over everything exceptional that thrusts itself to the fore. Every kind of priority gets silently suppressed. Overnight, everything that is primordial gets glossed over as something that has long been well known. Everything gained by a struggle becomes just something to be manipulated. Every secret loses its force. This care of averageness reveals in turn an essential tendency of *Dasein* which we call the 'levelling down' of all possibilities of being.

> Distantiality, averageness and levelling down, as ways of being for the *they*, constitute what we know as 'publicness'. Publicness proximally controls every way in which the world and *Dasein* get interpreted, and it is always right.

> Thus the particular *Dasein* in its everydayness is *disburdened* by the 'they'.[16]

As neuter, would the *they* thus be Blanchot's 'they die': which is to say, the impersonal that is equally concealed by being-towards-death as undetermined, but whose indeterminacy would thus equally be the neutrality of the impersonal? This very difficult question which joins the *they* to death, but not to being-towards-death in an 'attempt to determine the undetermined' by calculation (in *Besorgen*), is also the question of what links *the* death *to* the dead [*la mort au mort*], to what, as *what, is not living*, to what I call 'the dead' in the sense of the reign of what is not alive [*vivant*] and yet essential to what is living in life [*au vif de la vie*] that is constituted by the existence of the *who*: technics, and more precisely, technics in so far as it constitutes tertiary retention, in fact concealing the dead [*le mort*] in the living, in its very intimacy and as *ex-sistence*,[17] in its intimacy always already ex-claimed as being-in-the-world.

Thus, there are several dimensions of the *they*, which can also be understood as the *one* [*il*], as the impersonal, which is the condition of what Heidegger himself calls the *They*, but which would not be reduced to it. I have attempted elsewhere[18] to characterize this *one* as what I call here 'the dead': which is to say, also as the impersonal and equally as the condition of the *One* [*Il*] – which is to say, of the (mono)theological. But it is also the impersonal as in what Blanchot calls 'the impersonal knowledge of the book' in *The Beast of Lascaux*[19] and thus already the pre-individual. And it is indeed thus that Deleuze understands the *they* of Blanchot: 'Every event is like death, double and impersonal in its double.'[20]

> It is the abyss of the present, the time without present with which I have no relation, toward which I am unable to project myself. For in it *I* do not die. I forfeit the power of dying. In this abyss they (*on*) die – they never cease to die, and they never succeed in dying.)[21]

It is in this multidimensionality that the *they* is the neuter as this other plane of 'they die', *as if here dying were the return of the living to the dead*, which is to say, to the pre-individual reserve – the *they* of mortality where the *stupidity [bêtise] of death* supports as its point of flight and collapse the *idiocy of life*, which is to say, the singularity of the idiom.

However, Simondon's inattention to the entropic tendency of digital technology – not only to cybernetic technology, by the way, but also to digital technology, that is to the expansion into all the domains of logistical and computational technology, that thus imposes calculation on everything that constitutes the movement of life, that is also the development of technologies of the society of control, that is thus also the absorption of the symbolic into the sphere of production and merchandise and the liquidation of the difference that Marx thought he could make between infrastructure and superstructure – thus, Simondon's inattention and naiveté, which in fact strongly resemble a discourse of mastery, this inattention to an avatar of metaphysics in its modern version is the fact of *forgetting the question of support* and of *the question of forgetting support*: of the question of support in so far as it is what always forgets itself as a fish forgets the water.

Certainly, Simondon asserts that there can only be transindividuation on the condition of a material and artefactual conservation of its trace:

Through the intermediary of the technical object is created . . . an interhuman relation that is the model of transindividuality. [This relation puts individuals into a relation with one another] by means of this charge of pre-individual reality, this charge of nature that is conserved with the individual being and that contains potentials and virtuality. The object that comes out of technical invention carries with it something of the being that produced it.[22]

But at the same time he argues that information must be thought regardless of its supports; in order to oppose himself to Shannon, he turns to the illusions of Turing, Wiener and many others – including contemporary cognitivists: 'The notion of information should never be brought back to the signals, supports, or vehicles of information in a message, *as the technological theory of information, drawn by abstraction from the technology of transmissions, tends to d*".[23] In other words, *like Heidegger and yet entirely otherwise*, and against all expectations, Simondon does not see that the informational and computational support cannot be reduced by a mastery because it cannot be limited to a technicity that would only be *Besorgen* and non-originary, derivative facticity. He does not see, *like Heidegger and yet entirely otherwise*, that technicity, being constitutive and, in particular, constituting the condition of access to the past as pre-individuality is what opens temporality as such, the capacity for projecting the future, and it is also what opens up individuation to the question of death, in other words, of incompletion – being, after all, that which constitutes the very process of the phase-shift, as originary default of origin whose thanatological version is existential solitude. I will not develop these points, elaborated in *The Fault of Epimetheus*, any further.

Thus, this blindness will also have been that of Heidegger. But the same forgetting, as wavering in one and as in the other – since, just as Simondon underscores the place of prosthetic support, which is to say, of what I call tertiary retention in transindividuation, Heidegger dedicates long analyses to *Weltgeschichtlichkeit* – the same forgetting has as its consequences two different and even opposing types of forgetting in each of them: one forgets the *we* – this is Heidegger – and the other forgets the *they* – this is Simondon. This is also what renders impossible in both of them a thought of what I called overmortality; it is the history of being that is substituted for it in Heidegger – and as the abandonment of the initial ambition of the existential analytic. This is also what leads to the politics of the 'historial people'. The question of a possible completion of the process of Western psychic and collective individuation as the end of the history of being, the end of metaphysics, and the becoming of the *Gestell* in this sense, will appear later. But it is no longer as an *analytical* and *critical* question that this end presents itself, but as *Gelassenheit* in waiting for a god. Thus, the question of the loss of individuation becomes unthinkable both politically and apolitically (in the sense defined above).

The loss of individuation as the *possibility of a blockage of the process of Western psychic and collective individuation* is an eventuality that Simondon does not even envision and that he even rejects, adopting a discourse of mastery of a rather classical kind – the vocation of mechanology being to situate the human as the conductor of an orchestra of cybernetic machines. Simondon sees in the hylomorphic model the error of the techno-logical model of the artisan that one finds in Plato and Aristotle. As a result, it seems to me he loses, in turn, the technological question as the process of the individuation of the *what*, conditioning the individuation of the *who* as the *we* in a transductive maieutic. Thus, one will not be surprised to see him caught up in the illusion of the abstract machine, or, more precisely, of information without support, rendered possible by maintaining a certain dependence of the lived – a dependence he inherits from Bergson. Undoubtedly, Simondon stands *on the edge* of the question of the non-lived; he even addresses it thematically and recognizes it as an original fact. But he does not put it at the heart of the transduction of the psycho-collective and in this regard he still opposes the living [*le vital*] and the geometric.

Nevertheless, Simondon thinks signification starting with a concept of information that is neither that of Turing – *even though he shares with the latter the forgetting of the support* – nor that of the theory of information, of computer technology and sciences of information; Simondonian information is *improbabilistic*.[24] It is in this sense that his concept of information sustains a concept of *sense* that I present in the last volume of *Technics and Time* as *the process of individuation as signification* concretizing itself as *the deposit* of the transindividual; the transindividual is thus a process of concretion and concretization (it makes a system). In other words, *sense is essentially a process, movement, e-motion* (as an *act* of individuation, it moves [*é-meut*] individuation as the primary impassable motor, to be precise, of the sensible agent of the noetic soul). But it is necessary to appeal to the undetermined in the Heideggerian sense and to *différance* in the Derridean sense in order to 'bring a non-probabilistic term to the theory of information'. On the condition that it be thought as tension, information in the Simondonian sense functions as the textuality of a program that, in disseminating itself, catalyses the improbable, as the germ of sea water or mother water [*l'eau-mère*] triggers the process of individuation of a crystal:

> The hylomorphic schema or the notion of archetype possesses a high tension of information because they have elicited structures of significations over twenty-four centuries of very different cultures. The tension of information would be the property possessed by a schema of structuring a domain, of *propagating* itself through it, of *organizing* it.[25]

And information gives concretions because it is functional integration and concretization:

> The relation can never be conceived as a relation among preexisting terms, but rather as a reciprocal regime of the exchange of information and of causality in a system that individuates itself. The relation exists physically, biologically, psychologically, collectively as internal resonance of the individuated being; the relation expresses individuation and is at the heart of being. However, the *support* of the relation is missing here, the support that exists only technically and of which *On the Mode of Existence of Technical Objects* said that it was the *condition* of transindividuation, that precisely is described here.[26]

Of course, it is on the basis of the central concept of *metastability*, which I did not have time to analyse here, that the sense of these advances must be evaluated, just as the sense of these omissions or of these retreats. And when it concerns *psychic and collective* individuation, it is necessary to think metastability that is equilibrium at the limit of disequilibrium and disequilibrium at the limit of equilibrium, that precisely as such is the *mode of existence of the system's dynamic that is constituted by the process of individuation*, on the basis of *prostheticity* as *default of origin*. Which is to say, as *originary disequilibrium* in which prostheses consist, which is to say, as tertiary retentions supporting transindividuation as its crutches.

A translation of the question of metastability in the context of *Being and Time* would be possible as unstable equilibrium between *Besorgen*, understood as determination of the undetermined, and *Sorgen*, as the trial of the undetermined. The ipseity of *Dasein* would then become psycho-social individuation as unstable equilibrium of *Besorgen* and *Sorgen*. I tried to show that it is in fact the fixation and with that the determination of the already-there (which is to say, of that which in Simondon is called the pre-individual), constituted by *Weltgeschichtlichkeit* as well as by the hypomnesiac discretization of *logos* that form the condition of *différance* where sense individuates itself – the sense that intensifies individuation – which is to say, the quantum leap of *Entschlossenheit* and which I analysed as differing identification.[27] In other words, the determined and the undetermined are not opposed; it is a matter of tendencies that compose and this composition constitutes the metastable equilibrium of a process of individuation – which is to say, the individuation of an *I* in a *we* that the *they* endlessly threatens with decomposition.

This double economy constitutes being-towards-death in the Heideggerian sense as well as the structural incompletion of individuation in Simondon. Death itself is such an incompletion. But it is also a knowledge that forgets itself. Metastability is a *différance* in the sense that, incomplete by nature, it maintains itself only by composition. The determined and the undetermined are its strictly tied tendencies as the cross of *Dasein* and form its edges as well as its contradictory tendencies – which are at the same time its dynamic power and its possible fall, its movement as possibility always exposed to what I called a regression, thinking of Aristotle and Freud, rather than a fall or a collapse. However, it is as the weakness of the thinking of the economy of tendencies in which this dynamic consists that the thinking of Heidegger and the thinking of Simondon neglect – both of them and each respectively – the questions of the *we* and the *They*. I, however, believe that their conjunction renders thinkable a disjunction as a possibility of the opening of a new theatre of individuation: the conjunction between the Heideggerian question of the *they* and the Simondonian question of the *we* would be this composition that disjoins.

NOTES

1. Gérard Granel, *Le Sens du temps et de la perception chez Edmond Husserl* (Paris: Gallimard, 1968).
2. I have developed this question in *La Technique et le temps 3. Le Temps du cinéma et la question du mal-être* (Paris: Galilée, 2001).
3. This is certainly not the strict definition of the transductive relation according to Simondon; the latter *constitutes* its own terms, fully and entirely. However, internal resonance, as the progressive structuration of a milieu of individuation, is indeed a relation that *re*-constitutes its terms; in joining them, structuration transforms them. The terms, that here are texts, find themselves reinvented in this way.
4. See, for instance, Gilles Deleuze, *Pourparlers* (Paris: Minuit, 2003), p. 145: 'It's not the Greeks or Christians who are going to experience things for us these days' (*Negotiations, 1972–1990*, trans. Martin Joughin [New York: Columbia University Press, 1995], p. 106).
5. Martin Heidegger, *Being and Time*, trans. John Macquarrie and Edward Robinson (San Francisco: Harper San Francisco, 1962), p. 41.
6. Marc Crépon, *Terreur et poésie* (Paris: Galilée, 2003).

7. I have defended this point of view in Bernard Stiegler, *La Technique et le temps 1. La Faute d'Épiméthée* (Paris: Galilée, 1994); *Technics and Time 1: The Fault of Epimetheus*, trans. Richard Beardsworth and George Collins (Palo Alto: Stanford University Press, 1998).

8. And I owe much to François Laruelle who showed me the necessity of reading Simondon when, around 1984, I presented him a draft of what I call an 'idiotext'.

9. Bernard Stiegler, *La technique et le temps 3*.

10. Aristotle, *De Anima (On the Soul)*, trans. Richard McKeon, in *The Basic Works of Aristotle* (New York: Random House, 1941), 426b.

11. See Bernard Stiegler, *Passer à l'acte* (Paris: Galilée, 2003), p. 31.

12. Martin Heidegger, *Plato's Sophist*, trans. Richard Rojcewicz and André Schuwer (Bloomington: Indiana University Press, 2003), p. 92. Translation modified.

13. Aristotle, *Metaphysics*, Book A in *The Basic Works of Aristotle*, 982b 31.

14. Bernard Stiegler, *Le Temps du cinéma*, Chapters 1, 2 and 3.

15. Bernard Stiegler, *La Faute d'Épiméthée*, pp. 82–3. *Technics and Time 1: The Fault of Epimetheus*, pp. 68–9.

16. Heidegger, *Being and Time*, p. 165. Translation modified.

17. In primordial relation with what I call consistence and subsistence in Bernard Stiegler, *Mécréance et discrédit 1. La Décadence des démocraties industrielles* (Paris: Galilée, 2004).

18. In Bernard Stiegler, *Aimer, s'aimer, nous aimer. Du 11 septembre au 21 avril* (Paris: Galilée, 2003).

19. Maurice Blanchot, 'The Beast of Lascaux', trans. Leslie Hill, *Oxford Literary Review*, 22 (2000), pp. 9–18: 15.

20. Gilles Deleuze, *Logique du sens* (Paris: Minuit, 1969), p. 206; *The Logic of Sense*, trans. Mark Lester and Charles Stivale, ed. Constantin Boundas (Columbia: Columbia University Press, 1990), p. 152. In *Foucault*, Deleuze also writes:

> But all these positions are not the various forms of a primordial 'I' from which a statement stems: on the contrary, these positions stem from the statement itself and consequently become the categories of 'non-person', 'he', 'one', 'He speaks' or 'One speaks', which are defined by the family of statements. Here Foucault echoes Blanchot in denouncing all linguistic personology and seeing the different positions for the speaking subject as located within a deep anonymous murmur. It is within this murmur without beginning or end that Foucault would like to be situated, in the place assigned to him by statements. (Gilles Deleuze, *Foucault*, trans. Sean Hand [Minneapolis: University of Minnesota Press, 1988], p. 7.)

21. Maurice Blanchot, *L'Espace littéraire* (Paris: Gallimard, 1965), p. 160.

22. Gilbert Simondon, *Du mode d'existence des objets techniques* (Paris: Aubier Montaigne, 1969), p. 248.

23. Gilbert Simondon, *L'Individuation psychique et collective* (Paris: Aubier, 1989), p. 29.

24. Ibid., pp. 51–2.

25. Ibid., p. 54.

26. Ibid.

27. Bernard Stiegler, *La Technique et le temps 2. La Désorientation* (Paris: Galilée, 1996).

Fifty Key Terms in the Works of Gilbert Simondon

Jean-Hugues Barthélémy, translated by Arne De Boever

*Terms in **bold** are referenced elsewhere in the glossary.*

Alienation
In the second chapter of the second part of MEOT, as well as in this book's conclusion, Simondon reproaches Marx for not having thought through the 'psycho-physiological' alienation of the worker in the machine era. Indeed, behind 'economico-social' (MEOT 118) alienation – which is linked to the private ownership of the means of production that Marxists criticize – there exists a more fundamental alienation that is 'physical and mental'. Around the same time that Simondon is writing this, Georges Friedmann makes the same argument in his book *The Anatomy of Work* and then also in *Sept études sur l'homme et la technique* [Seven Studies on the Human Being and Technics], insisting on the presence of such alienation in the communist countries themselves. The worker, who has become a simple auxiliary of the machine, finds her- or himself reduced to a status that is inferior to that of the one who 'carries tools' – in other words, inferior to the status of the **technical individual** (see **Individual and technical individual**) – that used to characterize the worker.

But Simondon does not plead for a condemnation of machines. Instead, he calls for their 'liberation'. The *autonomization* of the work of machines in the new technical sets would enable the human being from now on to be above the status of a tool-carrier – with the machine *fully* becoming the 'technical individual' instead of the human being, and with the latter taking on the task of repairing and overseeing the machines. Such a conception of course presupposes a complete reform of the system of work – understood here in the narrow sense of the word, as a system of labour, since the latter would need to be *redivided* in order to let the machines do the work that until now alienated the human subject. Simondon thus inscribes himself in the movement of 'utopic socialism'. As Jeremy Rifkin's book *The End of Work* has shown, it may be that technical progress will force us to 'utopic socialism'. The utopia is therefore only properly 'utopian' for a human egoism that is *cut off from the technical conditions of social becoming*. In this sense, psycho-physiological alienation is reinforced by another, *cultural* alienation, since culture – and thus the holders of capital themselves, this time – has not yet understood the *new technical normativity*: 'The technical individual is not of the same age as the work that drives it and the capital that enframes it' (MEOT 119). For more on new technical normativity, see **Culture and technical culture** and **Technics / work (labour)**.

Allagmatics
This term is used as the title for one of the 'Supplements' that were added to the French editions of IGPB and ILFI. Allagmatics is 'the theory of operations'. For this reason, 'it is, in the order of the sciences, symmetrical to the theory of structures, constituted by a systematized set of particular sciences: astronomy, physics, chemistry, biology' (ILFI 559). One understands that the project of allagmatics, which is already formulated in ILFI and MEOT in passages where Simondon enters into a dialogue with cybernetics, brings the philosophical project in close connection with the idea of a science (see ILFI 561), even if this new philosophical science is by definition transversal and unifying; whereas each positive science is a science of *generic structures*, allagmatics is the science of *genetic operations*: 'the operation is that which makes a structure appear, or that which modifies a structure' (ILFI 559).

Analogy
In the same way that ILFI rehabilitates the philosophy of nature at a time (1958) when phenomenology (Merleau-Ponty) and existentialism (Sartre) are dominant in France, MEOT rehabilitates technics in a context that is largely technophobic. One of Simondon's major aims is in fact a third rehabilitation: *in philosophy*, he seeks to rehabilitate analogy, defined as 'identity of relations' (ILFI 563). *In the sciences*, however, analogy is not constitutive of knowledge itself but only *heuristic*. 'Theory of the analogical act', a text that is featured in the 'Supplements' to ILFI, makes this very point.

However, such a rehabilitation of analogy in philosophy cannot be accomplished without specifying its restrictive conditions of validity. In order to do so, Simondon distinguishes between *operatory* analogy and *structural* analogy. The first is the only one he holds on to; the second he leaves aside as mere 'resemblance' (ILFI 563). Philosophy, whose role it is to unify the sciences that lack unity (on this point, see **Allagmatics** and **Encyclopedism**), is analogical 'knowledge', to the extent that it ceases to objectify the real so as to set free the processes of genesis. It unifies these processes according to identities of operatory relations, and by providing as the *methodological ground* for these analogies between operations a *mental and reflexive* analogy between the genesis of beings *and the thought itself of this genesis.* Simondon calls this analogy between geneses *that is also the operation of genesis itself* '**transduction**'. On the non-objectifying reflexivity of philosophical 'knowledge', see also **Ontogenesis.**

Anthropology
Simondon gives a new double meaning to this notion, which becomes the name of his great adversary in the theorization of human and technical reality. Indeed, in Simondon's work the word 'anthropology' refers to two major Western tendencies that must both be resisted:

1. First of all, it refers to the tendency to separate the human being from the living, on the grounds that the human being would have an 'essence' that is either psychic (Freud) or social (Marx, Durkheim) – this is not to mention, even, the mythological human 'reason' (Aristotle, Descartes, Kant) that Simondon does not even discuss. Against this tendency, Simondon in IPC, and more particularly in the first chapter of this book's second part, wants to think the human being as a living being that has become centrally and indissolubly psycho-social, with the 'purely psychic' and the 'purely social' being only 'limit-cases' (IPC 209 or ILFI 313). On this basis, Simondon seeks in FIP to refound the human sciences so that it would become possible to unify psychology and sociology, which have been artificially separated from one another. On this count, see the words **Axiomatic** and **Transindividual.**

2. Second, 'Anthropology' refers to the tendency to reduce technics to a set of means in the service of human work. In MEOT, and more particularly in its Conclusion, the paradigm of work is thus criticized because it is this paradigm that has led to what the beginning of MEOT denounces: the forgetting of the proper technicity of technical objects – that is to say, their *functioning,* in aid of their *usage* (see MEOT 19–20). One can only condemn usages, and not technics in its technicity. The originality and force of this critique of

the 'anthropological' conception of technics is that it shows, in the second chapter of the second part of MEOT, that there is a valuable human dimension in the technical object, but that this dimension resides precisely there where one least expects it: in the functioning itself. *First of all*, this functioning of the object is analogous to mental schemas that act upon one another in the subject at the moment when she or he invents the object (see MEOT 138). *Second*, that which Simondon calls the 'normativity' of technics is that which reveals itself in the *contemporary* age of *informational sets*, in which the functioning itself of technical objects enables the construction of a transindividuality (see **Transindividual**) that is at the same time human and technical. It is the culture of work that obstructs the construction of this transindividuality. See also **Technics / work (labour)**.

Anxiety
In the second chapter of IPC, Simondon dedicates a decisive chapter section (IPC 111–14 or ILFI 255–7) to the anxiety that in Martin Heidegger's work is characteristic of *Dasein*. However, Simondon anchors this anxiety in the affectivity of the living animal. Anxiety is therefore this very particular emotion that calls for the realization – which is, however, most likely impossible – of the I without the We. This means that the passage from vital individuation to psycho-social or 'transindividual' individuation via the psychic 'transitory path' will have to be provoked by an emotion that is not anxiety. Unlike the latter, the emotion that opens on to the transindividual provokes a 'disindividuation' (see **Individuation / disindividuation**) that is merely *provisional* and that enables the **subject** to take hold of itself through the collective.

Art, aesthetic object and 'aesthetic thought'
In the first chapter of the third part of MEOT, art is presented as the 'neutral point' between technics and religion, with the latter two resulting from a **'phase-shift'** of the **'primitive magical unity'**. The function of such a neutral point is to recall, of course in an imperfect way, this lost unity of the 'being in the world' of the human being. 'Aesthetic thought' is therefore, in the second chapter of the same third part, that which precedes philosophical thought in the task of unifying the 'phases of culture'; like **philosophy**, aesthetic thought is intuitive, but this intuition is not yet *reflexive*.

The difference between technics as a 'phase of culture' and art as a 'neutral point' between the phases does not mean that the technical object could not be at the same time an aesthetic object:

> Any technical object, whether it be mobile or fixed, can have its aesthetic epiphany, to the extent to which it extends the world and inserts itself into it. But it is not only the technical object that is beautiful: it is the singular point of the world that is concretized by the technical object. (MEOT 185)

Reciprocally, 'it is the technicity of the artwork that prevents aesthetic reality from being confused with the function of universal totality' (MEOT 188). The aesthetic object in general 'is not properly speaking an object, but rather an extension of the natural world or the human world, which remains inserted in the reality that carries it' (MEOT 187).

Associated milieu

The thought of individuation cannot be constructed without taking into account the milieu that is associated with the individual, and this is why this notion of the associated milieu is of central importance in both ILFI and MEOT. Indeed, Simondon remarks in the introduction to ILFI that if **hylomorphism** presupposes a 'principle of individuation' – whether it is form or matter – that already comes from the mode of being of the individual that it was nevertheless supposed to explain, this is because hylomorphism sought to explain the genesis of the separate individual, without taking into account its associated milieu:

> If, on the other hand, one presupposed that individuation does not only produce the individual, one would not seek to pass quickly through the stage of individuation to arrive at this final individuality which is the individual: one would seek instead to seize ontogenesis in the entire unfolding of its reality, and *to know the individual through the individuation rather than the individuation starting from the individual* (ILFI 24, Simondon's emphasis)

One will observe that this is not a question of explaining the individual starting from its associated milieu, but of explaining *both* starting from a *pre*-**individual** reality.

With the living being, the associated milieu becomes the pole of a permanent exchange, whereas for the psycho-social personality (see **Personalization and personality**), the collective is no longer even a simple milieu but a group that has its proper unity and its proper personality, with which the personality of the individual is 'coextensive' (IPC 183 or ILFI 297). In so far as the 'technical individual' goes (see **Individual and technical individual**), it can be thought by analogy with the living to the extent that its **individualization** is 'recurrent causality' with an associated milieu.

Automaton / Open machine

This opposition is one of the keys for understanding MEOT. In this book, Simondon is in constant dialogue with cybernetics. The latter privileges the automaton. However, 'the meditation on automata is dangerous because it risks limiting itself to a study of the exterior characteristics and thus operates an abusive assimilation [of the machine to the living being]' (MEOT 48). Indeed, 'the notion of the perfect automaton' is definitely 'contradictory: *the automaton would be a machine that is so perfect that the margin of indeterminacy in its functioning would be non-existent, while it would still be able to receive, interpret, or send out information*' (MEOT 140, Simondon's emphasis). The perfect automaton is mythological, and quickly slips into the illusion of a possible identity with the living, whereas there is *analogy* between the technical object and the living being and *asymptotic* '**concretization**' of the 'technical individual' (see **Individual and technical individual**).

For Simondon, true technological progress therefore lies in the 'open machine': that is to say, in the machine which integrates into its functioning its '**associated milieu**'. That is the significance of the famous example of the 'Guimbal turbine' (see MEOT 54–5).

Axiomatic

In Simondon, this notion does not designate a formal system as in the case of logico-mathematical axiomatics, but simply a set of principles, or first propositions, that enable the linking of fundamental concepts. It is in this sense that Simondon, in IPC in general and more specifically in FIP, struggles to work out a 'common axiomatic' (FIP, in IPC 35 or ILFI 533) for the human sciences – which enables the unification of psychology and sociology.

Concretization

This notion is used as the title of the famous first chapter of MEOT. Concretization is a 'process' through which technical objects progress analogically to the living beings thought by ILFI, who are the only ones who are 'concrete from the beginning' (MEOT 49). Technical objects, on the other hand, are never *absolutely* concrete. The concretization of technical objects has several aspects, depending on whether one approaches it at the level of the elements, the individuals or the sets (see **Element / individual / set**). At the level of the elements, Simondon distinguishes two aspects:

1. The augmentation of the 'internal resonance' between elements that compose the object. This is the idea of a growing organicity, through which each piece 'cannot be other than it is' (MEOT 21).
2. The fact that an element of an object becomes *pluri-functional* instead of having a single function. Simondon develops here the example of cooling fans in the thermal internal combustion engine (MEOT 22–3).

A third aspect no longer pertains to the elements that compose the object, but to the relation of this object to its '**associated milieu**' in so far as the latter is *external* and not internal resonance. This is the process of the 'individualization' of technical objects which only fully accomplishes itself in the machines of modernity understood as 'technical individuals'. On this count, see **Individual** and **Individualization**.

Finally, in today's age of informational sets the *convergence between science and technics* – and therefore the naturalization of technical objects – is fully accomplished, which is the last aspect of concretization. The entry on **Naturalization** addresses this point as well.

Culture and technical culture

The *fundamental stake* of MEOT is to reconcile culture with technics by supporting the introduction of a 'technical culture', which is necessary today for the very equilibrium of culture: 'Culture must become general again, whereas now it is specialized and impoverished. Such an extension of culture, which would suppress one of the principle sources of **alienation** and would reestablish regulative information, has political and social value' (MEOT 14). Culture is defined as: 'that by which the human being regulates its relation to the world and its relation to itself' (MEOT 227). In order fundamentally to reconcile culture with technics, Simondon will embark in MEOT on a complex operation that consists in reconciling nature simultaneously and to an equal extent with both culture and technics. Such an operation, which is perfectly attuned to the spirit of the fight already waged by ILFI against **anthropology**, takes its meaning first of all from the fact that it was contradictory to oppose nature to technics and to culture, while also opposing technics and culture to each other. 'Technical culture' is therefore that which must be introduced into culture, because 'if culture would not incorporate **technology**, it would include an obscure zone and would be unable to make its regulative normativity bear on the coupling of the human being and the world' (MEOT 227). As one can see here, that which Simondon calls 'technical normativity' (see **Anthropology** and **Technics / work [labour]**) is always, as such, a normativity *of culture through technics* – in other words, it is a normativity of culture thanks to 'technical culture'.

Element / individual / set

These three notions have to do with technical reality and correspond at the same time to *levels of analysis* of this reality and to *tendential eras* of technical progress (see also **Progress and technical progress**):

1. The levels of analysis are classic; in MEOT, the elements compose the individual, and the individuals compose the set. Thus, 'the infra-individual technical objects can be called technical elements' (MEOT 65). As far as the sets are concerned, they do not *fully realize* themselves before the information age:

   > One can confirm in this sense that the birth of a technical philosophy at the level of the sets is only possible through the in-depth study of regulations, that is to say of information. True technical sets are not those that use technical individuals, but those that are a network of technical individuals in a relation of interconnection. Any philosophy of technics that moves away from the reality of sets using technical individuals without putting them in a relation of information, remains a philosophy of human power through technics, and is not a philosophy of technics. (MEOT 126)

   On the notion of the 'technical individual' in MEOT, see also **Individual and technical individual** and **Individualization**.

2. As far as the tendential eras are concerned, what precedes enables one to understand that

   > today, technicity has a tendency to reside in sets; it can therefore become a foundation of the culture to which it will bring a power of unity and stability, by rendering this culture adequate to the reality that it expresses and regulates. (MEOT 16)

   The technical individual, for its part, had expanded itself with the age of the machinic, industrial revolution. One should add that this thesis is not incompatible with the idea that the elements are the 'carriers of technicity' (MEOT 73 and 76) because by doing this, the elements merely *transmit*, at least today, the technicity they have acquired by way of the set. On the 'normativity' of *contemporary informational sets* that is glimpsed here, see also **Anthropology** and **Transindividual / interindividual.**

Encyclopedism

This notion is absolutely fundamental to characterize Simondon's project. Simondon's ambition is to initiate, in the twentieth century, a third type of encyclopedism after those of the Renaissance and the Enlightenment (on these three stages, see MEOT 96–106). The new encyclopedism is 'genetic', in the sense that it thinks the genesis of each thing (see **Individuation / disindividuation** and **Ontogenesis**). On the other hand, it resists a type of alienation that is different from those that its predecessors fought against:

> In the sixteenth century, human beings were enslaved to intellectual stereotypes; in the eighteenth century, they were limited by hierarchical aspects of social rigidity; in the twentieth century, they are the slave of their dependence on unknown and far-away powers that direct them [. . .]. Having become machines in a mechanized world, human beings can only find back their liberty by assuming their role and by surpassing it through an understanding of technical functions from the point of view of universality. Every encyclopedism is a humanism, if one understands by humanism the will to bring back to a status of liberty that aspect of the human being which has been alienated, so that nothing of the human would be foreign to the human being, (MEOT 101)

In addition to this essential link between encyclopedism and **humanism**, it seems that the 'relation of the encyclopedic spirit to the technical object' is 'one of the poles of all technological consciousness' (MEOT 94).

Humanism

Simondon's opposition to 'facile humanism' (MEOT 9) should not lead one to think that Simondon would be a representative of anti-humanism. First of all, the proposal of MEOT is to reconcile culture with technics; 'facile humanism' thus refers to the humanism that rejects technics as foreign to culture. Simondon shows that contemporary technics has entered into an 'age of sets' (see **Element / individual / set**), in which 'technical normativity' is revealed to be the cultural dignity of technics – in other words, the capacity of *coupling* the human being and technics so as to make possible a true *transindividuality* (see **Transindividual / interindividual**). It is only through the latter that the **alienation** that has characterized the world of work since the machinic industrial revolution will be overcome. Simondon thus seeks to found a new humanism, because 'humanism can never be a doctrine nor even an attitude that could define itself once and for all; each epoch must discover its humanism by orienting it towards the principal danger of alienation' (MEOT 102). On this count, see also **Encyclopedism.**

Hylomorphism

Simondon's critique of hylomorphism is fundamental. This is why Simondon presents it in the extraordinary first chapter of ILFI, which is also the first chapter of IGPB. Hylomorphism comes from Aristotle, and consists in explaining the 'genesis' of the individual starting from the union of a matter (*hyle*) with a form (*morphe*). Simondon argues that the hylomorphic schema is insufficient when it comes to thinking true genesis. In the case of hylomorphism, matter and form pre-exist their union; they are already of the same mode of being as the individual of which one is trying to give an account. Thus, Simondon shows that the hylomorphic schema has a *conscious* and an *unconscious* paradigm at the same time, and that the second is the one that led the first to be misunderstood and betrayed by the hylomorphic schema that claimed it. The conscious paradigm of Aristotle is in fact technical taking-form, of which the moulding of the brick is the classic example. However, this taking-form cannot be reduced to the union of a matter and a form. First of all, the matter introduced into the mould is already prepared or 'preformed'; in addition, and reciprocally, the form of the mould is already materialized; finally, the taking-form will be made possible by the specific energetic conditions that come from a *metastability*. If the hylomorphic schema has reduced its own paradigm of technical taking-form to a simple union of matter and form, this is because of another paradigm, and an unconscious one this time: the paradigm of the *impoverished social relation* between the slave who moulds the brick and the master who gives the order for the technical operation.

Imagination

In IMIN, Simondon proposes a new theory of the imagination, which is on every count opposed to Jean-Paul Sartre's: the imagination is neither always conscious, nor an 'irrealizing' function which should be opposed to **perception.** Indeed, Simondon shows that that which *precedes* perception – that is to say, the motricity of the living – is already the birth of a 'cycle of the image' that extends into perception itself in the form of 'intra-perceptive images', and then beyond perception through 'image-memories' which are called to become 'symbols', so as to finally 'concretize' the imagination into *invention*, founding a 'new cycle of relation to the real' (IMIN 138). On this last point, see **Invention**.

Individual and technical individual

Simondon distinguishes between '**regimes** of individuation' and thus between degrees of individuality of the individual, in such a way that

> one cannot, even with the highest rigour, speak of an individual, but only of individuation; one must go back to the activity, the genesis, instead of trying to apprehend the being as entirely made in order to discover the criteria by which one will know whether it is an individual or not. The individual is not a being but an act. [. . .] Individuality is an aspect of generation, can be explained by the genesis of a being, and lies in the perpetuation of this genesis. (ILFI 191)

This is why the crystal is not truly individual unless it is at the moment of crystallization. The living being, on the other hand, possesses a complex and durable individuality; its **associated milieu** participates in its being, which is therefore a 'theatre of individuation' rather than simply the 'result of individuation like the crystal or the molecule' (ILFI 27).

The machine is a 'technical individual' in so far as it 'carries its tools' and becomes capable even of doing without the human auxiliary (see **Alienation**). But the *individualization* of the technical object is also this aspect of the process of 'concretization' through which the technical object *calls forth* an associated milieu that it integrates into its functioning (see **Concretization, Individualization** and **Associated milieu**). Finally, in the order of the *levels of analysis* of the technical object, the technical individual is opposed to the *element*, which 'does not have an associated milieu' (MEOT 65) and transposes itself from one object to another.

Individualization

This notion applies at the same time to the living being (in ILFI) and to the technical object (in MEOT) because of an operative **analogy**: 'It is because the living is an individual being that carries with it its associated milieu that the living is capable of inventing: this capacity to condition itself is in the beginning the capacity to produce objects that condition themselves' (MEOT 58; see also MEOT 138–9).

With the living, individualization is, first, that which accompanies this 'perpetual individuation' which is life in so far as it is *continuous genesis*: Simondon has the tendency to reserve the notion of individua*liza*tion to the *somato-psychic splitting* of the living. Whence the fact that, for him, 'psychic individuation' is not, properly speaking, an individuation (see

IPC 132–4 or ILFI 267–8) but an individua*liza*tion and a 'transitory path' between vital individuation and psycho-social individuation (see **Regimes**).

In MEOT, then,

> the individualization of technical beings is the condition of technical progress. This individualization is possible through the recurrence of causality in a milieu that the technical being creates around itself and that conditions it in the same way that this milieu is conditioned by the technical being. This milieu, which is at the same time technical and natural, can be called the associated milieu. It is that by which the technical being conditions itself in its functioning. (MEOT 56–7)

It is because of such technical progress that 'human individuality finds itself more and more cut off from the technical function through the construction of technical individuals' (MEOT 80). This is why, 'when reflecting on the consequences of technical development in relation to the evolution of human societies, we must take into account the process of individualization of technical objects before everything else' (MEOT 80). On this point, see **Alienation**.

Individuation / disindividuation

'Genetic' **encyclopedism** is a philosophy of individuation, or, for Simondon, of *genesis*. Individuation is thus not differentiating individua*liza*tion, as was the case in the work of Carl Gustav Jung; for Simondon, individuation as genesis founds and encompasses the differentiation between individuals, which only becomes fully meaningful in the case of the living individual and its individuation. This is continuous and very different from the individuation of the physical individual (see **Individualization**). On individuation, see also **Ontogenesis**.

The term 'disindividuation' refers to a very particular phenomenon that can generate emotion in the *bio-psychic living*, and that makes possible in its turn, as long as this phenomenon is temporary, the passage to the psycho-social – or the **transindividual**. On the difference between temporary disindividuation and the disindividuation that generates *anxiety*, see **Anxiety**.

Information

This term is defined as the *centre* of a larger work of *conceptual reform* that Simondon is pursuing, because information can only become 'the formula of individuation' (ILFI 31) if it is first thought beyond what information theory has to say about it, and in which cybernetics has remained stuck (see **Universal cybernetics**). Information theory and cybernetics have understood information as 'negentropy': that is to say, inversion of the growth of disorder and therefore the possibility of biological life. At the same time, however, information theory has dissociated information and *signification*, because of a *technical and probabilistic paradigmatism* that is improper to the *universalization* of the notion of information. Simondon bet that he could make possible the application of the notion of information to psycho-social reality *by starting from a physical but autocomplexifiable paradigm* (see **Transduction**). At the same time, he was laying the foundations for bringing his reflection on information in relation with his reflection on *the wave-particle duality* in quantum physics. The reflection shows that both are *geneses* that can be theorized *at the same time* as probabilistic and *non-probabilistic*. This is the epistemological heart of his work, the insight with which it is shot through, which yields a programme rather than a complete theory.

Invention
Simondon is certainly the thinker not of innovation – the catchword of contemporary *technocracy*, which is not *technologist* – but of invention, a term he discusses in MEOT, IMIN and IT. In so far as the Simondonian analysis of technical becoming is established first and foremost in terms of *functioning* and by rejecting *usage* as extrinsic to technicity, properly speaking (see **Anthropology**), the analysis would appear to be under pressure, given that most inventions of functionings are made *with a preliminary view to a determinate usage*. Simondon is conscious of this, and it is for this reason that in the last subsection of MEOT's first chapter, he introduces an idea that he will expand on in IMIN in 1965 to 1966. It is in this expanded discussion that he will develop a response to the objection that was just raised:

> In MEOT, Simondon introduces the idea of 'an absolute origin of a technical lineage'. He specifies:

>> The beginning of a lineage of technical objects is marked by the synthetic act of the constitutive invention of a technical essence. Technical essence can be recognized by the fact that it remains stable across an evolutionary line, and not only stable, but also productive of structures and functions through internal development and progressive saturation. (MEOT 43)

> There thus exist lineages of technical objects that realize the becoming that is potentially contained in an 'essence'.

2. The consequence of this will be developed by Simondon in IMIN in the form of a transcendence of the invented object in relation to first intentions of usage that had nevertheless demanded the object's invention: 'It would be partially false to say that invention is made to obtain a goal, to realize an effect that was known in advance' because 'true invention contains a leap, a power that amplifies and surpasses simple finality and the limited search for an adaptation' (IMIN 171–2).

One will therefore distinguish between:

1. the first invention of a technical *essence*, as the absolute origin of a lineage, such as the technical essence of 'the internal combustion engine'
2. the *continuous*, minor optimizations that take place within this technical essence as it progressively realizes itself
3. the *discontinuous* invention made necessary by the 'saturation of the system' that results from a continuous series of minor optimizations (see MEOT 27 and 39–40). This discontinuous invention is that in which the technical object really 'concretizes' itself as reality of a progress, such as the invention of the diesel engine (MEOT 44) within the technical essence of the 'internal combustion engine'.

Machine
In addition to the opposition **Automaton / Open machine** in MEOT, one must refer to the classification of machines in IT. Let us recall that MEOT defined the machine as 'that which carries its tools and directs them' (MEOT 78). On this point, see also **Alienation, Individual and technical individual** and **Individualization**.

In IT, Simondon follows Jacques Lafitte's *Reflections on the Science of Machines* when he *expands* our understanding of the machine. First, he distinguishes between:

1. 'simple machines' like 'systems of the transformation of movement' such as 'the handle' (IT 97)
2. 'machine-tools' that are 'semi-autonomous, namely autonomous for their energy and heteronomous for information' (IT 98)
3. the 'true machine' which is 'autonomous for both alimentation and information during its functioning, with information being delivered as a ground before the functioning' (IT 98)

Then, Simondon takes up and *rethinks* the distinction operated by Lafitte between:

1. the 'passive machine' and its different degrees, such as the tool with a handle and the architectural vault
2. the 'active machine' and its different degrees, such as the oil lamp and the engine
3. the 'reflexive machine': that is to say, the auto-regulative machine or the 'information machine'.

See IT 158–226.

Metastability

This term, which is used by Norbert Wiener as well, refers in Simondon to a state that has been discovered by thermodynamics. It is a state that transcends the classical opposition between stability and instability, and that is charged with potentials for a becoming (see ILFI 26 or IGPB 24). The central importance that Simondon gave to this term is characteristic of the theoretical gesture that Gilles Deleuze so admired in IGPB:

> Few books, in any case, make felt to such an extent how a philosopher can take his inspiration from contemporary science, while at the same time dealing with the great, classical problems of philosophy by transforming them and renewing them. The new concepts established by Simondon are of extreme importance; their richness and their originality capture and influence the reader. (Deleuze, 'Gilbert Simondon, L'Individu et sa genèse physico-biologique' [Gilbert Simondon, The individual and its physico-biological genesis], *Revue philosophique de la France et de l'étranger*, vol. CLVI, 1–3, 118)

The difference between the physical individual and the living individual is therefore that the second entertains within it a metastability, whereas the first has become stable and has exhausted its potentials. Life is for Simondon a 'perpetual individuation' (ILFI 27 or IGPB 25). On metastability as condition for the processes of individuation, see also **Pre-individual**.

Naturalization

This term, which is absolutely foundational, comes after **concretization** and **individualization** in the first part of MEOT. The naturalization of technical objects is the result of technical progress, since 'the progressive evolution of technics, thanks to the increase in value of each invention constituting an object, brings about natural effects in the world of technics, all of which results in the fact that technics becomes progressively naturalized' (IMIN 175). For Simondon, the consequence of this with respect to *knowledge* is an ever-increasing convergence between technics and science. This convergence has two reciprocal and complementary aspects, which he deals with in MEOT and NC respectively:

1. In MEOT, the technical object is conceived of as a physico-chemical system in which reciprocal actions take place according to a growing number of natural laws that are scientifically known. This is why the construction of the technical object can only be perfect if it proceeds from what Simondon calls a 'universal scientific knowledge'. Such is the path of *technology*, which is defined as an asymptotic path to the extent that 'the scientific knowledge which serves as a guide to foresee the universality in mutual actions taking place in the technical system, remains affected by a certain imperfection' (MEOT 35).
2. In NC, it is scientific knowledge that depends on technical activity, to the extent that the growing integration of natural laws into technical functioning turns the technical object into a mediator between the human being and nature that remains to be discovered: 'True technical activity exists today in the domain of scientific research that, because it is research, is oriented towards objects or properties of objects that are still unknown' (IPC 263 or ILFI 512). Technical normativity expresses itself fully in scientific research, because the machine does not mediatize there the individual's relation to the community, but the relation of the *active subject* to the *object*. Such is the *phenomenotechnical* path that had already been defined by Bachelard. On this count, Simondon certainly is, together with Bachelard, the precursor of a philosophy of what will later be called 'techno-science'.

Neoteny (generalized neoteny)

In biology, neoteny is the paradoxical process of slowing down that enables an early phase of development in a species (for example, the primate) to develop itself further in the immediately superior species (for example, the human being). As the French embryologist Alain Prochiantz writes,

> the mature human being presents numerous characteristics that are also found in young chimpanzees but are absent in adult chimpanzees. [. . .] Certain of these characteristics may have played an important role in the human species' acquisition of properties as essential as standing upright

or cerebral development. (*Les Stratégies de l'embryon* [*Strategies of the Embryo*] [Paris: PUF 1988], pp. 137–8)

Simondon, who wants to overcome the opposition between *mechanism* and *vitalism* in a better way than Henri Bergson and Georges Canguilhem did, applies the term neoteny to the passage of the physical to the living:

> Physical individuation is considered here as an individuation that takes shortcuts, that does not remain in abeyance long enough at its origin. Vital individuation would be a dilatation of the inchoative stadium, enabling an organization and deepening of the extreme starting-point. (ILFI 233)

The physico-chemical would thus be the *condition* of the living without, however, being its *cause*, which is 'pre-physical and pre-vital' because it is **pre-individual**.

Ontogenesis

This term is first of all a synonym of **individuation**, because individuation, for Simondon, is genesis. In biology, ontogenesis is also the genesis of the individual; in this case, it is distinguished from 'phylogenesis', which is genesis of the species. However, Simondon also applies this term to philosophical theory itself, because the 'knowledge' of individuation is 'individuation of knowledge' (ILFI 36). This is the properly Simondonian mode of overcoming the subject / object opposition in view of a non-objectifying philosophical 'knowledge'.

One must point out that there exists a hesitation in Simondon when, in the introduction to ILFI, he writes that one must not '*consider individuation as only ontogenesis*' (ILFI 24, Simondon's emphasis); later, he writes that, in his theory, '*individuation is thus considered as the only operation that is truly ontogenetic, as the operation of complete being*' (ILFI 25, Simondon's emphasis). Ontogenesis – the French 'ontogenèse', which Simondon consistently spells as 'ontogénèse' – is *first* distinguished from individuation, to the extent that the latter is also the appearance of an **associated milieu** that one must take into account for a true explanation of the genesis of the individual. In the *second* instance, it is the term ontogenesis itself that is enlarged in order to refer to the 'becoming of being' (ILFI 25) in general, and thus to individuation as the genesis of the individual *and its associated milieu*.

Orders of magnitude

One of Simondon's most original and cutting-edge contributions is to pursue the effects of the relation between orders of magnitude – which are called 'scales' today – at the root of one's understanding of the real. Indeed, if the individual *is* relation and not merely *in* relation, as the Simondonian doctrine of the **realism of relations** proclaims, then the individual can only be relation between orders of magnitude. The individual enables these orders to communicate; in the *pre*-**individual** state, on the other hand, they do not. These orders of magnitude, to the extent that they only exist *relative* to each other, are not terms that pre-exist their relation. Therefore, they do not put the realism of relations in question.

Thus, for example, the vegetative is presented by ILFI as an individual that puts in relation the order of the cosmic grandeur of sunlight – necessary for photosynthesis – and the molecular order of mineral salts that nourish the vegetative. This relation that *is* the vegetative individual is itself in relation with an **associated milieu** that is of the same order of magnitude as the individual. In CSI, Simondon tries to apply the thought of orders of magnitude to the difficult question of the instinct.

Perception
Simondon dedicates the voluminous CSP to the problem of perception, which he also addresses in the earlier ILFI. Together with *action* and *emotion*, perception is one of the three dimensions of the living animal, and one cannot understand its functioning without thinking its interferences with the two other dimensions, as the fourth and fifth parts of CSP do. After ILFI had already contested the 'anthropological' cut (see **Anthropology**) that the philosophers make between the human being and the living, Simondon proposes in the third part of CSP to singularize the simple human *degree* by the capacity of abstraction and symbolization; this is the very meaning of human privilege in the perception of forms. Perception exists with animals, too, but it does not have the same 'semantic richness' (CSP 204). The first part of the book consists in a historical trajectory of theories of perception and ends with an exposé on *Gestalt* psychology, which had been Simondon's most important interlocutor on the theme of perception since ILFI.

Personalization and personality
After the individuation of the living as 'absolute origin' (ILFI 27 or IGPB 25), and its subsequent somato-psychic individua*liza*tion as perpetual genesis, comes *personalization*. Personalization makes possible the passage from the properly vital **regime** of individuation to the *psycho-social* regime; individual *personality* is construed within a group that has its own unity and its own group personality (see IPC 183–4 or

ILFI 297–8). Whereas individuation is 'unique' and individua*liz*ation 'continuous', personalization is 'discontinuous' (IPC 135 or ILFI 268); personality undergoes profound restructurations, but only periodical ones. See also **Transindividual / interindividual**.

Phases and phase-shift

First of all, the term 'phases' is always plural, because phases only exist in relation to each other. Thus, they are marked by their *relativity*. Second, the term also refers to *something other than a moment* within a temporal succession (see MEOT 159). Simondon highlights the *physical* origin of this term, which, together with the terms 'relation' (see **Realism of relations**) and 'orders of magnitude', lays down a new and difficult logic; if one does not want to misinterpret Simondon's discussion of a particular regime, one must always keep this in mind when the ontology of 'regimes of individuation' – physical, vital and psycho-social – is being constructed. This new logic is made explicit in a foundational passage of ILFI, the one that starts off the conclusion of this work:

> Here, the idea of a discontinuity [*discontinu*] becomes that of a discontinuity [*discontinuité*] of phases, which is linked to the hypothesis of the compatibility of successive phases of being: a being, considered as individuated, can in fact exist according to several phases that are present at the same time, and it can change phases in itself; there is a plurality in being that is not the plurality of parts (the plurality of parts would be below the level of the unity of being), but a plurality that is above this unity, because it is that of being as phase, in the relation of one phase of being to another phase of being. (ILFI 317).

The notion of 'phase-shift' refers to this process through which the phases are constituted. One finds its most extensive illustration in the 'phases of culture' in the third part of MEOT. See **Art**, **Religion** and **Primitive magical unity**.

Philosophy

Philosophy's specificity is to be able to take itself as object. This is why Simondon ends MEOT in the way he had started ILFI: that is to say, by announcing what he considers philosophy's role to be. From being 'knowledge of individuation' at the end of the introduction of ILFI (see **Ontogenesis**), philosophy becomes the 'intuition of the real' (MEOT 237) at the end of MEOT. These two definitions can shed light on each other when they are considered in the context of Simondon's dialogue with Henri Bergson. From now on, philosophical intuition is *reflexive*, and this is why 'philosophical thought can only constitute itself after having exhausted the possibilities of conceptual knowledge and knowledge through the idea. That is to say: after a technical and a religious becoming-conscious of the real' (MEOT 237).

Polarization

Like the term '**(generalized) neoteny**', Simondon uses this term to overcome, better than Henri Bergson did, the opposition between *mechanism* and *vitalism*. Mechanism reduces the living to physico-chemical processes; vitalism, on the other hand, renders the living incomprehensible by starting from the physical. In ILFI, Simondon takes up a decisive position in this debate, and he is in this sense the precursor of philosophies of 'emergence'; he conceives of the physical and the living as different types of the same process of polarization. The crystal is polarized, in the same way that the affectivity of the living animal is, and between the two there is a polarization of the cellular membrane, where the first difference between the physical and the living is marked. In the crystal on the path of formation, the limit that is in progress is the one that separates *the past from the future*. In the living cell, on the other hand, the membrane separates *the interior from the exterior* since the interior is *not past but contemporaneous to the membrane*.

Pre-individual

This term, which is crucial to Simondon's thought, refers to the state of **metastability** that makes possible each individuation. While metastability can exist within the process of individuation, as is the case with the living, the pure pre-individual actually exists 'before' this process – in an 'anteriority' that is not temporal, since time itself '*develops out of the pre-individual just like the other dimensions according to which the process of individuation takes place*' (ILFI 34, Simondon's emphasis). The conclusion of ILFI presents the pre-individual as a 'hypothesis' that is 'derived from a certain number of thought schemas borrowed from physics, biology, technology' (ILFI 327). It is important to specify that the pre-individual comes from physics – in IGPB and in IPC the *same* passage from the conclusion does not even mention biology or technology. Simondon's inspiration for the pre-individual comes from thermodynamic metastability, and also from the famous wave-particle duality in quantum physics, in so far as this duality is 'more than one' and in so far as the particle is, strictly speaking, not an individual. Only *contemporary micro*-physics can give an idea of this primordial state, which Simondon sometimes qualifies as 'pre-physical and pre-vital', with physical and vital individuation being only two *regimes* having the same source, and not two *substantial domains* of being (on this distinction, see **Regimes**).

Primitive magical unity
In the first chapter of the third part of MEOT, the theory of the 'phases of culture' leads religion and technics away from a 'primitive magical unity' that, in so far as it precedes them, is not yet a **phase**. The 'magical mode of existence' is 'just above a relation that would be simply that of the living to its milieu' (MEOT 156). In it, there only exist natural 'key points', such as the top of a mountain or the centre of a forest. This raises the question of whether, for Simondon, this means that artifacts are absent in the magical mode of existence – certain formulations in MEOT seem to indicate that this is the case – or whether artifacts are already present but not yet invested with the role of 'first objects' that they will have during the technical phase, which is complementary to the religious phase in which the first 'subjects' appear (see **Religion**). This debate may ultimately be irrelevant, given that, for Simondon, the *genesis* of phases is not a *history* (see **Phases and phase-shift**). This is an important question for the exegesis of an *œuvre* that has not completely made its aim explicit, but whose force of *invention* is matched only by its *actuality*.

Problematic
Simondon's originality in this case lies in the fact that he gives an objective reality to a term that traditionally refers to the result of an activity of the thinking subject. With Simondon, indeed, every reality has its problematic to the extent that the potentials are not yet actualized and demand to be so; the problematic is the configuration *starting from* which something can 'pose a problem' and provoke a becoming, as the resolution of the problem. Thus, for example, the 'problematic' of psychic individuation can only fully resolve itself through the passage to psycho-social individuation. This is why psychic individuation is merely a 'transitory path' between vital individuation and psycho-social individuation; it is first and foremost an *individualization* rather than a true individuation.

Progress and technical progress
In the fourth part of IMIN, which deals with invention, Simondon maintains that

> progress cannot be guaranteed as long as culture, on the one hand, and the production of objects, on the other, remain independent from one another. The created object is precisely an element of the organized real that is detachable because it has been produced following a code that is contained in a culture enabling one to use it at a distance from the place and time of its creation. (IMIN 164)

Culture and technics must therefore be linked in order to make progress possible. The stagnation of 'animal cultures' does not mean that they would not be cultures, nor even that they would not produce objects (primates produce objects). It simply means that this production of objects is not 'cumulative' (IMIN 163), and that it is not founded on the detachable character of the constituted object. Progress thus becomes synonymous with the *perpetual progress of humanization* [*hominisation*], and is defined as 'the character of the development that integrates into a whole the meaning of discontinuous successive discoveries and the stable unity of a community' (NC in IPC 267 or ILFI 515).

In MEOT, properly *technical* progress is thought in terms of the **concretization**, **individualization** and **naturalization** of technical objects. One should add that the *tendential eras* of technics will be redefined in IT, which will indeed divide the history of technics in two different ways, neither of which contradict the division proposed by the last page of the introduction to MEOT:

1. First, it divides the history of technics by distinguishing between four periods that are called, respectively, (1) 'anterior to the use of the tool and the instrument', (2) 'of the tool, the instrument', (3) 'of the machine-tool and the machine', and finally (4) of the 'reticulation' (IT 104).
2. Second, it also does so by distinguishing between three periods that are called (1) 'pre-scientific inventions', (2) 'inventions made or completed with the help of the sciences', and finally (3) a 'third group of inventions' in the 'information' age (IT 229 and 271–2).

The first division contains only four periods because the first of them precedes the artifact and concerns the very first 'techniques', understood here in the sense of *processes*: for example, 'a primitive technique of hunting such as that which consists in chasing the animals towards the rocky coasts and frightening them' (IT 86).

Real collective and community / society
The term 'real collective' can be used as another name for the **transindividual** when the latter is considered in its social rather than its psychic

aspect. Indeed, the paradox of the transindividual, as Simondon presents it in the second and third chapters of IPC, is that 'psychological individuality appears as that which elaborates itself while elaborating transindividuality; this elaboration rests on two connected dialectics, one that interiorizes the exterior, and another that exteriorizes the interior' (IPC 157 or ILFI 281). This means that where psychic individuality unfolds itself to the utmost, the collective equally becomes a 'real collective', immanent to each individuality. This paradox is an ontological consequence of the epistemological doctrine of the **realism of relations**.

It is by way of this paradox that one must understand the central distinction between 'society' and 'community' that Simondon makes in IPC and in MEOT. A community, such as the community of work, puts individuals in relation, but without founding itself on that which remains **pre-individual** in the **subjects** – that is to say, that which remains susceptible to individuating itself further to construct a transindividual reality through and beyond the individuals. It is the other way around in the case of the true society, and this is why Simondon refuses the distinction made by Bergson between 'closed' and 'open society'. If, in his own way, he returns this distinction to the community / society distinction, he does so precisely without succumbing to the prejudice of 'societies without history'. On this count, see also **Transindividual / interindividual**.

Real potential

This term refers to a potential that cannot be reduced to either the possible or the virtual. Instead, and paradoxically, it 'actually exist[s] as potential' (ILFI 313 or IPC 210). That is where the entire specificity of Simondon's reinterpretation of the physical notion of 'potential energy' lies. Simondon follows here the Nobel Prize-winning French physicist Louis de Broglie: 'The potential, conceived as potential energy, is *real*, because it expresses the reality of a metastable state, and its energetic situation' (FIP in Simondon ILFI 547 or IPC 68, Simondon's emphasis). See **Metastability**.

Realism of relations

This term refers to the epistemological doctrine of Simondon's work, which provides the core of his genetic ontology. The term – which was curiously lacking in IGPB – is most completely developed in the third chapter of ILFI. The *realism* of relations consists in *desubstantializing the individual without, however, derealizing it*. It posits that the individuality of the individual increases through the demultiplication of the relations that constitute the individual. This is why the individual does not dissolve in the relations that constitute it. Simondon's anti-substantialism thinks of relations as not being preceded by the terms that they relate. At the same time, it preserves the idea that the individual is the 'active centre' of the relation. For more on both these aspects, see **Orders of magnitude.**

The precursor of the realism of relations is Gaston Bachelard, the great French epistemologist and philosopher of physics, whose most important disciple was Georges Canguilhem, philosopher of biology, who was the director of both Simondon's main doctoral thesis and his secondary thesis.

Regimes (physical / vital / transindividual)
In contrast to Maurice Merleau-Ponty in *The Structure of Behavior*, Simondon does not distinguish between 'orders' of beings but between 'regimes' that, in line with the theory of the '**phases**' of being, are not substantial but *possible phases of every being*. In Simondon's work, the psycho-social regime of individuation takes up a privileged place with the human being. However, at times the latter is able – for example, through relations of work (in the sense that the ant works) – to function as a living individual, rather than as a **subject** individuating itself into a psycho-social or transindividuated personality. On the other hand (and vice versa), certain animals can, in a highly ephemeral but nevertheless real way, access the psycho-social or the **transindividual.**

Relaxation (the law of)
Simondon introduces the law of relaxation in the second chapter of MEOT. This law has to do with the tripartite division '**element / individual / set**'. It affirms that

> in the evolution of technical objects, one can witness a passage of causality that goes from the sets, which are anterior, to the elements, which are posterior. When these elements are introduced in an individual whose characteristics they modify, they enable technical causality to return from the level of the elements to the level of the individuals, and then from that of the individuals to that of the sets. From there, in a new cycle, technical causality descends through a process of production to the level of the elements again, where it reincarnates itself in new individuals, and then in new sets. (MEOT 66)

Such a law does not undermine the idea that there is an 'era of elements', an 'era of individuals' and an 'era of sets', since these denominations are in any case relative and only define the *successive, privileged* '*sites*' (the element, the individual or the set) of technical progress (see **Element / individual / set**).

Religion
In the first chapter of the third part of MEOT, religion is, together with technics, the result of a **phase-shift** of the **primitive magical unity**. It is therefore a phase of culture, and its particular function is to develop the 'background qualities' that, before this phase-shift, were still mixed up with the 'figures' in the primitive magical unity. This means that religion, due to its function of unifying totality, is complementary and symmetrical to technics, which for its part develops the 'figures' in the form of elements that are detachable from the foundation. It is in this way that religion and technics bring into the world the first *subjects* – the divine, the priest – and the first *objects* – the artifacts.

Spirituality
This notion has two meanings in IPC:

1. It is first of all – and surprisingly so – a synonym for 'having a psyche'. This is because Simondon considers the '*spirit*' to be the psyche (*mind as psyche*).
2. Spirituality is also the higher form of the **transindividual** and of the intuitive consciousness it has of its continuing 'pre-individual charge', and of the power that this charge represents for it always to overcome itself: 'Spirituality is the signification of the relation of the individuated being to the collective, and therefore also of the founda-tion of this relation, that is to say of the fact that the individuated being is not fully individuated. (IPC 105–6 or ILFI 252)

Subject
Simondon uses the term subject in the following three ways:

1. In a classical sense, the *subject* is the one who is capable of trans-forming the components of the world into *objects*. It is in this sense that the first chapter of the third part of MEOT thematizes technics and religion as two *complementary* **phases** of culture that make appear, respectively, the first objects and the first subjects (see **Religion**).
2. In his battle against the anthropological (see **Anthropology**) split of the human being from the living, Simondon uses the term 'subject' to refer to the *bio-psychic* being that results from the 'somato-psychic

splitting' that is internal to the *living*. The human being therefore does not have the monopoly of being a subject.
3. The 'subject' is also, and perhaps first and foremost, the *ensemble* constituted by the individual *and its pre-individual charge*.

The link between 2 and 3 is the following: by individualizing itself through somato-psychic splitting, the animal becomes a 'subject' that is no longer a simple individual, but the ensemble individual / pre-individual charge, with its psychic affectivity being capable of receiving the **metastability** maintained in the living from which this subject comes, and that it continues to be.

Substantialism
Simondon's strong opposition to **hylomorphism** is only one particular instance of his more general opposition to substantialism. Hylomorphism is a disguised or subtle figure of substantialism – because it pretends, against atomist substantialism, to account for the genesis of the individual. For Simondon, substantialism is the doctrine that posits a 'principle of individuation' without genesis, whether this principle be the individual itself as indivisible (*atomos*), or form, or matter. In HNI, Simondon turns Leibniz into substantialism's representative *par excellence*. This is because in Leibniz, 'the notion of the individual is universalized because everything is individual in the world: there are only individuals, and these individuals are substantial' (ILFI 454).

Technics / work (labour)
This opposition is fundamental, and captures the remarkable originality of Simondon's thought. Already in the second chapter of NC, which establishes the transition between ILFI and MEOT, Simondon asserts that "the specialists' are not truly technicians, but workers' (IPC 263 or ILFI 512). Work, in the narrow sense in which this term is understood in Simondon – namely, as labour – does not fall within transindividuality but within interindividuality (see **Transindividual / interindividual**). In the latter case, beings are not mobilized as 'subjects' in the sense that Simondon gives to this term since ILFI – that is to say, as carriers of a pre-individual charge of nature that enables them to transindividuate. The relation of labour merely puts individuals in relation with each other – it merely relates being as already individuated. Simondon adds another aspect to this first aspect of labour, which is meant to complete it but which remains, in truth, foreign to the transinvidual: in labour, the interindividual relation between the workers is also a relation of the

human species to nature. In each case, however, the transindividual is missed, because humanity precisely does not realize itself in labour. For labour understood in this way is always too poor to found a transindividuality; it adds the intrasocial to the interindividual, but even this conjunction does not engender transindividuality. It merely falls within the 'community' that Simondon criticizes in ILFI (see **Real collective and community / society**).

By contrast, the activity of technical invention provides the 'support' of a human relation that is the 'model of transindividuality' (MEOT 247). NC already turned the technician into a 'pure individual: in a community, the technician is part of another species [. . .] technical normativity is intrinsic and absolute; one can even remark that it is through technics that the emergence of a new normativity in a closed community is made possible' (IPC 263 and 265 or ILFI 512 and 514). That technical normativity be intrinsic and absolute means that the adoption or the refusal of a technical object by a society says nothing for or against the validity of that object, as Simondon explains in this decisive passage. Indeed, it is in these lines that Simondon's entire thought comes together, because in NC it was the same passage that, with respect to **naturalization**, addressed the convergence of science and technics. One cannot understand Simondon's affirmation of technical normativity if, on the one hand, one does not distinguish between transindividuality and community, and if, on the other hand, one does not think of technics as ultimately concretizing itself in the informational set of contemporary scientific instruments, through which a human transindividuality is realized whose relation to nature is mediatized by the machine: 'Free individuals are those who do research, and institute through it a relation with a non-social object' (NC, in IPC 263 or ILFI 512).

Technology and the technologist
The ordinary meaning of the word 'techno-*logy*' refers to modern technics in so far as it would be the application of the *logos* of science. Simondon reinterprets this word as the study (*logos*) of technics. One of the main theses of MEOT is that 'philosophical thought must achieve the integration of technical reality in universal culture by founding a technology' (the title of the last chapter in the second part). The *technologist* – also called 'mechanologist' (MEOT 13) by Simondon – is thus the human being who makes it possible to 'give back to culture the truly general character that it has lost'; it is through the technologist rather than through the psychologist or the sociologist that one can 'reintroduce into [culture] a consciousness of the nature of machines, of their

mutual relations and their relations with the human being, and of values implied in these relations' (MEOT 13). On this count, see also **Culture and technical culture.**

Transduction
Like Jean Piaget before him, Simondon uses this term, which is at the same time technological and biological, in order to give it a new meaning, one that will become absolutely central in the thought of individuation. In Piaget's work, transduction refers to a mental operation that is different from both the deductive and inductive operations. One finds the same understanding of transduction in Simondon, but just as with the term **ontogenesis,** the term 'transduction' refers first of all to the process of individuation of the real itself. This is why transduction is defined as 'a physical, biological, mental, social operation through which an activity propagates gradually within a domain, by founding this propagation on a structuration of the domain that is realized from one place to the next' (ILFI 32). The paradigm or exemplary case of transduction is therefore *crystallization*, in so far as it is 'the simplest image of the transductive operation' (ILFI 33). It is understood here that the notion of transduction is susceptible to *auto-complexification*, so that it can apply to different regimes of individuation. This is why the 'transposition' of physical schemata used by Simondon is at the same time a 'composition' (ILFI 319), which enables one to avoid *reduction-ism*. The notion of transduction also enables Simondon to found a new thought of **analogy.**

Transindividual / interindividual
This opposition is decisive for understanding the psycho-social or 'transindividual' **regime** of individuation, but also for understanding the value of technical invention:

1. The transindividual, first of all, is defined as 'the systematic unity of interior (psychic) individuation, and exterior (collective) individua-tion' (IPC 19; ILFI 29). Unlike the interindividual, it is therefore not simply a bringing-into-relation of the individuals. The transindivid-ual makes **subjects** intervene in so far as they carry a charge of **pre-individual** reality. The mistake of psychologism – which only sees the *interindividual* – as well as of sociologism – which merely sees the *intrasocial* – is to have forgotten this reality of the subject which is 'vaster than the individual' (MEOT 248) and which alone enables one to explain the birth of a **real collective** *and also* the ultimate

realization of the individual psychism that is becoming 'personality' (see **Personalization and personality**).

2. In addition, and this has already been explained in the context of the opposition '**Technics / work (labour)**', the paradigm of the transindividual is the human relation, which is 'supported' by the invented technical object, as Simondon says in MEOT. It should be added here that it is by virtue of the *contemporary informational sets* that the properly called 'modern' human society of work – which was born from the industrial revolution, and which was made up of merely *inter*individual relations and as a consequence sometimes found itself alienated (see **Alienation**) by the machine – can from now on construct itself as a *transindividuality* that is indissociably human and technical. Simondon was already proposing this in NC, where he wrote that the 'value of the dialogue of the individual with the technical object' was 'to create a domain of the transindividual, which is different from the community' (ILFI 515 or IPC 268).

Universal cybernetics
This term is a synonym of '**allagmatics**'. Thus, it refers to a reformed cybernetics because it is genetic – understood as referring to the notion of genesis – in view of encyclopedic universalization. For Simondon, the aim is always to enter in competition with the **hylomorphic** doctrine that has been dominant from Aristotle to Kant – thinker of the 'form' and 'matter' of knowledge – and whose strength was its capacity to universalize its schema in order to apply it to the entirety of reality. Cybernetics had the benefit for Simondon of already being an analogic and inter-scientific thought. At the same time, it was nourished by the theory of **information**, which Simondon wanted to discuss. 'Universal cybernetics' must ultimately succeed cybernetics, which is too technicist and reductionist, but it is in the important debate with cybernetics that the tensions that operate the very unity of Simondonian thought become manifest. MEOT qualifies Norbert Wiener's *Cybernetics* as 'a new discourse on method'. MT, on the other hand, is the most 'cybernetic' text of Simondon's.

Notes on Contributors

Jean-Hugues Barthélémy is Professor of Philosophy and Director of the Seminar 'Individuation and Technique' of the Maison des Sciences de l'Homme at Paris-Nord, Director of the *Cahiers Simondon*, main editor of the online journal *Appareil*, and Doctor in the Epistemology and History of Sciences and Techniques (Paris 7 University, 2003). He is the author of *Penser l'individuation: Simondon et la philosophie de la nature* (Paris: L'Harmattan, 2005), *Penser la connaissance et la technique après Simondon* (Paris: L'Harmattan, 2005) and *Simondon ou l'Encyclopédisme génétique* (Paris: PUF, 2008).

Marie-Pier Boucher is a PhD student in the Department of Art, Art History and Visual Studies at Duke University. Her work focuses on the concretization / individuation process of (bio)technical objects. She is currently investigating the potential for the integration of biological materials and processes into architecture to facilitate the emergence of living techniques (*techniques du faire vivant*). In 2006, she was a researcher in residence at *SymbioticA: The Art and Science Collaborative Research Laboratory* based at the University of Western Australia. She has presented her work in multiple venues across Canada, Australia, the UK, Spain and the Netherlands.

Sean Bowden is an Associate Lecturer at the University of Melbourne, Australia. He has published on contemporary French philosophy – and in particular on Deleuze and Badiou – in journals such as *Deleuze Studies, Bulletin de la Société Américaine de Philosophie de Langue Française, Parrhesia* and *Pli*. He is currently preparing a book manuscript on the concept of the event in Gilles Deleuze's *The Logic of Sense*.

Miguel de Beistegui is Professor of Philosophy at the University of Warwick. He is the author of *Truth and Genesis: Philosophy as Differential Ontology* (Indiana University Press, 2004); *The*

New Heidegger (Continuum, 2005) and *Immanence: Deleuze and Philosophy* (Edinburgh University Press, 2010).

Arne De Boever teaches American Studies in the School of Critical Studies at the California Institute of the Arts. He also directs the School's MA Program in Aesthetics and Politics. He has published numerous articles on literature, film and critical theory, and is editor of *Parrhesia: A Journal of Critical Philosophy*. He is the author of *States of Exception in the Contemporary Novel* (Continuum, 2012) and *Narrative Care: Biopolitics and the Novel* (Bloomsbury, 2013).

Elizabeth Grosz teaches in the Women's and Gender Studies Department at Rutgers University, New Jersey. She is the author, most recently, of *Chaos, Territory, Art: Deleuze and the Framing of the Earth* (Columbia University Press, 2008) and *Time Travels: Feminism, Nature, Power* (Duke University Press, 2005).

Igor Krtolica is a former student of the Ecole Normale Supérieure (Lettres et Sciences Humaines) and holds the *agrégation* in philosophy. Under the direction of Pierre-François Moreau, he is currently preparing a PhD thesis in political philosophy around the works of Karl Marx, Gilles Deleuze and Fernand Deligne. His research interests predominantly concern the intersection between twentieth-century French philosophy, the Marxist tradition and psychoanalysis.

Dominique Lecourt is Professor at the Université Paris Diderot–Paris 7. He also works for the human rights and social science divisions of UNESCO. With Jacques Derrida, François Chatelet and Jean Pierre Faye, he founded the Collège International de Philosophie. His work explores the scientific imaginary and investigates the evidence on which science is based. Gaston Bachelard and Georges Canguilhem are two of his major influences. He has published extensively on the intersection of science and philosophy.

Brian Massumi is the author of a number of works, including *Parables for the Virtual* (Duke University Press, 2002) and *A User's Guide to Capitalism and Schizophrenia* (MIT Press, 1992), and is the translator of Deleuze and Guattari's *A Thousand Plateaus* (University of Minnesota Press, 1987). Professor Massumi teaches at the Institute for Communication at the University of Montreal, where he is in charge of the Radical Empiricism Laboratory.

Yves Michaud graduated from the Sorbonne and Ecole Normale Supérieure in 1968, and since then has taught Philosophy at the Universities of Montpellier and Paris Panthéon Sorbonne. He was invited Professor at the University of Sao Paulo, Tunis University, Edinburgh University and the University of California at Berkeley. He has written extensively on Hume, Locke, the empiricist tradition and political philosophy. Also known as an art critic, he has published several books on aesthetics and contemporary art.

Alex Murray is a Lecturer in Twentieth-Century Literature at the University of Exeter. He is the author of *Giorgio Agamben* (Routledge, 2010) and *Recalling London* (Continuum, 2007). He edited *The Work of Giorgio Agamben: Law, Literature, Life* (Edinburgh University Press, 2008) with Justin Clemens and Nick Heron, and *The Modernism Handbook* (Continuum, 2009) with Philip Tew. He has recently edited *The Agamben Dictionary* with Jessica Whyte (Edinburgh University Press, 2011) and is writing a book on Decadent Space.

Jon Roffe is the Founding Convenor of, and a Lecturer at, the Melbourne School of Continental Philosophy. He is a Co-editor of *Understanding Derrida* (Continuum, 2004) and of *Deleuze's Philosophical Lineage* (Edinburgh University Press, 2009). He has published widely on contemporary European philosophy.

Anne Sauvagnargues is Professor at the Ecole Normale Supérieure in Lyon. A specialist on French contemporary philosophy, she has published extensively on Deleuze, Simondon, Guattari and Deligny. Her articles and books include 'Deleuze. De l'animal à l'art' (in Paola Marrati, Anne Sauvagnargues and François Zourabichvili (eds), *La Philosophie de Deleuze*, Paris: PUF, 2004), *Deleuze et l'art* (Paris: PUF, 2005) and *Deleuze. L'Empirisme transcendental* (Paris: PUF, 2010). She is a member of the editorial board of the journals *Chimères* and *Multitudes*. With Fabienne Brugère, she directs the collection 'Lignes d'art' with PUF.

Bernard Stiegler is Head of the Department of Cultural Development at the Pompidou Centre in Paris and co-founder of the political group *Ars Industrialis*. He is the author of many books in French, some of which have been translated into English, including *Technics and Time 1: The Fault of Epimetheus* (Stanford University Press, 1998), *Technics and Time 2: Disorientation* (Stanford University Press, 2009) and *Acting Out* (Stanford University Prress, 2009).

Ashley Woodward is a member of the Melbourne School of Continental Philosophy and an editor of *Parrhesia: A Journal of Critical Philosophy*. He is author of *Nihilism in Postmodernity* (Davis Group Publishing, 2009) and *Understanding Nietzscheanism* (McGill Queen's University Press, 2011), editor of *Interpreting Nietzsche* (Continuum, 2011) and Co-Editor of *Sensorium: Aesthetics, Art, Life* (Cambridge Scholars, 2007) and *The Continuum Companion to Existentialism* (Continuum, 2011).

Index

Ameisen, Jean-Claude, 117
Aristotle, 136, 183, 191, 192, 199, 201, 205, 212, 231
Avery, Oswald Theodore, 176

Bachelard, Gaston, xii, 89, 176, 218, 226, 233
Barbaras, Renauld, 158
Barthélémy, Jean-Hugues, 144
Bateson, Gregory, 32, 33
Bergson, Henri, 22, 33, 43, 46, 47, 58, 66, 70, 80, 103, 177, 186, 199, 219, 221, 222, 225
Bernard, Claude, 178, 180
Blache, Vidal de la, 179, 196
Blanchot, Maurice, 196–7
Broglie, Louis de, 225
Buytendijk, Frederik Jacobus Johannes, 181

Canguilhem, Georges, ix, xi, xii, 176–84, 219, 226, 233
Cicero, 177
Combes, Muriel, 88, 98, 151, 152
Compton, Arthur Holly; Compton effect, 5
Crépon Marc, 189
Curie, Pierre, 147

Darwin, Charles; Darwinian, 99, 179, 180
Deleuze, Gilles, ix, xi, x, 11, 22, 26, 31, 66, 67, 68, 69, 70, 103, 120, 135–53, 188, 193, 197, 202, 231, 232, 233, 234

Democritus, 177
Derrida, Jacques (Derridean), 199
Descartes, René; Cartesian, 23, 80, 157, 160, 219
Duchamp, Marcel, 130
Durkheim, Émile, 219

Eiffel, Alexandre Gustave; Eiffel tower, 9, 126, 131
Einstein, Albert, 163
Espinas, Alfred V., 177

Foucault, Michel, 182, 188, 193
Freud, Sigmund, 52, 88, 201, 205
Friedmann, Georges, 203

Galileo, 171
Goldstein, Kurt, 177–82
Granel Gérard, 185, 187
Greef, Étienne de, 14
Gros, François, 183
Gualandi, Alberto, 149, 152, 153
Guattari, Félix, 22, 31, 150
Guimbal, Jean; Guimbal turbine, 4, 23, 24, 28, 208

Heidegger, Martin, x, xi, xii, 114, 161, 162, 174, 185–202, 206
Heisenberg, Werner, 186
Hertz, Heinrich; Hertzian cables, 9
Hölderlin, Johann Christian Friedrich, 189
Hottois, Gilbert, 151
Husserl, Edmund, 155–6, 157, 159, 162–3, 172, 185–6

James, William, 27
Jung, Carl Gustav, 214

Kant, Immanuel, 58, 69, 160, 205, 231

Lafitte, Jacques, 216–17
Lamarck, Jean-Baptiste de, 180
Lautman, Albert, 146
Le Corbusier; the Le Corbusier
    monastery, 14, 126
Leduc, René; Leduc stato-reactor, 4
Leibniz, Gottfried Wilhelm, 144, 228
Leroi-Gourhan, André, 112, 178, 194

Maeterlinck, Maurice, 177
Marion, Jean-Luc, 190
Marx, Karl, 52, 110, 119, 193, 194,
    197, 203, 205
Massumi, Brian, ix, xi, xii, 55, 56, 96,
    101, 106
Merleau-Ponty, Maurice, ix, 114, 120,
    154–75, 177, 204, 226
Michaux, Henri, 66

Newton, Isaac, 157
Nietzsche, Friedrich, 83, 90, 182

Piaget, Jean, 230
Plato, 52, 55, 143, 156, 157, 199

Poincaré, Henri, 146
Prenant, Auguste, 177
Prochiantz, Alain, 183, 218

Raman, Chandrasekhara Venkata;
    Raman effect, 5
Rifkin, Jeremy, 204

Sartre, Jean-Paul, x, 88, 204, 212
Sauvagnargues, Anne, xi, 149, 153
Shannon, Claude E., 32, 198
Sokal, Alan, 20
Spencer, Herbert, 180
Spinoza, Baruch, 22
Stengers, Isabelle, xi, 22, 151
Stiegler, Bernard, xi, 55, 112, 116, 136,
    150

Taylor, Frederick Winslow; Taylorism,
    8, 35
Toscano, Alberto, ix, 149, 153
Turing, Alan, 198, 199

Uexküll, Jakob von, 179

Weierstrass, Karl, 146
Whitehead, Alfred North, 22, 26, 29,
    94, 106
Wiener, Norbert, 32, 198, 217, 231

EU Authorised Representative:

Easy Access System Europe Mustamäe tee 50, 10621 Tallinn, Estonia

gpsr.requests@easproject.com

Printed and bound by CPI Group (UK) Ltd, Croydon, CR0 4YY

03/10/2025

01968092-0006